D1594305

Beyond the Border

ALSO BY STEVEN E. ASCHHEIM

Brothers and Strangers: The East European Jew in German and German-Jewish Consciousness, 1800–1923

The Nietzsche Legacy in Germany, 1890–1990

Culture and Catastrophe: German and Jewish Confrontations with National Socialism and Other Crises

In Times of Crisis: Essays on European Culture, Germans, and Jews

Scholem, Arendt, Klemperer: Intimate Chronicles in Turbulent Times

Hannah Arendt in Jerusalem *(editor)*

Beyond the Border

THE GERMAN-JEWISH LEGACY ABROAD

Steven E. Aschheim

Princeton University Press *Princeton and Oxford*

Copyright © 2007 by Princeton University Press

Published by Princeton University Press, 41 William Street,
Princeton, New Jersey 08540
In the United Kingdom:
Princeton University Press, 3 Market Place,
Woodstock, Oxfordshire OX20 1SY

Library of Congress Cataloging-in-Publication Data
Aschheim, Steven E., 1942–
Beyond the border : the German-Jewish legacy abroad /
Steven E. Aschheim.
p.   cm.
Based on lectures delivered at the University
of California, Berkeley in October 2004.
Includes bibliographical references and index.
ISBN-13: 978-0-691-12223-6 (alk. paper)
ISBN-10: 0-691-12223-7 (alk. paper)
1. Jews—Germany—History—20th century. 2. Jews—Germany—
Intellectual life—20th century. 3. Jews, German—History—20th century.
4. Zionists—Germany—History—20th century. 5. Refugees, Jewish—Europe—
History—20th century. 6. Civilization, Modern—Jewish influences.
7. Germany—Ethnic relations. I. Title.
DS135.G33A758 2007
305.892′4043—dc22   2006049369

British Library Cataloging-in-Publication Data is available

This book has been composed in Adobe Caslon.

Printed on acid-free paper. ∞

pup.princeton.edu

Printed in the United States of America

1 3 5 7 9 10 8 6 4 2

To John Landau—even if he does not agree . . .

CONTENTS

Preface   ix

Introduction   1

1. *BILDUNG* IN PALESTINE
   Zionism, Binationalism, and
   the Strains of German-Jewish Humanism   6

2. THE TENSIONS OF HISTORICAL *WISSENSCHAFT*
   The Émigré Historians and the Making of
   German Cultural History   45

3. ICONS BEYOND THE BORDER
   Why Do We Love (Hate) Theodor Adorno,
   Hannah Arendt, Walter Benjamin, Franz Rosenzweig,
   Gershom Scholem, and Leo Strauss?   81

Notes   119
Index   189

PREFACE

The present work is replete with personal, existential concerns. For it delves into, and wrestles with, issues, loyalties, and conflicts that possess intense and ongoing autobiographical and emotional significance. The German-Jewish legacy and its movements beyond its original borders, it turns out, is surprisingly and rather profoundly tied up with these investments. It would be absurd to claim that my investigations of the possibilities, strains, and adventures of the Zionist binationalists in Palestine have no relationship to the perplexed contemporary plight of my home, Israel, its cruel conflict with the Palestinians, and the moral qualms that come in its wake. Similarly, as much as the chapter on the German-Jewish émigré cultural historians is intended to locate these scholars within their generational and border-crossing context and as an attempt to critically comprehend the role they have played in forging our understanding of German and German-Jewish history, it is also a kind of homage to those who have most powerfully influenced my own way of thinking and approaching historical problems. The personal and the general converge too in the last chapter. The attractive as well as the more problematic and dubious sides of Weimar Jewish intellectuals have always been a source of wonderment and fascination to me and in this chapter I try to examine why they seem to exert a surprisingly similar hold over much of our contemporary intellectual and academic culture and what such canonization implies about our own condition.

I am aware of the dangers that come with such personal engagement. Clearly, it renders the need for vigilant and critical analytical distance especially acute (and I have tried to exercise that responsibility here). Yet, it is also an indispensable animating force, the source of whatever energy and significance this work may possess. There is another sense in which the book, concerned as it is with the "German-Jewish intellectual legacy," disavows neutrality. The idea of "legacy," it is true, is lexically neutral with regard to value. By definition, it entails a bequest from the past that perseveres into the present, contains a certain contemporary reality, and presumably suggests guideposts to the future. In practice, however, legacies are always either positively or negatively conceived, presented in inspirational or admonitory fashion. There are many narratives that picture German Jewry and the lessons it has to teach us in a rather condemnatory mode, as paradigmatic of modern Jewish delusion, demoralization, and disfigurement. I have tried to deal with these questions elsewhere. The present work is concerned with some aspects of the German-Jewish legacy that I regard, at least in part, as admirable or positive and worth not merely analyzing but also preserving and—always in critical and appropriately modified ways—perhaps emulating.

This book is based upon, and is an elaboration of, the Joseph and Eda Pell Lectures that I delivered at the University of California, Berkeley, in October 2004. As always, the time spent in that university town was enormously pleasant, the hospitality generous, and the intellectual interchange intense and stimulating. I am very grateful to Robert Alter (whose ongoing friendship my wife, Hannah, and I continue to enjoy and cherish), John Efron, and Ron Hendel for inviting me to present these lectures. I also benefited from the warm welcome and critical comments of Berkeley faculty and friends such as David Biale, Erich Gruen, Robert Hollub, Tony Kaess, and Martin Jay.

All authorship is, in some way or another, shared. Many of the ideas contained in the following pages I have imbibed from, and discussed with, numerous colleagues and friends. They are to be credited for whatever merit this work may contain but not held responsible for its defects. Special thanks are due to Paul Mendes-Flohr for his careful, critical, and constructive reading of an earlier version of this book. I have corrected errors that he detected and incorporated many of his suggestions. Upon reading the manuscript (an unenviable task I always inflict upon him), my lifelong buddy John Landau was able to save me considerable embarrassment. It is to him that this book is dedicated. I would also like to record my appreciation for their comments and encouragement to Jeffrey Barash, Paul Breines, Rebecca Burlow, Dan Diner, Arik Dubnow, Saul

Friedländer, Ehud Greenberg, Adi Gordon, Atina Grossmann, Moshe Halbertal, Jennifer Jenkins, Michael Marrus, Ezra Mendelsohn, Jerry Z. Muller, David M. Myers, Daniel Pekarsky, Anson Rabinbach, Till van Rahden, Reinhard Rürup, Robert Sack, and Michael Steinberg. My apologies to those whom I may have unintentionally left out (perhaps they will find their names in the footnotes where I have endeavored to credit the help and advice I have received.)

Brigitta van Rheinberg is the most enterprising, caring, and knowledgeable editor that it has been my privilege to know. From the beginning she took a warm interest in this manuscript, encouraged its completion, and nudged its efficient passage through the publication process. Her involvement was never merely technical. Her sensitive, informed, and critical readings of the text were helpful at every step of the way. I am exceedingly grateful to her. My appreciation also goes to Jill Harris, Heath Renfroe, and Clara Platter of Princeton University Press. Marsha Kunin did a fine job of copyediting.

Writing is usually a lonely business demanding solitude and silence. But, in my case, it would not be possible without the din of a warm, nourishing family atmosphere. It also renders it a pleasure. The birth of a granddaughter, Yael, has added to this happy boisterousness. Family (and also friends and nice colleagues) make it all worthwhile.

Beyond the Border

INTRODUCTION

All such writing is an assault on the frontiers.

—Franz Kafka, *The Diaries, 1914–1923*

In 1956 Hannah Arendt wrote: "The German-speaking Jews and their history are an altogether unique phenomenon; nothing comparable to it is to be found even in the other areas of assimilation. To investigate this phenomenon, which among other things found expression in a literally astonishing wealth of talent and of scientific and intellectual productivity, constitutes a historical task of the first rank, and one which, of course, can be attacked only now, after the history of the German Jews has come to an end."[1]

The Nazi rise to power did indeed brutally cut short the compelling and complex story to which Arendt was alluding. Yet, in another sense the history of German-speaking Jewry did not, in her words, "come to an end." Albeit in splintered and fragmented form, that legacy remains palpable. In manifold and often quite surprising ways its—always ambiguous—influence continued (and continues) to be widespread and pervasive, mediated and incarnated by those intellectuals (such as Arendt herself) who departed from their Central European settings and moved beyond their borders mainly to Palestine/Israel, Britain, and the United States.

Few topics have been as exhaustively studied, and institutionally supported, as the history of German Jewry and its interactions with German society, politics, economy, and culture. But, viewed from the present standpoint, its legacy continues to be most resonant and immediately felt beyond its historical environment, in its outward movements. The current need, it seems to me, is to grasp in greater detail some of these twentieth-century migratory moments and to analyze the dynamics, interconnections, continuities, transformations, and problematic sides of these German-Jewish impulses as the dispersion from Central Europe took effect. This work is offered as a modest contribution toward that aim. It is certainly not intended to comprise a comprehensive, or even vaguely systematic, critical history of the German-Jewish intellectual migration. This has been, more or less well, done in a wide variety of studies.[2] Significantly, one of the subjects of this work, Walter Laqueur, has recently sketched a collective portrait of his entire generation and told the larger story of how refugees from Nazi Germany, with varying degrees of success and difficulty, made their way in different parts of the world.[3]

My aim here is far more limited. It is to examine three case studies in which, I believe, this transplanted and always complex hyphenated identity has played a crucial, and as yet insufficiently examined, role in issues and predicaments that continue to engage and perplex us. Chapter 1 examines the ultimately doomed (but still remarkably pertinent) odyssey of a fascinating group of German-speaking Zionists who, very much against the grain, sought to bring about a binationalist solution to the Arab-Jewish conflict in pre-Israel Palestine. Chapter 2 analyzes the emergence of a new kind of cultural history created by German-Jewish émigré historians against the background of their exile from Nazi Germany. In related fashion it seeks to analyze the—often unacknowledged—tensions and differences between them and those writing social history in Germany at the same time. Chapter 3 documents the background to, and thus far little understood reasons behind, the remarkable contemporary canonization of a group of Weimar Jewish intellectuals (Theodor Adorno, Hannah Arendt, Walter Benjamin, Franz Rosenzweig, Gershom Scholem, Leo Strauss) within Western academic and cultural life. These at times surprisingly intertwined cases will, hopefully, illuminate not merely the nature and dynamics of this intellectual sensibility and the migratory moment but also aspects of our own condition and predilections.

The title of this book refers, of course, to more than geographical mobility. German-Jewish intellectual dispersion, at least in its more potent moments, did not merely entail the self-evident movement of people and ideas across physical spaces. More significantly, it resulted in the imported questioning and reshaping of conventional and normative conceptual borders, numerous projects to reconfigure cultural and historical boundaries of thought and knowledge, and manifold attempts to remap the contours of political—and sometimes religious—possibility. In that sense it both continued and (under conditions of adversity, novelty, and crisis) sharpened the cultural and intellectual proclivities characteristic of the wider postemancipation German-Jewish historical experience.

For over a half-century now, fascinated scholars have been chronicling, mapping, and variously explaining—at times in sophisticated, occasionally in equally celebratory and ideological, manner—why German-speaking Jewish intellectuals were particularly endowed with these qualities (and why, in their view, these qualities continue to be worth emulating).[4] It is not within the purview of the present work to elaborate upon this post-Enlightenment explosion of creativity as Jewish intellectuals and artists encountered (and co-constituted) modern and German culture.[5] It is, however, worth noting that many of the most prominent accounts derive from the work of the thinkers who form part of the present story (and who themselves embodied these qualities).[6]

For all that, in our context, it is worth noting a certain paradoxical characteristic of the modern German-Jewish experience. On the one hand, aware of the conditionality and vulnerability of their status, German Jews often demanded rather timid and inconspicuous behavior from themselves. Respectability became built into their comportment, restraint regarded as a key to well-being. "Stepchildren," German-Jewish leaders stressed, "must be doubly good."[7] Even that supreme dissenter Walter Benjamin warned that Jews endangered "even the best German cause for which they stand up *publicly*."[8] German citizens of the Jewish faith were exhorted to take care not to go beyond the limits, not to tread across invisible yet clearly intuited lines.[9] In 1897 the young Walther Rathenau had railed against Jewish conspicuousness,[10] yet he himself later accepted the highly visible, vulnerable position of German foreign minister, and his 1922 murder sadly vindicated the warnings and imprecations of his friends to give up the office in the face of growing Weimarian anti-Semitism. One of these friends was Albert Einstein.[11] He later wrote: "I regretted the fact that he became a Minister. In view of the attitude which large numbers of the educated classes in Germany assume toward the Jews, I have always thought that their natural conduct in public should be one of proud reserve."[12]

Yet at the same time (and who more than Benjamin and Einstein themselves better exemplified this tendency), the history of modern German Jewry was distinguished by the remarkably adventurous nature of its cultural, scientific, and intellectual enterprises, animated by an especially open, critical, and experimental sensibility bent on questioning cognitive, artistic, and political borders—on a radical crossing and refiguring of mental and social frontiers.

Perhaps, after all, there is no paradox here. Could it be that this iconoclastic sensibility represented, at least in part, a kind of (conscious or unconscious) compensatory reaction to, a protest against, the conformist and behavioral constraints imposed upon and by German-speaking Jews? Certainly these thinkers were all confronted with the ever more problematic issue of their own Jewishness, and the tensions that this entailed must have surely figured in the ensuing critical and searching modes by which they questioned, and often sought to go beyond, conventional borders and generally accepted ways of thinking.

Whatever the correct explanation, the majority of figures who form the mosaic of this work fit this pattern. Their lives and work, however, also reveal another important double dimension. They were not just participants in and products of the German-Jewish story; they also became its historians and critical anatomists. As they proceeded beyond the borders of their birth—whether in voluntary, idealist fashion or in forced exile—they became its prime analysts, explicators, and mediators. Not all would necessarily have agreed with Fritz Stern's statement that: "The historical enterprise aims to restore to German Jewry the dignity of its history."[13] But all were mightily impelled to come to explanatory grips with that past and transmit its "lessons" and "legacies" whether in condemnatory, celebratory, or more balanced critical fashion. In their migration they formulated highly charged, often opposed historiographies and accounts of that experience. At its extreme poles stand Gershom Scholem's Zionist narrative of a disfigured, deluded, and demoralized "assimilationist" project[14] through to Peter Gay's impassioned liberal defense of it.[15] (These were by no means the only accounts, and during the course of this work, we shall have occasion to discuss some of their major outlines.)

At the same time, and in various settings and modes, the thinkers who feature in the present study themselves embodied and put into play the very sensibilities and qualities of German-speaking Jewish intellectuals whose history they so masterfully and critically analyzed. In more or less conscious ways they acted as legatees and incarnations of German Jewry's cultural proclivities abroad, exemplified its strengths, strains, bi-

ases, and weaknesses, demonstrated again its accomplishments and conflicts, and analyzed, overcame, or replicated its blind spots. Certainly a
crucial part of that (usually self-conscious) legacy corresponded to Kafka's
notion of writing as an "assault against the frontiers," a felt desire to re-
figure conventional cultural, political, and mental definitions and boundaries. It is to these border-crossing impulses and activities, to their ongoing transformations, strains, and resonances that we must now turn.

I

Bildung in Palestine

Zionism, Binationalism, and the Strains of German-Jewish Humanism

> . . . the last flicker of the humanist nationalist flame, at a historical moment when nationalism became amongst all the nations an anti-humanist movement.
>
> —Shmuel Hugo Bergman[1]

When we think of German-speaking Jewish intellectuals abroad, beyond their borders, we tend to think of them largely as exiles, refugees from Nazism. Our first case study, however, consists of a group of Central European thinkers who (with one or two exceptions) departed from Europe well before the Nazi onslaught. During the first three decades of the twentieth century, the center of their attention moved to Palestine. As second-generation Zionists, to be sure, Europe (and Germany in particular) was rejected as the site in which their Jewishness, as they conceived it, could be authentically validated. Yet this physical (and ideological) move beyond the borders of their birth did not mean that they necessarily wanted to, or indeed could, unload the fraught mental baggage they brought with them. The mixed European experience—for it was both negatively and positively conceived—marked and defined, molded, them for life. Some of its less noble ingredients—its intolerance, integral nationalism, and chauvinism—served as a negative foil for their own model of a spiritual, enlightened nationalism. At the same time, they also carried with them the positive values and nuances of a European tradition that could remain relatively authoritative because the Nazi experience had not yet rendered so much connected to that past sullied and questionable (something our later subjects could not automatically do.) They brought with them the sensibilities of what they took to be an amalgam of European humanism and Jewish religioethical values and sought to apply them within and reshape their new reality—a reality that inevitably tested and strained it to its outermost limits.

This small circle of German-speaking Zionist intellectuals—all three labels are equally pertinent—sought to subvert conventional notions of sovereign national identities and state-political boundaries. This was rather unique because their skepticism of political "ethnonationalism" and a majoritarian state proceeded from *within* a deeply felt nationalist commitment—and at a time when almost all nationalists belonged to the more militant, integral variety. From an early stage of Zionist settlement they devoted themselves to the cause of Arab-Jewish understanding and advocated a binational, common state or federative solution to the emerging conflict (producing, over the years, any number of detailed blueprints as to how this purportedly could be put into practice.) Throughout, and to the chagrin of others within their camp, they identified this issue as *the* central moral and political challenge to Zionism.

Not all German-speaking Zionists, of course, were binationalists, nor were all binationalists Central European intellectuals and university professors.[2] Indeed, the great moral hero of this group (though he was not himself a member nor did he ever endorse a binationalist path) was the Russian founder of modern "cultural" Zionism, Ahad Ha'am (Asher Ginzberg).[3] Moreover, a major mover and leader of this idea—especially in its later 1930s and 1940s "Ichud" guise—was the Oakland, California, rabbi and later president of Hebrew University Judah Magnes (although one may claim for him an honorary German pedigree—his mother was born in Germany, he studied in German universities, knew the language rather well and most of his trusted friends and colleagues in Jerusalem were these Central European intellectuals.)[4] Nevertheless, over time, the circle's Germanic provenance and preponderance was evident and significant both to its members and to their many derisive opponents who mockingly referred to "all these Arthurs, Hugos and Hans.'"[5]

The list of such acculturated Central European Jewish intellectuals involved, at one stage or another and in various degrees of activity, in the numerous institutional permutations of the binationalist idea—most prominently in Brit Shalom (Covenant of Peace) of the mid-1920s and early 1930s, the League for Arab-Jewish Understanding founded in 1939, and, during the 1940s and after, the "Ichud"[6]—is impressive and

no doubt, at least in part, accounts for the attention their ideas and activities attracted both then and now. While the total membership and
sympathizers of Brit Shalom itself never amounted to much more than
a hundred or so people, they produced a wealth of publications, and
their protestations resonated far beyond their numbers.[7] (It should be
pointed out, however, that the League for Arab-Jewish Understanding
was founded and sponsored by the left-oriented Ha-Shomer Ha-Tzair,
which at the time had tens of thousands of members.)

The leading early proponents of the binational idea were nearly all
distinguished thinkers and scholars in their own right.[8] Its most famous
exemplars include the Prague-born Hans Kohn (1891–1971), the pioneer of the theoretical and historical study of nationalism, who eventually severed his ties with the Zionist movement; Gershom Scholem
(1898–1982), founder of the modern study of Jewish mysticism and
one of the most fascinating intellectuals of the twentieth century; Martin Buber (1878–1965), the philosopher and theologian, who at the time,
was the most renowned and influential figure of the group and whose
writings endowed its positions with the stamp of moral authority (until
1938, it should be noted, Buber lived in Germany and thus functioned
as an overseas supporter); and, albeit at a later stage from afar and in a
more peripheral manner, Hannah Arendt (1906–1975).[9] Albert Einstein too was in touch with members of Brit Shalom. He took an intense interest in possible future schemes of shared Jewish-Arab political power and administration and in 1929 advocated the creation of "a
genuine symbiosis between Jews and Arabs in Palestine."[10]

Other members or supporters of the group, within or without Palestine, are perhaps less well known but no less interesting for that. Most
prominently these included the founder of Brit Shalom, the most moderate of the group and one who also became increasingly skeptical of
the possibility of a peaceful, amicable compromise, the Posen-born Arthur
Ruppin (1876–1943), a creator of Jewish demography and sociology
and a key figure in Zionist immigration, settlement, and land acquisition policies (activities that he constantly sought to square with his
changing views on Jewish-Arab relations); the philosopher, librarian
and first rector of Hebrew University, Shmuel Hugo Bergman (1883–
1975); Ernst Simon (1899–1988), the philosopher and educator; and
Robert Weltsch (1891–1983), the writer and editor (among other things)

of the German-Zionist organ, the Jüdische Rundschau, and author of the renowned "Wear the Yellow Star with Pride" article penned upon the Nazi assumption of power. Because they published less, other colorful figures such as Gabriel Stern (who was active later in the Ichud) have been almost totally forgotten.[11]

The role and status of the leading central European members of Brit Shalom were inherently paradoxical. If in certain ways they were "outsiders," they were also "insiders." We should not forget that, for all the differences, they were part of the intellectual and institutional Zionist establishment, both within and outside of Palestine. Their ideological dissent notwithstanding, this was possible because it was only in the 1940s that political statehood became the official goal of the Zionist movement. Until then the conceptually rather vague notion of a "Jewish National Home"—which permitted a degree of interpretive flexibility in a still historically open situation—prevailed. It was only the Revisionists— the avowed enemies of Brit Shalom—who openly proclaimed a majority Jewish state as the goal; Labor Zionism, of course, shared this desire but officially maintained a pragmatic neutrality in this regard. It was only just prior to, and obviously after, the creation of the Jewish state that opposition to it appeared tantamount to treason. In that sense the study of the binationalists may serve as a counterfactual exercise: it provides us with an alternative foundational perspective when not only was statehood not a certainty but other options did not seem to contradict historical reality and it was possible to envisage alternative future social orders.

Yet, if these intellectuals constituted part of the elite of the Yishuv (Jewish settlement in Palestine), they also acted as its gadflies, a source of constant critical irritation. This was dissent that proceeded from within.[12] Indeed, they very closely fit Michael Walzer's description of the "connected critic."[13] As highly committed Zionists they articulated positions based upon a sense of belonging and intense identification. This rendered their discontent and objections particularly relevant and irritating for, unlike enemies, their criticism possessed standing.[14]

Binational Zionism has been rather thoroughly researched. There is thus no need to comprehensively cover its political, institutional, and ideological history—others more competent than me have done this.[15] Here I want to limit the focus on the central theme of this book and explore the manifold, sometimes contradictory, ways in which the German-speaking contexts and cultures informed the ideas and biases of these binationalists; the modes in which they both perceived and sought to re-mold the new reality into which they had been transplanted; and the strengths, strains, and limits that were entailed in such border crossings.

What then are the links between an idealist binational Zionism, the rejection of "political" ethnonationalism, and the German-Jewish legacy abroad? Recently, scholars have correctly noted that generalized and rather abstract notions of the "influence" of a vaguely defined and positively conceived "German culture" leaves much to be desired. After all, normative German nationalism was more integral than cosmopolitan, and its dominant political culture cannot be labeled as liberal-humanist.[16] This, then, was hardly a direct, unmediated influence. Moreover, these researchers point out that, while these binationalists were indeed largely products of the German *Kulturbereich*, they came from politically and socially distinctive parts of Central Europe. The diverse realities of, and reactions to, the experiences of Prague (whence hailed Bergman, Kohn, and Weltsch); Rawitsch, in the southeast corner of Posen (Arthur Rup-pin); and Berlin (Scholem and Simon) cannot be simplistically reduced to one another.

Indeed, Yfaat Weiss has suggested that the varying inspirations be-hind Zionist binationalism did not emanate necessarily from culturally elevated notions and positive experiences: The binationalists, she de-clares, could hardly derive their ideas from a tradition of tolerant "lib-eral Central European moderation, because no such thing existed."[17] Local knowledge and experience of a differentiated and mainly negative kind, she argues, was a crucial factor in the genesis and relocation of such views. Thus, the more mainstream (and later disillusioned) bina-tional position of Arthur Ruppin was a translation into Palestine of the distinctively illiberal settlement model of the Prussian colonization of his native Posen. He projected the Posen experience, and replicated its German-Polish division, onto Palestine and envisaged the coexistence of the two groups (Arabs and Jewish) as proceeding within quite sepa-rate territorial, spatial frames. "I see as the only solution in the future," he wrote in 1923, "the territorial limitations of the Jews with autonomy on the plains, the Arabs in the mountains and the lower Jordan valley."[18]

Moreover, in making his early move from Germany to Palestine, Ruppin's baggage included few classic liberal precepts, and much of the

eugenic and racial discourse of his time (which he believed would provide the tools for combating what he took to be the real dangers of Jewish assimilation and even "degeneration")[19] was hardly in tune with the
classical precepts of liberalism. But, it should be clear, these racial views
had nothing to do with doctrines of hierarchy and domination. Indeed,
at least initially, Ruppin dreamed not so much of Jewish-Arab separation but of an ultimate and higher integration. In certain moods, he
imagined the nascent Jewish commonwealth as destined to become an
integral part of the new Near East, a vital part of the modern flowering
of a greater Arab civilization. "We must place ourselves again in the
Oriental circle of peoples," he declared in 1923, "and together with our
racial brothers, the Arabs (and Armenians) create a new cultural community of the near East. More than ever, it seems to me that Zionism
can be justified only in terms of the racial belonging of the Jews to the
peoples of the near Orient."[20]

An examination of Ruppin's writings indicates that his notions of division seem to be predicated less upon the illiberal colonial Posen model
than upon the need not to trample upon the rights and needs of the
Arabs. Early on—his optimism was later dashed—his hopes for accom-
modating both groups (conditioned on the good behavior of both sides)
were based upon the fact that through World War I the population
(750,000) was sparse, and available unused arable land still relatively
plentiful. "There need not be a struggle over shortage of land between
Arab and Jew—there is place for all."[21] As the spatial and political realities increasingly pressed upon him, it is true, Ruppin ultimately came
down on the side of an equitable territorial division (and later despaired
even of this).

The more radical binationalists, on the other hand, developed a cultural rather than a physical conception of separation and coexistence.
They too, Weiss argues, forged their ideas not via any native humanist
liberalism but essentially as responses to the essentially negative experiences of ethnonationalism in Central and Eastern Europe. The mal-
treatment of minorities and the intolerance of ruling national majori-
ties was what Zionism had to avoid (apart from anti-Semitic instances, the
Czech-German, Italian–South Tyrol, and Polish-Ukrainian examples
were most often invoked). Thus Hans Kohn, witnessing the escalation
between Czechs and Germans (and the move from what he took to be

an inclusive to an exclusive nationalism), sought to avert this fate and save Zionism by means of a binational solution that would facilitate both mutually respecting separate cultural national existences and shared political power.[22]

In the view of this new scholarship, then, Zionist binationalism, as it moved beyond its originating borders, was hardly the importation into Palestine of a European-based liberalism and humanism but rather the negative projection outward of problematic local models and situations. Clearly, too there were also wider deleterious continental developments. The shock and lessons of the brutalizing Great War, in which unrestrained nationalisms had gone murderously berserk, must be considered as a crucial animating force. Most of the people who were later to form the binational nucleus joined the initial overall enthusiasm for the war, but eventually understood its disastrous magnitude (Gershom Scholem's opposition to the war from the beginning was an honorable exception, though it must be said, his stance derived not so much from humanitarian as nationalist reasons—this was not a "Jewish" war, he declared, and thus a dividing line between Europe and the Jews had to be drawn).[23]

At any rate, out of the ashes of war, it was clear, a more refined, positive counterconception of nationalism—one that was less power politically oriented and more ethically anchored—had to be formulated.[24] This postwar reformation, as Hans Kohn put it in 1921, would usher in an age "when 'national sovereign independence,' the goal of the age of political nationalism, will vanish because mankind will have realized that, just as individual men can never be fully sovereign and must be bound by myriad dependencies and obligations and, for the sake of solidarity, must put up with restrictions . . . so national independence, the nonintervention of the 'foreigner' in 'our' affairs is a dangerous phantom. . . . Enthusiastic and soul-felt and fervent as any article of faith at its inception, through its attachment to politics and violence and rights, this one has become emptier and emptier, more and more deathlike."[25] It is not surprising then that for Kohn and others the critical ethical litmus test of such a nationalism consisted in what became known as the "Araberfrage," the Arab Question. Moreover, notions of autonomy and nonsovereign nationalism were also very much afloat in postwar discussions and treaties concerning minority rights.[26]

The new scholarly emphases on "negative" models and the critique of previously rather unexamined assertions as to the unmediated transmission of European humanist influences do, indeed, provide valuable correctives. Yet another important contribution to the debate, by the young scholar Dimitry Shumsky, also insists on the centrality of the local as a molding force of the binationalist outlook but, contrarily, insists on the "positive" dimensions of that experience. He argues that in the case of the early twentieth-century Bar Kochba Circle (to which Bergman and Kohn enthusiastically belonged and whose central inspiring force was Martin Buber), the specific "in-between" situation of Prague Jews, the quest for a cultural negotiation between the Gentile (Czech and German) and Jewish cultures, rendered the search for a kind of everyday multicultural accommodation, both natural and necessary. This accommodatory impulse, Shumsky argues, animated their critique of ethnonationalism and thus also their subsequent binational approach to Zionism.[27] This was not, as has been claimed, a retreat into idealistic, "de-territorialized" thinking but grounded in the prosaic realities of the Czech-German experience.[28] It resulted, he claims, in an open national identity whose content was not threatened but enriched by a plurality of cultural affinities and informed by a cosmopolitan belief in the ultimate unity of mankind.

Toward the end of his long life, Hugo Bergman essentially articulated this thesis: "More and more do I regard this synthesis as the specific task of Jews for humanity. We grew up in the city of Prague, in which three peoples, the Czechs, Germans and Jews lived and despite all the differences lived *together*. It was the greatest service of the Bohemian Jews to the two other people to act as *bridges*. . . . We took Prague into our hearts as a bridge city and assumed the function of trying to overcome the antagonisms. It is probably no coincidence that Bohemian Jews were the carriers of the Brit-Shalom ideas. That, it seems to me, is the teaching that we should pass on to our descendants."[29]

Yet, when all is said and done, "local" emphases of either the negative or positive variety, can go too far. Despite all their differences, these men were shaped within a recognizably similar cultural universe; in many ways they shared a common worldview and outlook. If they cannot be said to emerge from a generalized "German" culture, their intellectual formation did take place within the contours of a specific, historically conditioned German-speaking Jewish world, characterized, more often than not, by its common ideals and sensitivities.[30] Broadly speaking, the Zionist binationalists, while rejecting the domestic, liberal-integrationist impulses of their fellow German Jews, shared other parts of their normative and conceptual baggage. This consisted of a set of rather rarefied Enlightenment attitudes and *Bildungs* values and biases, that George L. Mosse has argued—for reasons associated with their struggle for emancipation—became built into the core of a new German-Jewish identity: a belief in critical reason; a certain moral, humanist posture; the cultivating centrality of "culture"; an idealist bias; and a downplaying or underestimation of the power-political realm; and so on.[31] Not a hypostatized German culture in itself, but rather, its historically specific Jewish appropriations and emphases played into their binationalist sensibilities.

If these Zionists rejected their parents bourgeois culture and what they took to be the "assimilationist," hyperrationalistic, and quietist aspects of the original *Bildungs* idea, they retained its cultivating ethical and spiritual dimensions and rendered its humanist and cultural impulses central to both their radicalism and their specific brand of nationalism.[32] If they regarded themselves essentially as Jews in Germany, in many ways they were Germans in Palestine.[33] Certainly they were perceived as such.[34] In the Yishuv, it was these propensities that were integral to their self-definition, and that tied them together as a social group and indeed marked them off. Here it was of little importance if one hailed from Prague, Rawitsch, or Berlin. In a curiously ambiguous way, half admiring and half contemptuous for those who observed it, this German *Kultur* and language constituted a kind of mental and social border.

These borders were palpable to both sides. Many of their mainly East European Yishuv contemporaries regarded these German intellectuals as stiff, buttoned-up "Yekkes,"[35] unworldly professors perched in their ivory towers at Hebrew University and closely and comfortably concentrated in the Jerusalem neighborhoods of Rechavia and Talbieh. To be sure, this perception often went together with a certain bemused attraction. Nowhere has this been better captured than in S. Y. Agnon's classic novel *Shira,* with its gentle mingling of satire and respect, and its ironic rendering of these putatively over-refined subjects by endowing them with everyday carnal desires.[36]

Yet this separation also expressed itself in hostile political terms. Adherents of Brit Shalom and the Ichud were often portrayed as deracinated and irresponsible elitist intellectuals, seeking to import alien and naively utopian schemes to Palestinian shores (a prevalent image to this day). The official organ of the Labor party, *Davar,* declared that these Germans had no "part in the people; they are atomized, individualized, confined to their small groups . . . [they] fear everything associated with the masses, power, force."[37] In a 1930 attack on what he took to be their meddling, unpatriotic politics, Menachem Ussischkin simply conflated "Brit Shalom" with "the Germans" arguing that the organization reflected a peculiar "criminal" mentality.[38]

One does not want to make too much of it, but such attitudes were in many ways a surprising carry-over of the old *Ost-Westjude* tension, but within a new context and with the power relation reversed—the *German,* not the East European, Jews were now a kind of misplaced cultural minority.[39] Both sides were aware of this. "I have the feeling," one binationalist wrote in 1928, "that we are all too negatively integrated. . . . We are not positively enough engaged with the country and bound to Hebrew culture etc. We are really . . . 'uprooted' (*Entwurzelte*). We live spiritually/intellectually (*geistig*) in Germany and not here. . . . Hebrew is alien to us, thus we are able to follow Hebrew literature only through the daily press and not the literature itself. . . . [W]e know far better about an article in *'Tagebuch'* or the *'Weltbühne'* than an article in *'Ketuwim'*."[40] Even the most mainstream member of this circle, Arthur Ruppin, well after he had moved to Palestine, confided to the novelist Emil Ludwig (who was visiting in 1924): "My whole personality is tied into the German language. I can be effective in German, not another language. It occurs to me that recently people have the wrong impression of me and [because of this] I can't make friends even if I want to."[41] Moreover, after four decades of life in Palestine/Israel, Hugo Bergman still associated intolerance with Eastern European Jewish attitudes toward the non-Jew. In 1964, after listening to a particularly chauvinistic sermon, he returned home and told his wife Escha, "I went to such lengths to integrate myself into *Ostjudentum,* and in the end I feel entirely foreign. How can the Jewish people cure itself of all this? And can we exist at all as a Volk and also as a religion, without this chauvinism?"[42]

Even within their own mental and social borders, an interesting ambiguity applied to these circles. They almost perfectly embodied the tension between a broadening, open-minded "Bildung" and a narrowing concern for "respectability" characteristic of the German and German-

Jewish bourgeoisie in general.[43] This split may go some way toward an-
swering Tom Segev's excellent question as to "how it happened that people
who were so sedate . . . law-abiding, moderate, some of them very conservative and religious, adopted ideas that most other people considered
so radical, subversive, even traitorous."[44] In their personal habits and
everyday behavior they were pedantic, exemplars of conventional morals
and manners (*Sittlichkeit*); in their intellectual and public worlds they
combined Bildung with a religioethical sensibility that strived always to
go beyond the stifling borders of conformity and open up new areas of
experience and possibility.[45]

This, then, was a nationalism that was guided essentially by inner cultural standards and conceptions of morality rather than considerations
of power and singular group interest. Its exponents were united—as
many saw it, in hopelessly naive fashion—by their opposition to Herzl's
brand of "political" Zionism[46] both because they had a distaste for his
strategy of alliances with external and imperial powers and because they
did not hold the political realm or "statehood" to be an ultimate value:
their main goal was the spiritual and humanist revival of Judaism and
the creation of a moral community or commonwealth in which this
mission could be authentically realized. To be sure, it is not always easy
to separate the more general German and "cosmopolitan" ingredients
from the recovered, specifically Jewish and religious dimensions of their
vision.[47] The two were often unselfconsciously combined, although occasionally the possible tensions between them surfaced. Thus, after Hans
Kohn had bitterly left Brit Shalom and the Zionist movement as a whole,
Hugo Bergman—who sadly proclaimed that Kohn's departure was a
case of "disappointed love"—self-critically examined these tensions in a
letter addressed to Kohn:

> And while you, unconcerned by all that has happened, hold fast
> to your cosmopolitan worldview, I see myself as increasingly
> drawn to a Jewish one and try to bury myself more and more in
> our teachings and heritage and must—no other way exists—take
> on the paradoxical teaching of Israel's election (which so com-
> pletely contradicts everything that was inculcated in me by Marty-
> Brentano from my youth on) and from there, out of religious Ju-
> daism, build my worldview anew. Because of your cosmopolitanism,

you have treated our own heritage as a stepmother, knew French
and English literature better than the Hebrew; I too, at least as
far as philosophy was concerned—the only literature that I really
know—went the same way and still do; thus, for instance, I have
still not read the "Kuzari." But I see that all this—the direction
in which German Zionism seduced us—was the wrong way.[48]

One way or another, their approach to nationalism remained suspicious of the "ethnosovereign" sort. Ernst Simon typified this approach.
"The Jewish State," he declared in 1943, "means Jewish domination over
the Arabs, just as an Arab State means domination over the Jews."[49]
While he affirmed "the vitality of Jewish politics and the building up of
the country that is connected with it," he insisted that these actions
would be judged "by a moral-religious standard that is over and above
politics itself."[50] As Hans Kohn put it in 1929, the Zionism he champi-
oned was not political in the conventional sense of power: "I and a group
of my friends regarded Zionism as a moral cum spiritual movement
within which we could realize our most fundamental humane convictions, our pacifism, liberalism and humanism."[51]

Men like Bergman were convinced that such a Bildungs insistence on
personalizing relationships could humanize the harshness of prevalent
nationalist politics and conflict. When, one morning, he passed by an
Arab village with his son Uriel but did not return with him in the
evening, the Arab women on the side of the road asked after Uriel with
such "a heartily human concern, no different from that of the Czech
peasants did with us. I felt suddenly again, how close human beings are,
just as much as politics estranges them. The experience of having a child
binds me clearly . . . with all fathers and mothers of Bet Iksa and all the
other villages."[52] This—touching but increasingly desperate—emphasis
on personalized trust between Arabs and Jews increased as political
hope declined. In later years, these circles would increasingly seek ways
in which such personal bonds of national understanding could be created and reinforced. A glimpse of such (perhaps naive) plans and ap-
peals in their journals makes for both painful and sad reading.[53]

It is true that this Bildungs sensibility occasionally entailed a certain
patronizing, clearly Eurocentric, attitude toward the Arabs (as did other
Zionists). "The estrangement between Arab and Jew," wrote Ruppin,

can only be made to disappear when the Arabs are raised to the same cultural level of the Jewish immigrants. The Arabs are by nature intellectually well endowed and their mentality closely related to the Jewish one, so it seems certain that with an equal school education the emerging Arab generation will achieve the same cultural level as the Jews. We will strive to mediate European culture to the Arabs.[54]

For all that, these binationalists (moderate and radical alike) were all characterized by an inbred distaste for chauvinism and intolerance. This certainly includes the allegedly "illiberal" Arthur Ruppin. If his policy of separation appears at least in retrospect to be more "realistic," it was also explicitly opposed to domination and expropriation. His diaries are shot through with such concerns, indeed they constituted the reason for his founding of Brit Shalom (as a study circle rather than a politically activist group) in 1925:

> The Arab question lies heavily on my soul. I am no chauvinist and do not dream of Jewish rule (*Herrschaft*) or a Jewish State in Palestine. I want the Jews to have equal rights with the Arabs living in Palestine and regard with concern the gulf that exists between the two peoples, the growing enmity on the side of the Arabs and the chauvinistic and uncomprehending attitude of many Jews to the Arabs. With a few like-minded people I have founded a club to further these goals of better relationships, but for the present see no clear way before us.[55]

This lack of clarity gave way to despair as the situation worsened and the premonition that the very structure of the situation may have made such chauvinism inevitable: "Will Zionism really deteriorate into a meaningless form of chauvinism?" Ruppin asked in 1928.

> Is there really no way to set aside an area in Palestine where an increasing number of Jews can operate without exploiting the Arabs? I see the limited geographical territory as a particular problem. The day is undoubtedly not far off when no more land will be available, and settling a Jew will necessarily cause the removal of a fellah. . . . And what will happen then?[56]

These circles noted—and rather helplessly tried to resist—the increasingly militant nationalist atmosphere. As one of them reported as early as 1922: "Jewish children fight these days with Arab children and say: just wait, tomorrow Palestine will belong to us. In the Gymnasium recently a teacher gave a talk about the Arabs and said: this people is not worthy of cleaning our shoes."[57] Particularly worrying and perhaps typical were the sentiments of none other than the son of their guiding spirit, Achad Ha'am. In 1928 he declared that he was against Brit Shalom and would rather emigrate from a land in which Muslim Arabs rather than Jews dominated. Brit Shalom, he argued, was not being honest with itself—it was absurd to interpret Zionism in idealist terms. Zionism was simply a race for Palestine, and this did not depend upon how fast we run, but, rather, on how slowly the others moved. That is why we had to be honest and declare that the high mortality rate of Arab children was welcome to us, indeed was absolutely necessary, and every attempt on the Jewish side to alleviate this mortality rate through child welfare, had to be condemned from a Zionist standpoint. One could not say this publicly but that was the truth.[58]

Such attitudes came even closer to home, when for instance, Arthur Ruppin had his first political conversation with his son, Rafi:

> He wanted to know what "Brit Shalom" is. I told him it was a society for making peace between Jews and Arabs. He did not like that. He revealed himself as a small chauvinist. There should only be Jews and Hebrew spoken in Palestine. When I asked him what the Arabs should do, he said that they should go to Arabia. He asked me to leave "Brit Shalom," for otherwise people would laugh at me. He told me that a child at school told him he should be ashamed that his father belonged to "Brit Shalom."[59]

Perhaps what set these men apart from most German Jews was the way in which this Bildung sat comfortably side by side with their own recovery of Jewish tradition and informed their project of a personal and collective renaissance of Judaism. Hugo Bergman's letters and diaries are studded with such unselfconscious entries. In January 1918 he wrote: "Proceeded with the study of Talmud, read most of the Odyssey in Greek, began Dante's Vita nuova and Divinia Comedia."[60] A far later entry, for December 2 1959, reveals a similar, almost innocent, catholic-ity: "[Heard] a lecture by Scholem on Pantheism. . . . worked well in the evening: Fichte, Natural right and the derivation of the Individual. Bought a new tefillin [phylacteries] for 8 pounds."[61]

Yet the fit was never complete; a certain strain remained. Thus, Berg-man despaired over the difficulties of rendering the radically different atmospherics of the German Jewish experience into Hebrew.[62] Was he aware, one wonders, of the irony when he complained that the translation into Hebrew *from German* of his piece on *Hebrew Humanism* required constant reworking and was giving him any number of difficulties![63] His commitment to German, even after the Holocaust, remained, if any-thing, even firmer. Indeed, for Bergman, German was itself a kind of Jewish language. Responding to anti-German agitation, he wrote in 1971, that especially for a Jew, who sought access to *Weltkultur,* reject-ing that language and culture, was no option:

> We university teachers must endeavor to tell our students, morn-ing and evening: learn German! Not just for German alone, rather because your ignorance of German cuts you off from six generations of Jewish culture. Without knowledge of German you cannot read the most important thinkers of the eighteenth and nineteenth centuries, cannot read Herzl's diaries, protocols of Zionist congresses, [Pinsker's] Auto-Emancipation, nor Kafka, nor Max Brod and naturally, not Schelling and not Kant and not Goethe and not Schopenhauer and not Fichte and not . . . and not (without end).[64]

The Eurocentric emphasis was, of course, quite explicit. Buber, Simon, and Bergman were all concerned with what they took to be the bar-barizing conditions of youth in the Palestine of 1928. As Bergman put it to Robert Weltsch: Without books and the countless European Bil-dung influences, "and when our European generation makes its exit, Jewry here will become like those today in Bagdad."[65] Indeed, it is not surprising, that—the study of Arabic apart—Bergman regarded the common acquisition of precisely these sources of Bildung to be a cru-cial component of Arab-Jewish understanding. In 1926 he reported upon the "small joy" he experienced when the director of the Arabic teachers seminary and some of his students came to the library in order to borrow books by Freud and Jung, and other similar visits and concludes: "So I sometimes have the feeling that we are tearing down the walls that separate people and in this place of fanaticism creating a human abode."[66]

For all that, the gulfs and incomprehensions pertaining to this meeting of Arabs, Jews, and European culture in Palestine are succinctly exemplified by a scene depicted by Bergman as, in a period of particular tension in May 1936, he waited for a bus connection to Jerusalem: "I had to wait in Lod for two hours together with uninterested Arabs, who obviously had no idea how dangerous they were while I sat quietly on a bench reading. I used the time to peruse something from Locke!"[67]

The binationalists were certainly committed Zionists but they opposed Zionist theories of "normalization," notions that Jews should become "like all other nations" and uncritically assimilate their accompanying ethos and deployment of political power and violence. Jewish nationalism, nurtured by the Jewish prophetic tradition, they insisted, had to retain Judaism's special ethical core. Most nationalisms, Hans Kohn wrote in 1925, manifested self-intoxication, were indulgent in self-praise and intent on hearing only the worst about their enemies. Truth was inevitably their victim. Jewish nationalism had to be different—self-criticism and conscience were at its heart and it was the intellectuals who were to be "responsible for the spiritual physiognomy of our Nationalism."[68] (Kohn's readers no doubt would have received something of a jolt when—in praise of self-critique—he commented: "There lies a deeper meaning, as Gorelik once said, that we should build a monument to Otto Weininger."[69] Such comments concerning a man who was widely considered to be a Jewish anti-Semite surely reinforced the continuing image of these men as a species of bleeding-heart, self-hating Jewish intellectuals.)

These critical tendencies become especially noteworthy in light of the fact that the members of Brit Shalom (and, later, the Ichud) were intense, deeply idealistic nationalists strongly and in some cases, almost fanatically committed to the personal and collective renaissance of Judaism and the Jewish People in their ancestral homeland. As Gershom Scholem noted in November 1916:

I am occupying myself always and at every time with Zion: in my work and my thoughts and my walks and also, when I dream. . . . All in all, I find myself in an advanced state of Zionisation, a Zionisation of the most innermost kind. I measure everything by Zion.[70]

Arthur Ruppin. Courtesy of the Zionist Archives.

We should not, therefore, be ahistorical and confuse this bi*nationalist* position with later postnationalist emphases on "a state for all its citizens," even though there were rather surprising moments when the possibility, albeit fleetingly, was broached. Thus in a 1928 conversation with Edwin Samuel, Bergman proposed a general "Palestinian land-consciousness [*Landesbewusstein*]" that would

> break the particularism of the various communities and create a place open to the Jew, the Arab, the English, the German, the American . . . and where things were not viewed from the stand-

Seated portrait of Ernst Simon writing. Courtesy of the Leo Baeck Institute, New York.

point of the particular communities, but rather judged from the perspective of the whole country.[71]

The "nationalist" credentials of these figures are clear enough, integral indeed to their very self-definition. Their humanist or ethical version of nationalism becomes even more noteworthy in view of the fact that their ideas, sentiments, and convictions were shot through with any

number of mystical, neoromantic, and "irrationalist" fin de siècle and
Weimarian impulses.[72] Indeed, it is one of the more interesting paradoxes of this group that the most nonchauvinist Zionist nationalism
was closely associated with various forms of organic, existential, and to-
talistic *Völkisch* visions and ideology.[73] The binationalists were able to
fuse the two by dismissing the hierarchical and power-political *Herrschaft*
dimensions of Völkisch ideology and deploying it in the direction of
"culture" and spirit, the moral and inner-directed realm (propensities that
characterized the German-Jewish intellectual legacy as a whole).[74]

Given the acute sensitivity of these intellectuals to the prior presence
of Arabs and their dismissal of conventional national considerations,
how, nevertheless, did they justify the Zionist project? It is worth quoting at length from a revealing 1919–20 text by Hans Kohn. "To refer to
historical rights," he wrote,

> seems impossible. . . . "Historic rights" can be used to justify every
> injustice. . . . Such justifications can vindicate princes or kings in
> levying a head tax and towns in shutting us in ghettos. . . . History
> continues to have an effect on us, but it does not give us rights.
> Only the living present gives us rights. . . . Nor did today's Arabs
> take the country from us by force or by cunning. Even their fa-
> thers did not do so, they did not oppress us, and thus this does
> not even give us the indignation of pathos and revolt. . . . [W]e
> have no historic right to Palestine. But though we do not have
> this, we have never neglected to exert our real right to Palestine.
> Since the destruction of our independence by the Romans, we
> have never ceased to live in that country for any length of time.
> There have been considerable Jewish colonies there, and the Jew-
> ish spirit has brought forth unique fruit. In this way, the country
> was always not only Arab but also Jewish, not as a historic right,
> but in the living present.
>
> But what draws us to Palestine, and will slowly change an
> Arab Palestine into a Palestine of Arabs and Jews, and later a
> Palestine of Jews and Arabs (nobody can predict the future de-
> velopment) is our love for this country, a love which in history
> surely continues to have an effect, as well as the needs of our
> time. Although the country is now Arab, this does not at all

imply that it is the exclusive property of the nation. No nation
has the right to a country in such an exclusive sense. The country
belongs to those who make it so fertile through the strength of
their minds and their hands that they can make their living
there. Palestine, a region of approximately 27,000 km is too
large for its present population of 700,000. It is very thinly
populated; there is no industry that could support a large number of workers; agriculture is primitive; and wide expanses have
not been reclaimed. That is why Palestine needs massive immigration so that it can achieve its potential for humanity and
the world economy. . . . The Arabs cannot provide this at the
moment.[75]

While Kohn did indeed indicate that he expected the Arab-Jewish
demographic and linguistic relationship to be reversed,[76] he also insisted
upon defining the nature of the nascent society in ways that definitively
departed from any integral or exclusive conception. "This future state,"
he declared,

> will not be a national state for an indefinite period, but a multi-
> national one. If we do not realize this in all seriousness, we shall
> always suffer from the Arab-Jewish problem. . . . No country be-
> longs to one nation, it belongs to the people who live there and
> work peacefully—and in Palestine that will always be not only
> the Jews, but also the Arabs. Our state institutions must take this
> into account, they must give both Jews and Arabs the broadest
> autonomy and self-determination so as to diminish friction. We
> will have the difficult (but not insoluble) task of settling two
> non-territorial, non-coherent national communities on one com-
> mon state-run territory, whose national functions amount to
> nothing more than the regulation of certain general economic
> questions. The problem of nationality would otherwise turn into
> a serious disease affecting our state, which could destroy it, as it
> has other states.

Both Arab and Jewish exclusivism and domination were unacceptable.
Beware, he wrote, "of the fetishism of a master-race!" Kohn concluded
with a literal call to go "beyond borders": "Only when mankind's ideas

Portrait of Hans Kohn. Courtesy of the Leo Baeck Institute, New York.

change and a new spirit fills it, when the League of Nations—a free association of all peoples—has blown open the state frontiers, will the nations' lust for power and greed for acquisition fade away."[77]

For a variety of—mainly unjustified—reasons (among them, this unpopular political stance), Martin Buber is very much an ignored (though not forgotten) thinker in contemporary Israel. Yet at the time, his writings and backing gave the ideas of these circles a stature and inter-

Shmuel Hugo Bergman. Courtesy of the Zionist Archives.

national dimension they would otherwise have lacked. Time and time again, Buber sought to theoretically balance the claims of his dual commitment to Zionism and the rights of the Arabs.[78] Morality, he argued, was meaningful only within, not above, the public battle; moral principles were pertinent only to corrupt not perfect worlds. Moreover, they had to be applied to each given, unique situation. Ontological truths were bound to time and history and were established through dialogue. Buber thus still upheld Jewish national claims yet remained convinced that this did not necessarily have to negate the rights of the Arabs. Even

Portrait of Robert Weltsch; 1935 (Photograph by Herbert
Sonnenfeld; Berlin). Courtesy of the Leo Baeck Institute,
New York.

for the great pioneering idealists, he wrote in retrospect, "the finest
people among us did not pretend to remain guiltless, we were perforce
reducing the space for future generations of the Arab nation." Yet he
rejected the *Realpolitik* zero-sum power logic of this position. While
Jewish needs and national aspirations, their connections to the land, remained legitimate, even urgent, one had to remain cognizant of the
effect of one's own community and actions on others. We will, he de-

Standing portrait of Martin Buber; 1930. Courtesy of the Leo
Baeck Institute, New York.

clared, "say to ourselves: we will do no more injustice to others than we
are forced to do in order to exist."

In later 1956 musings he argued that by rejecting the program for a
binational state and the later suggestion for a federation of Near Eastern countries, "the ground was prepared for the [Arab] refugee program

and thus for an enormous increase in our objective guilt."[79] In an earlier essay he wrote:

> The migration and resettlement of a nation, or of large parts of a nation, in the conditions of the world today, a world in which there are apparently no viable empty regions, necessarily entail obvious "injustices" to another population, whose living space has been encroached upon—if not in the present generation, at any rate for future generations. With regard to the issue of "necessity," there is a crucial difference between expansive settlement, seeking to enlarge the borders of the property and rule of the colonizing nation, and concentrative settlement, in which a nation which has lost its organic center seeks to return to its origins. We, whose settlement is concentrative may weigh our "righteousness" in the scales against the "injustice" which we give rise to, especially in this crucial moment [April 1945], unprecedented in human history. For since large portions of our people's expanse were shattered, the task of renewal, the need for regeneration which is the property of an organic center, has become correspondingly greater. But here again, the main point is recognizing limits. If one has the intention of driving people who are bound to the soil out of their homeland, then one has exceeded those limits. Here we confront an inalienable right, the right of a man who cultivates the earth to remain upon it. I shall never agree that in this matter it is possible to justify injustice by pleading values or destinies. If there is in history a power of righteousness that punishes evil-doing, it will intervene here and react. Transfers of population effectuated by conquerors have always been avenged; and this shall be done to the nation that attempts to answer evil with evil. I will seek to protect my nation by keeping it from setting false limits.[80]

We should note that what distinguished these binationalists from other Zionists was not necessarily the mainstream's refusal to acknowledge or recognize an Arab presence. Contemporary historiography has effectively refuted that widespread notion. Zionists of all stripes were indeed aware of this, but given the fact that they saw no way of solving the conflict and that their most central preoccupation was with what

they regarded to be the overwhelmingly urgent needs and interests of the
Jewish people, they could or would "not allow the moral dilemmas at-
tendant to the Arab question to affect in any fundamental way the political priorities of the movement."[81] Paul Mendes-Flohr has argued that
it was not ethical sensitivity per se that marked out the binationalists but
rather their insistence upon the political centrality and relevance of the
moral aspect of the Arab question. They consistently refused, as much
as the mainstream tried, to minimize or elide or sidetrack the issue. The
ideological framework and existential sensibilities of the binationalists
threatened or at least moderated the prevalent mechanisms of elision or
repression of the "Arab question."

To be sure, their positions were often based upon what they believed
to be the imperatives of ethical principles and not necessarily upon personal crises of conscience that followed real encounters with Arabs on
the ground. Hans Kohn wrote that his position was "not prompted by
any particular sympathy for the Arabs. . . . I was not concerned with the
Arabs but with the Jews, their Jewishness, and the confirmation of their
[humane] values."[82] Similarly, Gershom Scholem—whose highly Judeo-
centric worldview makes his early adherence to binationalism especially
intriguing and in need of special explanation[83]—envisaged an esoteric,
highly charged theological and metaphysical form of Zionism, one "which
God knows, originally had nothing to do with Englishmen or Arabs."[84]
In retrospect, Scholem candidly admitted that his membership in Brit
Shalom

> was for "external" purposes. "Domestically," I was something else.
> The Arab question was a controversial one, and our approach to it
> caused us to be suspected of liquidating Zionism—a charge that I
> think is unjustified. The debate will not be easily be settled. . . .
> But this matter has never been crucial for me. For me it was a
> matter of conduct.[85]

But among other binationalists existential crises of conscience were
palpable and persistent.[86] Throughout his 1927 visit to Palestine, Martin Buber reported

> the heavy feeling that our work was fateful/disastrous (*verhaeng-
> nisvolles*), an unintended sin. We inserted ourselves into the

house of other people, in which there were a few other rooms, without speaking to them. Yes, through the Balfour Declaration we are in the situation of soldiers who have been quartered in a stranger's house. Given such an unintended sin the Bible enjoins a sacrifice, but what sacrifice should we bring?[87]

For Hugo Bergman, the anguish entered into the depth of his dreams. "Yesterday," he reported in September 1950,

> I had a dream about the atrocities the Jews committed against the Arabs. . . . I stand in an open carriage at a train station in Israel. The train is still stationary and in front of it on the platform stands an Arab woman and begs. She was dressed in black and turned away from me. I said to myself: I'll give her a handout and then she turns to me. Then the train starts moving and I cannot carry out my intention. . . . I interpreted my dream thus: one should not defer giving help to the Arabs or one will lose the opportunity to perform a good deed. Frau Schärff thinks this is a completely false interpretation. My unconscious had the intention to compensate for my conscious outlook. She shows me that the Arab woman was *turned away* from me, and as long as this was true, there was nothing I could do. The unconscious was here ironising my "good heart."[88]

(What could better illustrate the Central European "beyond the border" consciousness than this psychoanalytic sensibility, the subtle awareness of the self-ironizing dynamics of the unconscious and the search for more and more inclusive metaperspectives?)[89]

But regardless of individual differences, and whether this was experientially or only theoretically articulated, the common concerns and emphases of these circles did render their mental and moral radars unusually empathic, sensitive to the concerns of the other side. (For their critics, this was a disastrously naive, altruistic position in a conflict in which there was no possibility of meaningful compromise and that demanded intense self-interest. They would, doubtless, have approved the contemporary witticism that these were liberals who could not even take their own side in an argument.) Many of their declarations still have a strikingly contemporary resonance (where empathy and the "humanization" of the enemy and the "other" still remain strikingly difficult). In the face of Arab outrages in 1929, Hans Kohn wrote: "Of course the Arabs attacked us in August. Since they have no armies, they could not obey the rules of war. They perpetrated all the barbaric acts that are characteristic of a colonial revolt."[90] Even in the face of the atrocities they had committed, Bergman declared, no one should hate the Arab nation. Indeed, "our heart aches when we hear that the army has detonated Arab homes or when we hear about young Arabs who have fallen in battle."[91] It is, wrote Robert Weltsch in 1925 "a horribly fatal situation that Jewish festivals in the country are automatically seen as days of mourning for the Arabs. This brings with it the danger that one will experience the Jewish festival as a kind of 'triumph' over one's opponent and he will also feel this."[92] The binationalists resisted this zero-sum consciousness, the almost reflexive figuration of the "other" as necessarily alien and enemy, a consciousness that prevails so strongly through to today.

By probing the limits and proper boundaries of a justified nationalism, Buber and the binationalists went against the normative grain. But clearly the application of this legacy was bound to undergo strain (at times to the breaking point) as it came into contact with the realities and exigencies of this new world. The Arab-Zionist conflict and its proper diagnosis has always been an enormously complicated issue, and even if these circles more or less mapped out the moral guidelines, in response to changing situations and their own perceived needs, they were not always consistent and, indeed, were more often than not confused as to the nature and directions of policy that should be adopted. These circles, let us not forget, were for the creation of a Jewish national home (however understood) and for Jewish settlement and immigration (if not statehood)—although the location of such settlement within Palestine and the numbers that should be allowed were always a matter of debate. These aims did not always sit easily with events on the ground or even with their views on the Arabs. Thus, especially in the face of intermittent Arab resistance, rioting, and violence, they often adopted the line that only *greater* immigration would render the Jewish presence as an established reality, and demonstrate that the Jews could not be shocked into submission. Only through the power of numbers, some argued, would Arab-Jewish accommodation eventually become possible.[93] This was as true for Bergman in 1921 as it was for Gershom Scholem in the wake of a

crucial turning point, the Arab riots of 1929. In a series of letters to his
mother, Scholem—who, rather surprisingly, was at the time galvanized
into more, not less, radical Brit Shalom activity by these traumatizing
events[94]—wrote: "What will be, one cannot yet say. What is certain is
that if the Jewish settlement was double in size, the Arabs would not
have risked this matter."[95]

Viewed with hindsight, the various scenarios and blueprints envisaged by the binationalists reveal a curious mix of ingenuity—and naïveté.
Many of their earlier ruminations centered around the critique of European imperialism, the nascent rise of Arab nationalism, and the possible role that Jews in Palestine could assume within this "awakening of
the Eastern Peoples."[96] They drew up plans for reciprocal municipal and
communal autonomy, a common parliament, various possible federative
arrangements—a difficult task, indeed, in the face of the absence of positive heterogeneous national Western models, as Yfaat Weiss has pointed
out. And when, as they often did, their deliberations hit the usual stum-
bling block—that there were no Arabs willing to negotiate even the
most minimal of Jewish national positions—their "beyond the border"
sophistication occasionally helped them to rationalize their plight. Thus
Scholem sometimes invoked his lifelong reliance upon a kind of salva-
tional dialectics: the very presentation of Brit Shalom's program and its
negation by the Arabs, he argued, would certainly usher in a historical
dialectic in which an internal Arab opposition to that negation would
emerge and eventually accept these conditions. In so doing, Brit Shalom
would itself create the needed negotiating partner.[97] Reflections such as
these were characteristic of these circles whose meetings increasingly expressed an almost equal measure of conviction and confusion.

Indeed, the exponents of binationalism were increasingly and acutely
aware of their own failings and impotence. In 1941 Magnes sadly and
bitterly complained to the circle "about our lack of activity, our lack of
courage. . . . [W]e have become old and have not acquired young members who are prepared to go down our path."[98] This was a concern that
some of the "old faithful" members carried with them even after the
proclamation of statehood. After an Ichud gathering in September
1951, Bergman noted: "I left the meeting with a bitter feeling. On the
one hand, the burden of responsibility for what was happening to the
Arabs in Israel, on the other, the total impotence of this circle. And so

I spent the entire day with the feeling of weakness and inadequacy."[99]
The canny, Salman Schocken, who was the patron of many of Brit
Shalom's leading members, early on shrewdly questioned

> the political savvy of professors and scholars who at best knew
> the Arab masses as their gardeners or day laborers, and whose
> ethical notions came from textbooks. His hunch was that only
> people who actually worked side by side with Arabs, namely the
> Russians, could forge a relationship with them—and one based
> less on condescending morality than on mutual self-interest and
> respect.

Perhaps he got at the nub of the strain of this transplanted German-
Jewish humanism in its new, rough environment when he told his colleagues: "You'll never win a political fight for power because you'll never
muster the will for it."[100] Not surprisingly he told them to go back to
what they knew best: *Kultur.*

But such confusion and self-doubt was only a small component of
the strains that attached to the binationalist position. Connected critics
may be admirable creatures but they are vulnerable ones. They always
have to carefully balance criticism with their own sense of belonging. As
Ernst Simon later put it: "Critique without solidarity is rootless. Solidarity without critique lacks direction."[101] In this case, the tension, finding the balance, was especially problematic because these figures were
operating within a still insecure, developing national movement where
solidarity was at a premium, as was sensitivity to group loyalty. Issues of
possible betrayal were always close to the surface.[102] Was it not funda-
mentally dishonest, one of them wondered in 1929, to sit on the soil and
reap the benefits of Zionist national funds and at the same time rail
against the repressive Arab policies of those very funds?[103]

Many of the binationalist stresses and strains were connected to their
fragile status as intellectuals and academics at Hebrew University. Indeed, since its founding there has been an inbuilt, continuing tension
between the university, on the one hand, as an essentially "national" institution serving the Zionist cause and the Jewish People, and, on the
other hand, as one dedicated to more universal principles and general
societal needs. Advocates of the former position argued that "the university is no institution for itself, but rather a part of our aspirations to

create a national home. Any matter that could harm that new life should not be advocated by the university."[104] The binationalists affirmed that a central role of the university was indeed to serve the Jewish People, but they insisted that it also act as the site of tolerance. The university, unlike church or state, wrote Judah Magnes, had no dogmas, was the natural home of minorities and had the right to say *no.*[105] Bergman and Weltsch envisaged a Hebrew-Arabic university where Arabs and Arab studies could assume their due place.[106] Their political opponents (especially the Revisionists) accused them of a kind of a detached, moralistic, appeasement mentality.

> With respect to the problems that face the nation and its youth, the professorial denizens of Mount Scopus [Har Hatzofim, site of the Hebrew University] are indeed observers [*tzofim*]. Their conscience is quiet; their soul is tranquil. . . . They are not party to what takes place below: they reside above on the heights of a moral Olympus.[107]

(These kinds of criticisms persist to this day. Indeed, they have grown even more extreme. Using statehood as the unquestionable, absolute measure, Yoram Hazony has recently mounted an injudicious attack on these German intellectuals as betrayers of the Zionist cause.)[108]

These were all irritations but the major binationalist strain consisted of the meeting of their ideas and sensibilities with the political realities of Palestine. Critics of the binationalist position—from Ze'ev Jabotinsky leftward—had always maintained that, given the acknowledged or implicit Zionist desire to create a Jewish majority in Palestine, the Arab-Jewish conflict was inevitable and not amenable to moderate or patchwork compromises.[109] One of the most effective German-Zionist opponents of the binational position was the revisionist Richard Lichtheim (1885–1963). Father of the famous Marxist scholar George Lichtheim, he articulated some of the most pungent criticisms that, to this day, constitute the fundamentals of the argument. In a political debate with other German Zionists at the end of 1929, he declared:

> It is false to say that the Arabs have exactly the same rights in Palestine. We do not contest their rights as inhabitants of the land, but it is impossible to compare the historic rights of the

Jewish people with that of the fellach on his soil. . . . The world accepts Zionism as a grand historical project that must be implemented with real means, or not at all. . . . One must understand that the Arabs are against Zionism. For where in all the world has it happened, that a population inhabiting a half-empty land, looks positively upon a Volk of a quite different historical development—for we are going to Palestine as Europeans—stream in great numbers, buy land as much as they can, occupy economic positions and bring in as many people as they can. An understanding with the Arabs will come when, under the protection of the Mandate, we have become so strong in the country that the Arabs will have to accept the National Home as a fait accompli. Before that, not. And that is why it is completely true, but unavoidable, that we colonize Palestine on the grounds of *power*. We cannot retreat from this line of politics now, or else all will be ruined. Only on the ground of power will the Jewish National Home be developed. When the Jewish commonwealth is a fait accompli, when we eventually become a majority, then I too will fight all Jewish chauvinism."[110]

It was most probably inevitable that in the course of time, and the hardening of conflict, there would be various changes of heart and disappointment among those who were centrally involved with the binationalist moment. For many, let it be noted, this occurred before the Nazi threat became apparent (not to mention the declaration of the State in 1948). Already by 1928–29, on the two extreme edges of the movement, these strains led either to a sad rejection of the ideas of Brit Shalom as unrealistic (as in the case of Arthur Ruppin) or to resignation from the Zionist movement for not taking these ideas seriously and not attempting to actually put them into effect (as in the case of Hans Kohn).[111] It is a measure of the uncertainty and ongoing nature of the conflict, and the competing narratives that seek to understand and shape it, that both these positions still resonate with a rather depressing familiarity.

By 1929 Ruppin, who originally believed that through rational settlement planning, mutual economic interests, and racial affinities, a common interest between Arabs and Jews could be forged, now declared the conflict insoluble. The disputes over land, labor, and immigration were so basic that all ideas of a common constitution, parliament, or federation were, he felt, simply fantasies.[112] "My attitude to Zionism," he declared later, "has changed in the last ten years. I always recognized the importance of a solution to the Arab question, but didn't think the Arabs would so quickly acquire power and that *so* bitter an enmity between them and the Jews would develop."[113] In a candid 1931 letter to Victor Jacobson, he summed up the Arab-Zionist situation thus: "*What we can get from them we cannot use, and what we need we cannot get*" (Ruppin's emphasis). Much of the problem revolved around the question of the vulnerability of minority rights and the desire for an ultimate majority state (which Ruppin, rather revealingly, characterized as an East European Zionist aim!): "The Arabs," he wrote,

> would allow us in the best of cases the protection of national minority rights in an Arab State according to the model of nationality rights in Eastern Europe. But we know from the situation in Eastern Europe how little incentive there is for a majority that has State power in its hands, to actually grant the minority full national equality. The fate of the Jewish minority in Palestine will always depend upon the goodwill of the Arab majority, which sits at the rudder of State. For the East European Jews that constitute the overwhelming majority of all Zionists, this would be entirely unsatisfactory and would kill enthusiasm for the Zionist matter and for Palestine. A Zionism that would agree to such a compromise would not have the East European Jews behind it and would quickly become a *Zionism without Zionists*.[114]

Ruppin understood that the mass attraction to Zionism resided in the desire and demand for a sovereign majority state (for a historically vulnerable minority this catered as much to deeply felt psychological needs as it did to political ones). One of the more striking aspects of the radical binationalist position was either to surrender this demand, and limit, while not ceding, the right to immigration, or to formulate political and constitutional arrangements in which neither side could dominate. While Ruppin, in the face of greater polarization, came to reject these notions as both impractical and undesirable, and quite unacceptable to the Arabs in the wake of the 1929 riots, Hans Kohn protested that the problem was not the binationalist humanist sensibility but rather the

Zionist indifference to it, and the reluctance even of the adherents of Brit Shalom to seriously pursue this alternative. "In the midst of this crisis," he wrote,

> it was still possible to turn over a new leaf and to adopt a fresh attitude after the [initial] shock. . . . This opportunity has been missed. The overwhelming majority of Zionists feel justified in pursuing a course which I cannot follow. . . . We have been in Palestine for twelve years without having even once made a serious attempt at seeking through negotiations the consent of the indigenous people. We have been relying upon Great Britain's military might. We have set ourselves goals which by their very nature had to lead to conflict with the Arabs. We ought to have recognized that these goals would be the cause, the just cause, of a national uprising against us. . . . Having come to this country [as immigrants], we were duty bound to come up with constitutional proposals which, without doing serious harm to Arab rights and liberty, would have also allowed for our free cultural and social development. But for twelve years we pretended that the Arabs did not exist and were glad when we were not reminded of their existence. . . . The old beaten paths of national policy as they were followed by the European peoples in the nineteenth century, the Eastern people in the twentieth century and now by the Jewish people, are for me no longer valid. We must search for completely new and different paths. Sometimes I still retain a proud hope that the Jews—nationally conscious Jews—might forge these new paths.[115]

By October 1929, just before he left Brit Shalom and the Zionist movement as a whole, he was prepared to argue only for protected minority status for the Jews in Palestine.[116]

But these were the two extreme edges of the movement. For others, clearly, the most significant strains and shifts in their positions occurred a little later and were a function of the dramatic historical events of the 1930s and 1940s—the rise of Nazism, the destruction of European Jewry, the establishment of the State of Israel and the ensuing 1948 war. Gershom Scholem (whose intense immanent philosophy of Judaism in any case fairly canceled out the liberal-cosmopolitan sensibility so marked in other members of these circles) is a case in point. Scholem was, throughout, aware of the strains entailed in his Brit Shalom stance. "We are aware," he wrote together with Bergman and Simon in the wake of the 1929 Arab riots,

> what a very difficult undertaking it is, under the prevailing political and psychological conditions, to simultaneously pursue a reconciliatory politics with the Arabs and to ensure our defense against attacks of the kind that we have just experienced. It seems to us, however, that there is no other way.[117]

As late as 1937, he reported to Walter Benjamin, that he was "personally against partition as such, since I believe joint Arab-Jewish sovereignty in the whole of Palestine to be the more ideal solution." Yet, given the depressing weight of events and policies, he added: "but this opportunity is one we will probably never be granted."[118]

Scholem's views hardened as circumstances worsened. His 1946 letter to Hannah Arendt (whose binationalist views strengthened during that time)[119]—given the intractable issues and arguments it contains—strikes a depressingly familiar contemporary chord:

> My political faith, if it exists at all is—anarchistic. But I cannot take offence with the Jews when they do not take into consideration progressive theories that no one else practices. I would vote with an equally heavy heart for the binational State as for partition. . . . The Arabs have not agreed to any single solution, whether federative, State or bi-national, insofar as it connected with Jewish immigration. And I am convinced that the confrontation with the Arabs on the basis of a fait accompli like partition will make things easier than without it. In any event, I have no idea how the Zionists could go about obtaining an agreement with the Arabs. . . . Unfortunately, it is by no means idiotic when the Zionist politicians declare that, given the sabotage events made by the British administration, there is no chance of reaching any agreement, however formulated. Certainly, as an old Brit Shalom man, I have heard the precise opposite argued. But I am not sufficiently presumptuous to maintain that our politics would likewise not have found precisely the same opponents, for they

are not interested in our moral or political sentiments, but rather in the question whether or not we are present here at all."[120]

Subsequently, Scholem conceded (in a 1972 letter to George Licht-heim) that Brit Shalom had falsely read the historical situation, "admit-tedly only when one takes into account that Hitler totally changed the perspective." Given the benefit of hindsight, however, Scholem added: "Whether we could have achieved more had Hitler not come to power, I still today doubt." History, he wrote elsewhere, had mocked his dreams.[121] During the 1948 war, Scholem upbraided Ernst Simon for not enlisting his son in the army (and leaving the country in order to do this), precisely because he *was* a leading member of the Ichud.[122] Scholem clearly made his peace with the State and many (though not all) of its empirical realities. Indeed, over the years—especially with his supposedly more cosmopolitan friends—his posture became decidedly more defen-sive, even patriotic. Increasingly he defined himself as an unabashed sectarian who saw no reason to submit to universal standards that no one, except the Jews, was expected to follow.[123]

There were others in the ranks of the binationalists like Georg Lan-dauer, Max Kreuzberger, and Robert Weltsch who viewed things with less equanimity and regarded statehood as a kind of betrayal of the best humanist ideals of Zionism and emigrated.[124] Others, like Buber and Bergman remained, accepted statehood, and adapted their critique to the new circumstances, keeping the plight of the refugees and the Arabs in Israel at the center of much of their work and thought.[125] And while all these binationalists were faced with the foundational question posed by Buber in 1949—"Should the Ichud Accept the Decree of History?"[126]— it is noteworthy that even for those who answered in the negative, none of them became virulent antinationalists, but instead, clung to their humanist cultural versions of the Zionist ideal (in their view it was the power-political, territorial and state-oriented Jewish nationalism that was deviant).[127]

By the time statehood was declared, the binationalists were of course quite aware that historical events had invalidated most of their assump-tions and predictions (as Ernst Simon put it in his masterly summing up of what he called their "moral politics"). The Ichud, he wrote, had erred in assuming that in any military confrontation with the Arabs, the Jews would lose; they had failed to recognize the fundamental changes and urgency for the Zionist movement brought about by the Holocaust[128] and, above all,

> underestimated the desire and determination of the Jewish na-
> tion to establish a state of its own. Ihud was composed of intel-
> lectuals who in their political thinking had gone beyond the no-
> tion of the state, believing that the social and political conditions
> of modern life required broader and more comprehensive forms
> of national and social organization. They did not understand the
> inner logic of a nationalist movement that was seeking belatedly
> to obtain what other peoples had long enjoyed: the concentration
> of its people in some one territory with at least a minimum of
> political "sovereignty."[129]

Now that the State had been created, Simon added, there was "the great moral opportunity of showing to what extent we seriously be-lieve in those claims for universal right and justice which we have never tired of making on other peoples during the long years of our Diaspora existence."[130]

The mistaken, often naive, assessments, and the moralistic postures and elitism of the binationalist intellectuals, were apparent, then, not only to their opponents but to them as well. Thus, as a rather sad and resigned Bergman put it to a guest in 1964 concerning the lessons of Cyprus:

> [T]he strivings for a bi-national State were doomed in the face of
> what we now experience as a flaming nationalism. . . . I believe in
> man, I believe too that nationalism is only a transitional phenome-
> non. Yet it is a fact today. It would be better for people of differ-
> ent nations to live side by side, to live together, to learn together.
> But if peaceful emigration/removal (*Übersiedlung*) was possible
> [the Sudeten Germans are here intended] wouldn't this be a bet-
> ter solution? . . . It is at base the same problem as separation in
> marriage. Should we force people to live together and to make
> their lives hell, when another solution exists? Assuming admit-
> tedly, that the separation is voluntary, and if it is possible, to do it
> so that those who have been moved suffer as little as possible.[131]

Yet, how wrong—or merely defeatist—was Simon when he wrote: "We always feared that the establishment of a Jewish state would sharply reduce the chances of a Jewish-Arab understanding or even render it impossible"? There are those, of course, who say that it is precisely the State—and its factual, unvanquishable power—that is the only guarantor of such a future eventuality. Sadly, the conflict continues and the decision is not yet in. But it is clear that many of the concerns raised by these Central European intellectuals continue to haunt us.

Binationalism has once again, although in altered form, become the topic of intense scholarly, intellectual, and political interest and debate.[132] The new turns in, and contemporary crisis of, Israeli-Palestinian relations, the search for—as well as perceived threat of—alternative scenarios, has, of course, much to do with this.[133] There is also some truth in Hagit Lavsky's observation that Brit Shalom has received so much historiographic attention precisely because it furnishes a simultaneously consoling and apologetic narrative: it at once reinforces the Zionist self-image as humane and moral, in search of genuine peace, while at the same time demonstrating the utopian nature of the binational dream as having been politically unrealizable from the outset—thereby justifying the path that the Zionist movement ultimately took.[134]

Yet, very much in the tradition of these intellectuals who went beyond the geographical borders of their birth and who questioned conventional conceptual and political ones, their legacy may help us not to rationalize and justify past actions but to retain a critical and humanizing impulse in the midst of increasing desperation, violence, and inhumanity. These thinkers sought not to abolish nationalism but rather provide it with a more tolerant, gentle face—a goal that, in the present circumstances, may be exceedingly difficult but is no less admirable for that.[135] George Mosse once declared that the nationalism of those we have discussed here was "a unique phenomenon in our own century and the only attempt I know of not to abolish but to humanize nationalism in an ever more nationalistic age."[136]

Among others, it fell to Mosse and a generation of émigré historians to analyze and transmit that variegated yet identifiably German-Jewish legacy to the world, a legacy that the Nazis did everything to destroy. But these historians personally experienced the Nazi rise to power, and

thus were also determined to unravel the origins, nature, and conse-
quence of National Socialism—in such a way that they themselves embodied the same humanizing cultural sensibility that they so masterfully
depicted in their work. Theirs was a sensibility that subtly, but clearly,
demarcated them from the German social historians engaged in the
same investigation. It is to the adventures of these émigré historians,
who left their old borders behind them and in the process created new
intellectual frontiers, that we must now turn.

2

The Tensions of Historical *Wissenschaft*

The Émigré Historians and the Making of German Cultural History

Whoever deals with the past, will always have to confront himself.
—Reinhart Koselleck[1]

Most of the intellectuals we encountered in the last chapter left their Central European geographical borders well before the Nazi rise to power. As ideological Zionists, indeed, their early migration to Palestine was marked by commitment and enthusiasm. For them, this was not exile but its overcoming; a return, as it were, to one's natural borders—even if, at the same time, they continually questioned and subverted conventional understandings of those mental and physical boundaries. The cultural historians who are the comparative subject of this chapter constitute a quite different case. A generation or two younger than the Zionist binationalists, their lives were directly affected by the experience of National Socialism. Their migration—to Britain, Palestine, and the United States—was neither voluntary nor ideological but, rather, an immediate product of the Nazi persecution of the Jews. It was as refugees that they left their old borders behind, integrated into new ones and in so doing (among other things) pondered and redefined the history of the country that they had left behind.

Theodor Adorno (to whom we shall return in the next chapter) once commented that part of the damage inflicted on intellectuals in the course of their emigration consisted in the sapping of the historical dimension that previously nourished their knowledge.[2] It is an open question as to whether the historians to be considered here were, indeed, "mutilated" in the sense Adorno intends. What is certain, however, is that these historians were young enough to allow their border crossing not so much to diminish them but rather to creatively enrich and enlarge their historical perspectives on a contemporary experience crucially in need of critical evaluation. Indeed, my claim is that in this process, historians like Peter Gay (1923), Walter Laqueur (1921), George Mosse (1919–1999), and Fritz Stern (1926) virtually reinvented German cultural and intellectual history and recast our understanding of it.[3] They did so in the 1960s, long before the "linguistic turn," and on the basis of epistemological assumptions and contextual emphases quite different from the "constructivist" and textual insistencies of the later "new cultural history," a point to which we shall later return.

I want to approach this theme comparatively by contrasting this cultural and intellectual approach with the more or less simultaneous emergence—from the 1960s on—of a new, committed "social" history developed in Germany by young German historians (exemplified by Hans-Ulrich Wehler, Jürgen Kocka, the Mommsen brothers—Hans and Wolfgang—Reinhard Rürup, Martin Brozsat, Heinrich Winkler, Wolfgang Schieder, and others). This will hopefully shed light not only on the biographical influences on the production of historical knowledge but also on the ways in which different ethnonational identities, generations, and geographical locations tend to color our biases and nudge historical emphases in one direction or another. It may perhaps, too, shed light—rather unexpectedly—on what, somewhat clumsily, has become known as "the German-Jewish" dialogue. In its post–Second World War guise, that dialogue, I suggest, becomes especially interesting not when the differences are great and obvious, but when, at least on the surface, they appear to be almost nonexistent. Indeed, it becomes most intriguing when the tensions are largely unacknowledged and unspoken (perhaps, even unconscious), when the discursive differences and relationships are at their most subtle. It is then that the charged moral, emotional, and intellectual stakes around the "German" and "Jewish" pasts become paradoxically most apparent.

It is, of course, a truism to state that the modern German past is a particularly explosive, emotionally loaded subject, one peculiarly prone to all kinds of interested projections and transferences. As one of the subjects of this chapter, Peter Gay, has written:

> [T]he German historian, however bravely he attempts to see the whole picture and to see it plain . . . is bound to be emotionally involved in, and often crippled by his materials. He, more than most historians, is exposed to the risk that psychoanalysts, wary of permitting their work to be distorted by feelings of affection or aversion toward their analysands, call counter-transference. The writing of German history is laden with, mainly unexamined, counter-transferences."[4]

At first glance, the comparative subjects of this chapter—the German social historians and the German-Jewish émigré cultural and intellectual historians—appear to be particularly inappropriate exemplifications of these tendencies. For they all must be considered postwar "good guys." Both groups defined themselves squarely within the liberal or Social Democratic "progressive" camps. Their reconfigurations of German history sought to throw off the apologetic yoke of a nationalist, politically and methodologically conservative *Zunft* (guild). The social and cultural historians alike were galvanized by the need to overcome the idealist, historicist tradition and to evaluate the past in essentially distanced, *critical* terms.[5] There could be no question of composing, in historicist spirit, an empathic, epic narrative of the Third Reich or *identifying* with it. Above all, their commonalities sprung from, and were animated by, a single great quest: to comprehend the unprecedented rise and nature of Nazism.

To be sure, earlier on within Germany, the patricians of the Zunft, Friedrich Meinecke[6] and Gerhard Ritter[7] (to name but the most prominent) and Hannah Arendt[8] (from without), had also undertaken such investigations. For them, indigenous German traditions and developments played only a minor role in explaining the etiology and disposition of National Socialism: the real causes (and blame) were deflected outward onto post-1789 Europe, where the origins of a formless mass society and totalitarian democracy were to be found.

Both the social and the cultural-intellectual historians rejected these accounts as defensive and apologetic, and insisted upon intimately linking the Third Reich to immanent elements within German society itself. Both, each in their own ways, indeed formulated what became a kind of historical orthodoxy: the critical *Sonderweg* version of German history. This (by now familiar) narrative held that modern German historical and political development was fatefully peculiar, illiberal, and misshapen. It argued that an obstinately and anachronistically authoritarian society would bring forth Nazism as the extreme manifestation, the last fruits of a foiled and disfiguring modernization process. (Like all orthodoxies this was eventually to be seriously challenged, and even revised by some of the proponents themselves—but, for present purposes, that is beside the point.)[9]

Given the rather basic commonalities between the social and the cultural historians, what is at issue? Inbuilt into all historical methods and approaches are certain principles of selection, emphases, and omissions. These, consciously or unconsciously, contain numerous narrative biases, interpretive strategies, and ideological preferences.[10] I would like to argue here that, despite their surface similarities, the more or less simultaneous emergence in the 1960s of the increasingly influential, tone-setting school of the "social history" of modern Germany and the—less studied and remarked[11]—émigré "cultural-intellectual" equivalent, emerged from significantly different, emotionally fraught textures of feeling, experience, and perception and resulted in rather differently nuanced representations of that traumatizing past. Their respective biographies, group membership, geographical location, and generational experiences played a crucial role in shaping these connected yet contrasting narratives. The resulting historiographies ultimately reflected divergent experiences and interests that went far beyond mere methodological differences.[12] What I am suggesting is that at some—not always conscious (and almost never explicit)—level these can be also be read as interested "German" and "Jewish" counternarratives, histories written within or beyond the geographical limits and mental boundaries of the Federal Republic, divergent readings of a contested and threatening past.[13]

Both groups focused on the same period (the *Kaiserreich* through the end of the Weimar Republic); both sought to grasp the historical roots of Nazism; both ended up with some kind of Sonderweg thesis. Yet, their respective foci, the centers of attention, were strikingly different. The German social historians were overwhelmingly concerned with the conditions that resulted in the collapse of the Weimar Republic; their works analyzed in great detail the social, economic, and political structures that eventuated in the breakdown of democratic rule.[14] Their great symbolic date, the major event to be explained—and avoided in the future—centered around 1933.[15] This date was important too for the cultural historians, but for them the implicit epicenter, the nodal point, the scandal in need of accounting, was 1941–42. Although (certainly at the beginning) they seldom directly dealt with the Holocaust per se, their emphasis on ideology, stereotypes, anti-Semitism, cultural breakdown, and the complex machinations of German-Jewish relations, rendered that event historically, one might say ontologically, crucial.[16] For the social historians, if I may put it this way, the Sonderweg was the collapse of liberal democracy; for the cultural historians it was anti-Semitism, genocide, and related Nazi atrocities. The two may have been related but they were neither conceptually nor existentially identical.

I am aware that defining these as "German" and "Jewish"—or "home" versus "refugee"—narratives is problematic. In the first place, if anyone adopted a highly critical attitude toward their own national past, it was the German social historians. That, indeed, was their defining credo. It is clear too, that the hermetic "German"-"Jewish" distinction, apart from its potentially essentialist connotations, blurs an important datum: The cultural historians all heralded from highly acculturated, liberal German backgrounds that would have dismissed out of hand any such elemental division. Fritz Stern came from a family that had converted from Judaism to Lutheranism and was baptized at birth. The Mosse family constituted an integral part of the German-Jewish cultural and economic elite, identified with the Jewish community and the Reform movement, but always with a quintessentially liberal and integrationist emphasis. Peter Gay once placed himself at

one end on the spectrum of the German-Jewish experience. . . . My parents saw themselves as wholly assimilated into German society. Both were principled, and in the case of my father, aggressive atheists. The earliest "information" I got about religion was anticlerical humor, and since the only religious people my father, who had grown up in a small town in Upper Silesia, had known were Jews, his stories were anti-Jewish stories. . . . Not surprisingly, my parents had officially left the Jewish faith, and lived in the Weimar Republic as "konfessionslos." So, of course, did I, and without difficulties. Only Hitler made me into a Jew and, it turned out, not a very good one."[17]

Indeed, after settling in the United States, Gay "was accused more than once of not being 'Jewish enough.'"[18] If Walter Laqueur's youthful attitudes were less extreme than Gay's, they were not entirely dissimilar: "My education," he writes, "was not Jewish, I did not attend a Jewish school, and most of my early friends were not Jewish either. I knew little about Judaism and was not particularly interested in the subject."[19]

It is thus certainly not my intention to simplistically reduce the respective historiography of my subjects to their national or confessional provenance. After all, the early functional-structural study of Nazism was formulated by Ernst Frankel and Franz Neumann, and an important pioneer of German social history was Hans Rosenberg—all German-Jewish émigrés—while certain postwar German historians such as Thomas Nipperdey and Reinhart Koselleck demonstrated a fine sensitivity to the "cultural" and ideational dimensions of their history. It would thus be absurd to argue that the German social historians and the Jewish cultural historians under discussion were somehow determined, ethnically driven, to argue in the way they did. What I am suggesting, however, is that divergent experiential, situational, and identificatory factors played an important role in the genesis, nature, and emphases of their work and that any assessment of their respective achievements and biases, their historical location and legacy, will have to take these dimensions into account.

Let us turn first to the social historians. There is an admirable, self-conscious generation of German left-liberal public intellectuals—the names Jürgen Habermas, Günther Grass, Ralf Dahrendorff, Rainer Lepsius, Walter Jens spring immediately to mind—a self-constituted, by now patriarchal, elite which, for over thirty years, has shaped much of the intellectual, cultural, and perhaps even political tone of the Bundesrepublik.[20] It is largely they who created its intensely critical atmosphere, insisted upon a radical break from the country's questionable past, and contributed to the creation and maintenance of its constitutional, democratic norms.[21] For our purposes it is important to note that many of those involved in social history's rise to prominence belong squarely to, and played leading roles within, this cohort. Beginning as young radicals, opposed to the old mandarins of the Zunft, they themselves became the tone setters, *the* Establishment—even if they often presented themselves as an embattled minority.[22] Hans-Ulrich Wehler is only the best-known and most influential of these. (They are themselves presently becoming the subjects of research and assessment, and, as we shall shortly see, have become the targets of generational attack by younger German scholars and historians).[23]

In retrospect, it seems clear that their historical emphases—on 1933, foiled and failed modernization processes, and the stubborn hold of authoritarian and conservative structures—reflected an urgent concern just as much with the contemporary and forward-looking needs of the nascent *Bundesrepublik,* as with the past.[24] Their great concern, the imperative of the hour, was the democratic shaping of the Federal Republic. History was mobilized to learn the lessons of the failures of German democracy in the recent past and to safely guide it into the future. Reformist and democratic inclinations thus clearly and legitimately entered their historiographical quest. But there were also other biographical circumstances that in some way or another were bound to leave a more problematic imprint.

This was a generation born between 1925 and 1938. All its members were young enough to experience growing up in the Third Reich. The Second World War and ensuing total defeat occurred, for the most part, between their fifteenth and twenty-second year. They were too young to be at the front, but they were inevitably socialized into National Socialist institutions; some, at the end of the war became antiaircraft gunners (*Flakhelfer*), even members of the party.[25] There was, of course, nothing exceptional in all of this—this was the fate of all German citizens during this period. Like many other Germans, those who were destined to become historians also had to grapple with the fact that their fathers and teachers, families and friends, were—in various ways and degrees— somehow implicated in Nazi society and policy.[26]

What I am suggesting here is that this issue of the implicated "fathers"— both literal and metaphorical[27]—has immediate relevance to the kind of social history that these historians subsequently produced. The rise of social history in the 1960s was, of course, a general phenomenon in the world of Western historiography, a left-leaning, putatively democratizing project that sought to go beyond the traditional elitist biases of narrow political narratives and extend the scope of attention to previously

neglected, less articulate sectors of society. It began as a dissenting movement but, within a strikingly short time, achieved a kind of professional
and epistemological hegemony that encompassed the United States,
Britain, and France, as well as Germany. During that period, it essentially dominated the terms of historiographical discourse. Social history
took the profession into ever more quantified and abstract directions,
characteristically assuming ontological priority of "social structure" over
concrete and contingent events, personal agency, "culture," and "ideas."[28]
(Fernand Braudel has recounted how, in his Second World War years as
a prisoner of war, he turned to social history and its long, impersonal
view as a means of getting away from, of denying, the unpleasant events
and depressing realities around him![29])

    The international nature and dominance of social history during this
time undoubtedly also facilitated its rise in Germany but in the light of
that country's charged past, it assumed a specific coloring, one particularly suited to contemporary psychopolitical needs.[30] For an extraordinary and uniquely German tension helped to shape a species of social
history that was at once *skeptical and protective*. For the putatively progressive, new paradigm of German social history sought somehow to
negotiate and integrate this strangely conflicted situation: a highly critical, reformist impulse with an unacknowledged, perhaps unconscious,
filial loyalty. Wehler has recently rendered this tension explicit: "We owe
loyalty to the dead with whom we spent good years—but also in tension
to another loyalty—the victims and the persecuted."[31] The "structural"
and "systemic" history of the kind practiced by this generation of social
historians encoded but also contained and domesticated this tension.[32]
Retrospectively this brand of social history can be read as a kind of—
subtle and not necessarily conscious—navigation exercise: formulating
a necessarily critical narrative of the past while at the same time leaving
questions of personal complicity and ideological and intellectual convictions relatively untouched.[33] An approach that placed transpersonal
structures and processes and curiously bloodless social formations at the
center—jagged economic growth, class polarization, authoritarian "structures," unresponsive "political processes"—and that typically gave short
shrift to the role of particular events and personalities, to culture, attitudes, and ideology, was admirably suited to fill this mediating function.[34] As Hartmut Lehmann strikingly put it, many chose "to discuss

problems of social history and structural history, as if deliberately to evade questions of moral responsibility and guilt."[35]

This methodological bias and the question of fathers were given sharp focus in the famous 1998 meeting of German historians, at their *Historikertag* and the heated debate that ensued thereafter. There it was alleged that the vaunted origins of German social history, far from the progressive pedigree to which it had laid claim,[36] had its roots in a dry-cleaned version of a conservative and thereafter Nazi-related *Volksgeschichte*, a discipline propounded by the spiritual (and in some cases literal) fathers of the social historians, most prominently Otto Brunner, Werner Conze, and Theodor Schieder.[37] It turns out that Brunner, Conze, and Schieder, who went on to become leading members of the German historical profession during the 1950s, were not only active during the Third Reich but had been enthusiastically engaged in Nazi *Ostpolitik* research and energetically advocated pernicious anti-Semitic policies.

Critics, eager to pin down continuities, also pointed out that the scholarly, personal, and research links between the generations were thickly intertwined. The younger social historians—almost to a man—were doctoral students of these professors and much of their early research was spent in combined projects. Thus Wehler, Hans Mommsen, Martin Brozsat were all involved, in one way or another, with the first German postwar exercise in "contemporary history" directed by Theodor Schieder—the massive *Vertreibungs* project, tracing in chronological and biographical detail, especially through eyewitness accounts, the persecution and expulsion of Germans from the East. Very obviously German victimhood, rather than perpetrator history, stood at the center.[38]

This is not the place to review the debate.[39] Suffice it to say that I do not find the attempt to taint or delegitimize "social history" by virtue of its alleged categorical and personal kinship to a Nazi-like Volksgeschichte particularly persuasive or helpful.[40] There is not much intellectual honesty or force in such ad hominem arguments of guilt by association (paradoxically they mirror the dubious attempt by social historians to delegitimize Kulturgeschichte in light of the fact that many of its proponents professed conservative views).

This being said, the issue nevertheless raises some troubling and relevant questions in the present context. These concern the silence, disinclination, indifference, or inability of the younger historians to face their

fathers and teachers and to ask pertinent questions, to delve into the untouched shadows of the past. To be sure this was part of a larger phenomenon, a generalized disinclination by no means limited to the group
in question.[41] What the present controversy has done, nevertheless, is to
force this generation of historians to acknowledge and confront or at
least explain these omissions—indeed a whole volume documenting
these missed opportunities and addressing the implications of these silences has recently appeared.[42] Those interviewed have furnished various explanations and provided numerous mitigating circumstances. Above
all, they point to a powerful taboo that prohibited broaching such deeply
sensitive, personal matters—especially by dependent young scholars![43]
Half admiringly and half resentfully, they advert to the fact that only recently has a younger generation, freed from these powerful prohibitions,
been able to puncture the silence and put the issue on the table.

One way or another there is a certain irony in the ways in which
the social historians have sought to account for their own elisions. Strikingly, they invoke contextual, individual, subjective, and psychobio-
graphical factors of *Verstehen* ("understanding") and *Einfuehlung* ("empathy") that they previously denigrated and conspicuously excluded from
the structural emphases of their work. Only through an "inner" understanding of the particularities of their experience and the difficulties of
transmitting it, they presently argue, can the silences—of both the "sons"
and "fathers"—be made comprehensible.[44] In these accounts the much
vaunted independent and "critical" function of the historian, the need
for a measured distance, seems to disappear. As Hans Mommsen would
now have it, historians cannot be distinguished from any other group,
but are merely mirrors, little less than reflections, typifications, of their
own society.[45]

In Germany the salience of this recent confrontation was partly linked
to a generational conflict, a younger group of historians challenging
their fathers, part of the changing of the guard. The debate has relevance here only to the extent that it may help to account for the peculiar narrative biases and emphases of postwar German social history and
the differences with the nascent cultural-intellectual history of the time.
For, in establishing the legitimacy of their own paradigm, the social
historians somehow consigned the stress on "Ideas" to necessarily reac-
tionary and conservative methodologies and influences. Social history,

as William H. Sewell Jr. has argued, in general, privileged "an under-lying ontological distinction between a determining social structure and a determined politics and culture."[46] Yet this did not in principle entail an *adversarial* relationship to "culture" and "experience." This was cer-tainly not always the case in Anglo-American circles where, for in-stance, the Marxist-oriented E. P. Thompson's *The Making of the En-glish Working Class* (1963)—a work replete with cultural resonances and experiential material—became canonical.[47] It was only in Germany that idealism and historicism were mistakenly identified with all of cultural and intellectual history. Indeed, the idealist and historicist traditions were often portrayed as complicit in National Socialism itself. Instead of being a tool for helping us to grasp the nature of Nazism, Kulturgeschichte was transformed into a kind of instrument or symptom of it.

There was also the converse (though never really explained) assump-tion that analyses of "society" and social structure were somehow more critical and "progressive" than older approaches.[48] The role of belief, perceptions, the creation and contestations of meaning, collective and personal identity and desires, resentments, symbols, indeed action and experience itself could not be considered "hard" data but rather a spe-cies of epiphenomena masking real, underlying material factors.

By highlighting previously neglected areas of class and interest poli-tics, the socioeconomic maneuverings and manipulations of elites, this historiography no doubt filled an important lacuna. A distinguishing (and admirable) component of German social history was, without doubt, its determined emphasis on the political dimension. But its narrative and methodological guidelines elided independent investigation of choices, motivations, beliefs, and actions. The existential crises and moral dimen-sions, the dynamics that endowed people's lives with meaning and di-rection, that imposed upon them decisions and responsibility—in other words, issues of agency—if present at all, lay buried, hidden in deper-sonalized economic structures, social systems, and political processes.[49] Reflecting later on these biases, one of the leading proponents of the new social history, Jürgen Kocka, suggested a sophisticated rationale: "It was particularly important to grasp the processes and structures that were not present in motives, preconceptions and experiences," he wrote, "but that were important as conditions and consequences of experiences and actions."[50] Yet, as Heinz Wolf has pointed out, the notion that

structures somehow "cause" people to act the way they do, unless intimately linked with aspects of experience and agency, remains itself a
kind of unexamined metaphysics.[51]

One way or the other, the biases and omissions of the social historians help to explain why for many of us trained in cultural and intellectual history (and perhaps beyond, for a wider reading public), these
vaunted major works of "*Gesellschaftsgeschichte*" or "*Historische Sozialwissenschaft*"[52] simply lacked existential resonance, urgency, electricity, relevance.[53] They always seemed to fall short, never reaching the core of
their self-proclaimed target: "to investigate," as Wehler put it in his influential work on *The German Empire 1871–1918,*

> why Hitler's National Socialist regime came to power some dozen
> years after the end of the monarchy; why this regime succeeded
> in establishing a system of unprecedented terror and barbaric
> mass extermination; and why it proved capable of conducting a
> second total war."[54]

More often than not, these works, in the words of Dan Diner, read like,
and functioned as, "neutralized" productions.[55] The mechanics of process and the forces of structure seemed to overwhelm events and intentionality.[56] Paul Nolte has tellingly noted that the image of society created in this mold is curiously devoid of "history," indeed becomes a kind
of substitute for it.[57]

We must turn now to a different kind of history—written beyond
these geographical and conceptual borders—to the émigré German-
Jewish cultural-intellectual historians. To be sure, the experiential and
biogenerational links to their work are both more obvious and (I would
argue) less problematic than those of the German social historians. Of
course, this does not render their personal or professional profiles less
interesting or complex. Indeed, the contrary may be true. When I remarked to Reinhard Rürup that while the émigré historians have all
provided us with autobiographical material—they are to be sure, of a
slightly older generation—there is virtually nothing by the social historians, he commented that, unlike their German counterparts, the émigré historians had all lived much more eventful and richer lives![58]

Peter Gay, Walter Laqueur, George Mosse, and Fritz Stern have all,
by now, in one way or another, published memoir material in which the

match between their forced emigration and historiography, their works and lives becomes clear enough.[59] They were never, to be sure, a coherent or academically organized group (such as the Bielefeld School of German social historians). There was only one institutional link between them: Mosse and Laqueur were the founders and, for many years, the editors of the London-based *Journal of Contemporary History*.[60] In the main, however, these historians pursued their own separate careers, and their personal relations proceeded on a spectrum ranging from close friendship to thinly veiled dislike. Nevertheless, the experiential, generational, and conceptual commonalities of their projects seem clear and that is what I shall emphasize here (it awaits a later study to underline the individual richness, variety, the obvious and important differences and deficiencies in their respective oeuvres). To be sure, neither their work nor their persons can or should be limited or reduced to their émigré experience. Their range makes this apparent.

Of the four, Fritz Stern has remained most closely within the ambit of German cultural and political history; Mosse and Gay can rightly be considered historians of a much wider "European" experience, while Walter Laqueur—thus far not given sufficient consideration, perhaps because of his autodidacticism and his only occasional formal attachments to university positions—has written extremely broadly on topics far removed from German and West European history. His works encompass tracts on the Soviet Union and Russian history, the Middle East, the history of Zionism, terrorism, guerilla warfare, and international relations.[61]

Whatever their differences, the commonalities are evident. Although they are a slightly older cohort than the social historians—they were born between 1918 and 1926—their early lives too were indelibly shaped by the breakdown of Weimar democracy and the advent of Nazism. But here of course their stories diverge, for all were (or were considered to be) Jews.[62] All were forced to become refugees or exiles or émigrés—the choice of appellation is significant, for the reactions of these historians to this event were very different. Although they eventually worked this through, Peter Gay and Fritz Stern, regarded that experience with a sense of deep, lingering resentment. In his memoir, *My German Question*, Gay speaks of it as "the story of a poisoning and how I deal with it," and Stern states, "I was no freer than others of hatred for what Germans had done,"[63] while for Laqueur and Mosse it was, ironically, akin to liberation, an opening up to the world. "The loss of my native country at the age of seventeen," Laqueur writes,

> hurt me considerably less than the loss of those I loved. Perhaps
> I felt, even vaguely, that the Nazis were leading the country to
> ruin and that the place where I was born and [had] grown up
> would be lost in any case. If my country did not want me, I was
> reasonably sure that I could find my place elsewhere."[64]

Mosse describes his last journey, as a fourteen year-old from an exceedingly wealthy home, in Germany thus: "Despite everything I regarded this journey not as something sad, as a blow of fate, no, I was happy to be able to see new places, ready for new adventures." Many years later he declared that he regarded his departure from Germany "as merciful providence. . . . Why such a way of thinking that goes against all clichés of Exile? Because exile tore me from wealth and left me no other choice but to make myself."[65]

However differently they may have experienced it, Nazism indelibly marked all their lives. As Gay put it:

> More than a half-century after the collapse of Hitler's Thousand
> Year Reich, every surviving refugee remains to some extent one
> of his victims. In recent years, the status of victim has become
> widely popular, I know, exploited to elicit sympathy and sustain
> claims for reparation. I make no such demands. My point is a
> simple factual one: even the most fortunate Jew who lived under
> Hitler has never completely shaken off that experience.[66]

Indeed, it is important to note that, like Gay, none of these historians have defined themselves as "survivors" or claimed "victim" status. Mosse put it thus: "I do not belong to a more recent generation where victimization is a badge of pride rather than a frustration or a test of character."[67] Yet, even though all left Germany in the 1930s, Nazi barbarity and the Holocaust became an existential conundrum, 1941–42 the implicit but deeply traumatic starting and end point of many of their longer-term historical investigations. In summing up his life, Mosse wrote:

> I suppose that I am a member of the Holocaust generation and
> have constantly tried to understand an event too monstrous to

contemplate. All my studies in the history of racism and volkish thought, and also those dealing with outsiderdom and stereotypes, though sometimes not directly related to the Holocaust, have tried to find the answer to how it could have happened; finding an explanation has been vital not only for the understanding of modern history, but also for my own peace of mind.[68]

This group shared other defining characteristics. "All," as Jerry Z. Muller notes, "were all old enough to have experienced the rise and regime of Nazism but young enough to complete their studies abroad," and thus cultivated the "ability to speak and write both German and English with style and verve, a talent that is difficult to acquire for those who move into a new linguistic culture after adolescence."[69] (The first generation of—both Jewish and non-Jewish—émigré historians, Felix Gilbert, Hajo Holborn, Hans Rothfels, Veit Valentin, Arthur and Hans Rosenberg, and Gustav Meyer, we should note, were all trained within Germany itself.)[70]

All the cultural historians who are the subjects of this chapter underwent significant transformations of identifications and identities. The different nuances are interesting: Fritz Stern went on to embody a kind of critical, yet sympathetic commitment to both (a reformed) Germany and the United States and the dialogue between them; Laqueur with his Israeli, British, and American career, retains perhaps the most internationalist profile; and while Peter Gay described his integration into his new homeland as "a beneficent transformation" and demonstratively entitled one of his papers, "At Home in America,"[71] a series of 1991 interviews with Mosse were published under the name, *Ich bleibe Emigrant*. ("I Remain an Emigrant").[72] Upon his migration to Palestine, Walter Laqueur added Zeʿev as his middle name; Gerhard became George Mosse, and, most enthusiastically, Peter Joachim Froehlich became Peter Jack Gay.[73]

"I believe," writes Walter Laqueur, "that I understood Germany better than France or Britain, even though I have spent much more time there than in Germany. This is largely a matter of instinct, of feeling in one's bones how people will react in a certain situation. But what is instinct? A little inspiration based on experience."[74] Their peculiar circumstances thus allowed these younger historians to combine tacit understanding of, and an "inside" feel for, German society with the measured distance of an external perspective.[75] (That "feel" comprised not just high but also popular culture. As Laqueur, whose memoir itself is replete with sporting events and accomplishments, comments: "Henry Kissinger or Peter Gay . . . would be able to recite fifty years later the composition of a leading German or Austrian team confronting England or Hungary or Italy."[76]) One positive legacy of exile, Mosse proclaimed, was a certain sense of overall "outsiderdom" that enabled the historian to bring to bear alternative perspectives.[77] "Perhaps," Fritz Stern reflected, "I gradually acquired something like bifocal views—others might call it impaired vision: I tend to see things German with American eyes, and things American also with German eyes."[78]

Experience encouraged a kind of insider-outsider perspective, one that crossed and at times transgressed physical and conceptual borders rather than being fixed within them. For instance, George Mosse's penchant for hilarity, his eye for the exotic and the outrageous, and his ongoing, always provocative critique of "normalcy" and "respectability" derived from a personal awareness of his marginal Jewishness and homosexuality—but his deliberate cultivation of outsiderdom was also obviously related to a more general location beyond or between these national German, American (and Israeli) borders.[79]

These, then, were the young émigrés who would go on to invent a new kind of German cultural and intellectual history—unburdened by the obvious inadequacies of traditional idealist assumptions and historicist narratives—able to shed novel light upon, and place into different perspective, the history of modern Germany and the shock of Nazism.

To be sure, there was a period of latency. Before turning to German history (in the 1960s) most first pursued other academic interests partly out of a need to more firmly establish their new careers and identities,[80] partly because they—like others around them—were not yet psychically and socially ready for such a confrontation. In the 1950s, as has been well documented, it was not polite to talk of such things.[81] These historians thus explored other fields. Fritz Stern edited a work on general trends in historiography;[82] Mosse first acquired his reputation as a leading scholar of early modern English history and the Reformation;[83] Laqueur published works on Communism and the Middle East;[84] and Peter Gay initially concentrated on the Enlightenment and American history[85] (it is true that he wrote his doctoral dissertation, which he later

Seated portrait of Walter Laqueur. Courtesy of the Leo
Baeck Institute, New York.

published, on Eduard Bernstein the German Social Democratic theo-
rist, but he did so at the time expressly because, as he put it, "Bernstein
had been an outsider to German society both as a Jew and as an erst-
while Marxist").[86] Eventually, however, they all turned, in one way or
another and in varying degrees of intensity, to a direct investigation of
the troubled German past. "Nearly two decades had passed," Mosse
noted, "since I had arrived in the United States and there was no more

George Mosse. Courtesy of the Estate of
George L. Mosse.

need to immerse myself in a respectable Anglo-Saxon subject in order
to distance myself from my past as an outsider."[87]

When—in their new homes—these émigrés found themselves investigating matters closer to their own personal pasts, they instinctively
turned to "culture" (in its broadest sense) as an explanatory key, to ideology, issues of self-definition and identity under crisis. Fritz Stern has
stated this bias in a way that contrasts quite obviously with the social
historians: "As an historian I was more interested in political culture—
an American concept—than in structure, more in individual people
than in classes or parties, with chance, but also with solid interests and
deeply layered tradition, with the gestures and often unspoken premises

Fritz Stern. Courtesy of the Leo Baeck Institute, New York.

of public transactions."[88] Formally, the notion of "political culture" may have been an American concept, but the turn to "culture" was also deeply connected to an awareness of the enormous power of ideological and symbolic forces within German history and National Socialism. These émigrés had, after all, experienced the weight of these forces directly on their own persons.

But these emphases were not limited to the study of negative forces only. Perhaps just as crucially, as acculturated young German Jews raised in a particular tradition of humanist Bildung, they shared the German-Jewish bias for "culture" not just as an explanatory key but as a constitutive value and a core ingredient of their own personalities. In effect the kind of history they composed was an expression of this inherited sensibility. George Mosse's classic 1983 *German Jews beyond Judaism* is simultaneously an identification, analysis, critique, and personal credo of

Portrait of Peter Gay; 1967 (Photograph by Paul Wehn). Courtesy of the
Leo Baeck Institute, New York.

this mindset and disposition. That disposition is surely an important source of Peter Gay's continuing immersion in, and defense of, the Enlightenment,[89] and even in his earlier works on that subject, he "managed to integrate Germany and Germans into the culture of modern Western civilization, which had become my favorite hunting ground."[90] Little wonder, too, that in addition both Mosse and Fritz Stern have written critically, appreciatively, and extensively on different strands, strengths, and weaknesses of the German intelligentsia and its engagement with politics and culture.[91] Gay and Laqueur, it will be remembered, wrote among the very earliest and valuable syntheses of Weimar culture—admiring if critical elegies that identified that culture's brilliant creativity, its impossible politics, and the fateful dialectic between them.[92] In retrospect these works helped to shape later perceptions of a still current celebratory "myth of Weimar" (a matter to which we will return in the next chapter).

If, across the border, these scholars were in some way not merely the mediators but also the repositories, exemplifications of the legacy and the traditions they analyzed—presumably a source of the attractiveness these European scholars possessed for many of their American students[93]— they also engaged in criticism of this overestimation of culture. As Laqueur put it in his *Weimar Culture:*

> German writers, including Thomas Mann and other leading
> spirits of the age, tended to attribute too much significance to
> *Bildung;* it dawned on them only gradually that illiterate people
> could be humanists and democrats by instinct whereas highly
> educated men could advocate cannibalistic ideologies and even
> become commanders of SS *Einsatzgruppen.*[94]

This was cultural and intellectual history that operated against the idealist current, critical of various aspects of both "culture" and intellectuals and yet always convinced of the motivating importance of meaning-bestowing ideas and symbolism in human affairs. This became most clearly and classically apparent in Stern's *Politics of Cultural Despair* and Mosse's *Crisis of German Ideology* (both published in the early sixties). These works outline the machinations and fantasies of middle-range pamphleteers and publicists in the formulation of a (late) nineteenth-century counterliberal Völkisch ideology and trace the multiple ways in which this semimystic, organic nationalist weltanschauung penetrated German politics and informed various strands of its high and popular culture.[95] This applies too to Mosse's and Laqueur's probings of the myopia of the youth movements and misjudgments of the educated and politically active intellectual classes, Stern's critique of the "Unpolitical German," and Peter Gay's dissection of the consequences of the "hunger for wholeness."[96]

In all this, the innovative nature of their enterprise became increasingly apparent. In their reinvention of German cultural and intellectual history these émigrés veered away from both the historicist legacy and the rather detached rationalist "history of ideas" tradition (a fact either not registered or not understood by the social historians who, while willfully ignoring their work, continued to label and dismiss Kulturgeschichte according to its superseded conservative pedigree). Having experienced Nazism and gone beyond the border, no trace of the epic, empathic, and idealist historicist narrative could be found among these émigré historians. Rather, they radically enlarged the meaning, definition, and scope of the "cultural." No longer was the concept reserved for matters high and cultivated; for Mosse, indeed, it became broadly "anthropological." He defined culture, in its Western historical context, extensively "as a state or habit of mind which is apt to become a way of life intimately linked to the challenges and dilemmas of contemporary society."[97] In this guise cultural and intellectual history was no longer purely elite oriented—and when it was, it was largely critical—but extended to a vast range of aspects of popular culture previously untouched: the content and diffusion of racism and stereotypes; strategies of class, religious, national, ethnic, and (later with Mosse) sexual, inclusion and exclusion; anti-Semitism; political myths and mass symbolism.[98]

Moreover, the work of these cultural historians betrayed few signs of a detached Lovejoyian "chain of ideas" that somehow floated above the historical process. These were always context-sensitive presentations rooted in particular historical circumstances. For example, the emergence and percolation of Völkish ideology as a habit of thought, feeling, and perception was closely tied to crises of the Kaiserreich, analyzed as a response, generated by the perplexities and singularities of the German modernization experience during the latter part of the nineteenth century and radicalized and reinforced by World War I and its traumatic aftermath. These were not presented as epiphenomena, mere reflections of class and other material interests, but as active—and interactive— forces in their own right.[99]

Given the catastrophic and unprecedented nature of their subject matter, these historians—precisely because they were liberals and men of the Enlightenment—were constrained to deal with material usually quite foreign to students of the mind and in so doing virtually rein- vented the study of German cultural and intellectual history. For the émigrés, Nazism and genocide rendered ideologies and the modalities of "irrationalism" (however understood) as a central issue, as an essen- tial, and indeed extremely appealing driving force of mass culture and politics. They plumbed the histories of the late nineteenth and early twentieth century in search of their manifold manifestations and sought to account for their genesis and dynamics. Indeed, they became its master analysts, dissecting its various forms and trajectories. Stern's reflections on his own work applies equally to the other émigré historians discussed here: "I only wanted to emphasize that history must scientifically and rationally also research the role of the irrational, that these factors are just as real, true and objective as the interest-politics of industry or the claims of the military or the bureaucracy."[100] As opposed to the social historians, the subjects of their history were endowed with ideas, prejudices, myths, stereotypes, emotions, and, indeed, minds—even, per- haps especially, when these sometimes went astray. Precisely as unrepen- tant liberal humanists and adherents of the Enlightenment, they sought to more deeply probe—and tame—the sources of nineteenth- and twentieth- century "irrationalism" that they believed had so threatened that vision. This surely is a major motivating force behind Peter Gay's intense pre- occupation with Sigmund Freud.[101] Similarly, Mosse's assertion that the essence of the German-Jewish intellectual legacy was to "exorcise the ir- rational, to render it harmless by filtering it through the rational mind" applies as much to his own project as to the subjects he was analyzing.[102]

We have already adverted to the fact that while in Germany the so- cial historians more or less excluded the cultural, experiential, and phe- nomenological from their purview, this German-Jewish émigré group placed such issues at the center. It was, after all, at this immediate ideo- logical and existential level that they had also personally experienced these events. The virtual exclusion of the ideational dimension from the purview of the social historians, as we have seen, had numerous sources. Perhaps, additionally, when it came to issues related to National Socialism, German Jews, both because they were above suspicion and beyond the border, could openly address these ideological issues, the putative magnetism of right-wing radicalism and Nazi politics, in a way that would have been taboo for Germans in Germany. Concerning the content and attraction of such ideas, it was both politic and a matter of good taste to be mute and discreet.[103] George Mosse, on the other hand, felt free to, and would often describe to his students the tremendous personal and group appeal of the myths of German nationalism and the pull of Nazi mass meetings. In his memoirs he describes how his school at Salem "gave me a first taste of nationalism, which at the time I found congenial; there was a danger that it might provide the belief system that I so badly lacked. . . . When as a historian much later I wrote about German nationalism, I did have an insight into its truly seductive nature."[104] When he was about fifteen years old, he watched a Nazi demonstration in front of his home in Berlin. "The impression was so great," he later recalled, " . . . that I ran away from home, it must have been in 1932, and went to a Hitler rally. I must admit, even today, that it was an experience. I was swept away. First there were the masses of people; that was very captivating to be in the middle of it all. But it was also Hitler."[105] Fritz Stern has claimed that as a "victim" he is able to say what few German historians could allow themselves to say. In his lecture on "National Socialism as Temptation," he was able to cheerfully acknowledge that he was saved from that temptation by dint of not being a full-blooded Aryan.[106]

Clearly, then, this reconfiguration of modern German cultural and intellectual history reflected, to some degree, the personal memories and trajectory of its creators. "I vividly remember the speeches," Laqueur has written, "the demonstrations, the torchlight parades that hailed the dawn of the new era. The teachers told us, with varying degrees of conviction, what bliss it was to be alive in that dawn." "Gibbon," he commented later, "once said that his service as captain of the Hampshire grenadiers had not been useless to the historian of the Roman Empire; attending school from 1933 to 1938 was of use to the future student of the Third Reich and totalitarianism."[107]

Employing, explicitly or implicitly, the same Sonderweg model (of a

flawed modernization process that deviated from Western liberal, democratic, and Enlightenment models) the works of the émigrés actually
complemented analyses of the sociopolitical processes studied by the
social historians (indeed what they sought to do with their insistently
contextual approach was what Peter Gay described as a "social history of
ideas").[108] Yet—presumably because the cultural historians were invok-
ing an ideological, implicitly intentionalist and decisionist framework,
one that emphasized "lived experience"—the former almost completely
ignored them.[109] This nonreception, a kind of "scientific blindness," is
made even more poignant by the fact that these two groups were bound
together by numerous friendships and personal and professional contacts while little or no dialogical incorporation or integration of the work
occurred.[110]

It would not be true to say that German scholars from the 1960s on
did not pay any attention to anti-Semitism as a factor within pre-1933
Germany. There were, indeed, numerous works on the subject.[111] Reinhard Ruerup's pioneering analyses merit special mention in this regard.[112] Nevertheless, in more general histories, the phenomenon was
too often consigned an epiphenomenal status and not integrated into
the larger narrative. Thus, in Wehler's volume on the Kaiserreich, anti-
Semitism is discussed but ultimately understood merely as a form of
manipulation from above and, in effect, isolated from the larger motivating forces of the historical process.[113] The result of this compart-
mentalization, as Shulamit Volkov has perceptively noted, is to leave the
mystery unanswered: how could such an apparently harmless, latent pre-
disposition have achieved such power and influence under the Nazis and
provided the driving animus behind its murderous policies?[114]

The émigré scholars, on the other hand, recognized this mutual complicity. In its changing forms and functions, anti-Semitism (and other
forms of exclusion and outsiderdom), they insisted, was in various ways
and degrees tied into numerous and basic strands of German self-
definition. Thus, for the early Mosse it was through Völkisch ideology
that conceptions of nineteenth- and twentieth-century German identity became so critically linked with the "Jewish Question." The central
foil, the salient antitype of this sensibility and its imagery—with its
metaphysic of national roots; its symbolism of blood, soil and will; its
antiurban and antiliberal bias—focused most naturally upon the Jew.

Who better fit the requisite stereotype of rootlessness and foreignness and of liberalism and restless modernity than the Jew? For Mosse, therefore, the eventual development of Nazism into an "anti-Jewish revolution" became comprehensible largely within the wider context of an ongoing Völkisch disposition.[115]

Mosse later extended his historical net to an analysis of the pernicious dynamics of what he termed "bourgeois respectability" and the infiltration of middle-class morality into national self-definition, with its exclusionary constructions of insiders and outsiders, its dichotomies of normalcy and abnormality, health and disease, beauty and ugliness. Startlingly he proclaimed that "the new man of national socialism was the ideal bourgeois."[116] In his *Nationalism and Sexuality* (1985), the victimization of the Jew remains both central and most extreme but is comprehensible as part of a continuum and dynamic affecting the stereotypical bourgeois creation of other outsiders.[117] "The Jewish stereotype," Mosse proclaimed,

> is . . . the same as the stereotype of all outsiders: sexual deviants, gypsies, the permanently insane, people who have hereditary diseases. They all look alike. . . . And, of course, these are all the people Hitler wanted to exterminate and whom he did exterminate. They all look the opposite of the middle-class, self-controlled idea of beauty, energy, all of this sort of thing.[118]

This is not the place to analyze and critique Mosse's changing view of the role of the bourgeoisie within the disposition of National Socialism—from his early depiction of the bourgeoisie as victim to his later position that Nazi ideology was essentially an expression of its values and worldview.[119] The point here is the cultural historian's emphasis on the co-implication of these anti-Jewish and other exclusionary themes, their centrality to the ontologies and economies of the broader societies out of which they emerged. This emphasis is common to all the émigré historians. Thus, Fritz Stern's subtle ruminations on the "anguished ambiguity of Jewish success" and its consequences as evidenced in the most elevated corridors of German power—the charged Bismarck-Bleichröder relationship[120]—his notion that Jewish prosperity in Germany was achieved "at great psychic cost. . . . In no other country were Jews met with so peculiar a mixture of hospitality and hostility."[121]

It is clear that the narrative biases of these historians, their emphases on "culture," exclusion, and the ideological dimension, sprang, at least in part, from their liberal Jewish backgrounds and émigré experience. Yet they were careful not to allow dislocating personal experience to warp their viewpoint. They remained acutely aware of the dangers of teleology, and warned against linear history: Auschwitz was not a necessary inscription of an incurably infected past, not inherent in Germany's cultural and political fabric.[122] Peter Gay put it thus: "To say that the Third Reich was grounded in the German past is true enough; to say that it was the inescapable result of that past, the only fruit that the German tree would grow is false."[123] Rather, with differing emphases, they sought to identity potentialities, the multiple forces, and building blocks that moved the society in the direction it did without ever reducing it to it. Contingency too played a role. Thus George Mosse never tired of asserting that if, at the beginning of the twentieth century, one were to predict which Central or West European country would perpetrate a Holocaust against the Jews, the answer, in all likelihood, would have been France![124] It was absolutely crucial to trace the steps that led to Auschwitz—while always remembering that the road leading there was never simply straight, but twisted and quite unpredictable.

Not surprisingly, these émigrés, more than any other group of scholars, did not limit themselves to the study of anti-Semitism but sought to grasp the wider history of German-Jewish relations as such, consistently and insistently bringing to light their complex and subtle nature, stressing always the co-implicated nature of the nexus, its ironies, limitations, and problems but also its achievements, possibilities, and richness. These writings, let me suggest, represent in part a commemorative project written after the catastrophe and, in every way, from beyond the border. "The historical enterprise," Fritz Stern once declared, "aims to restore to German Jewry the dignity of its history."[125] This applies not only to their various forays into pre-1933 Germany. Walter Laqueur has recently become the biographer—in *Generation Exodus: The Fate of Young Jews from Nazi Germany*—of his own generation's collective displacement and relocation, the role of luck in its members' survival and their (not always) successful, highly diverse adaptation throughout the world (ranging from stories like that of Henry Kissinger through a German-Jewish "Benedictine Abbot, Hindu guru, and West African chieftain").[126]

Yet the commemorative seldom lost sight of the critical. Mosse's ironic piece on Jewish internalizations of the Völkisch idea; Stern's depiction of the intricate and loaded modes of Jewish entry into the higher realms of German economic, political, and scientific life; Gay's ruminations on the complex relations between German Jews and modernism; Walter Laqueur's biting assessment of the insensitivity and irresponsibility of Jewish radicals such as Kurt Tucholsky represent only a few examples of this kind of work.[127]

None of the émigrés claimed to be internal "Jewish" historians; they could hardly be said to be familiar with, or particularly interested in, traditional Jewish texts (although he has not dwelled upon the tradition, Walter Laqueur may be a partial exception here; by virtue of his early emigration to Palestine, he is the only one of these historians with a thorough knowledge of Hebrew). Their Jewishness did not reside in their tie to Jewish religion or ritual but rather—like Freud and Einstein and other German-Jewish intellectuals whom they both studied and admired—in a sense of identification through common descent, historical circumstance, and cultural achievement. In many ways their liberal, acculturated backgrounds are reflected in their historiographical emphases and accounts. They all exemplify what Dan Diner has called the individualist, emancipated, Western European Jewish narrative as against the collective, pre-emancipationist East European Jewish conceptual framework.[128] For, all sought, as it were, to "deghettoize" Jewish existence while at the same time making European history sensitive to that Jewish presence. As Peter Gay put it, "Jews lived in a world larger than themselves, and just as it is impossible to understand that larger world without its Jews, it is impossible to understand its Jews without that larger world."[129]

Their perspectives were always based upon the same—albeit self-critical—liberal and acculturated Bildung assumptions with which they were raised. Perhaps because of this, in differing degrees of intensity, they confronted, rejected, or, at the very least, modified and refined, or sought to find some saving grace in, the uncompromisingly Zionist terms of Gershom Scholem's tone-setting and highly controversial thesis— that the German-Jewish project, the putative "dialogue" and "symbiosis," had been doomed from the outset and was a purely one-sided delusion.[130] Thus Fritz Stern could comment "that though the 'German-Jewish partnership or collaboration' may have been an illusion, it was an enticing illusion, an illusion productive of greatness."[131] For Mosse, the dialogue (with its ideals of self-cultivation and liberal outlook on society and politics, and based upon the need to transcend the gulf between the history of the Jews and the German tradition) "became an integral part of the European intellectual tradition . . . served to produce a unique heritage for the Jews themselves and for intellectuals all over Europe, but also became a part of the German Jewish identity, infiltrating . . . most aspects of Jewish life in Germany."[132] Similarly, Walter Laqueur has declared that, "Without the Jews there would have been no 'Weimar culture.'"[133]

Peter Gay, of course, has been the most vehement opponent of the Scholem thesis. In his view Jewish integration was at the very least a partial reality, and the rise of Nazism was not inevitable nor was the Holocaust predictable. Accusing German Jews of self-delusion, he argues, is really "an attack, an accusation. . . . What Hitler did to the Jews so goes the reproach—they deserved."[134] In this debate, it is difficult to separate historical analysis from personal experience. Thus, Scholem, caustically dismissing his father's belief in the purported symbiosis, reports that he had no real non-Jewish friends, nor had any non-Jews ever entered their house. As if in direct riposte, Gay declared that his "father found his closest friends in business and sports, and his professional associates and the soccer players and sprinters he knew and liked were nearly all gentiles. And without the help of some of them, we would probably have ended up in the gas chambers."[135]

It is worth noting parenthetically, however, that whatever their views on Scholem's thesis, the particular refugee and generational experience of these cultural historians inclined them toward a certain sympathy for—a liberally conceived—Zionism and the State of Israel.[136] Clearly, the degree and intensity of such a commitment differs considerably among them. It is well known that Laqueur and Mosse, though critical of certain aspects of Zionist history and Israeli attitudes, have been actively identified with its political and intellectual life. Laqueur was the only member of this cohort to emigrate to Palestine, where he spent seventeen years (before moving on to London and Washington, D.C.) first on a kibbutz and then as a well-known journalist (some years later he also taught at Tel Aviv University). "I was not a Zionist in the usual sense of the term when I went to Palestine in 1938," writes Laqueur.

"There was a bitter joke told in Jerusalem and Tel Aviv in the 1930s: New immigrants were asked, 'Are you here out of conviction—or do you come from Germany?' I certainly was not there out of conviction."[137] Yet he did become an acknowledged authority on Zionism—he penned a classic history of the movement and its idea,[138] has written extensively on the Middle East and the Arab-Israel conflict, and recently published a memoirlike historical and contemporary tract, *Dying for Jerusalem.*[139] (While his historical analyses demonstrate a shrewd political sense and a judiciously impartial approach, like so many other German Jews who comprise this volume, his early Zionist sympathies were also humanist and binationalist in nature,[140] though he grew increasingly skeptical as to its chances in this conflict-charged political reality.)[141]

With George Mosse this commitment is rendered even more powerful by the tensions between his intellectual predispositions and his biographically laden emotional attachment, "a sense of belonging, close even to love," as he put it. As we noted in chapter 1, Mosse, among other things, wrote incisively about and identified with the humanism of the Zionist binationalists. To be sure, he always questioned conventional conceptual borders, yet his emigrant history rendered the need for secure physical ones palpable. "There was always a certain pull toward realism," he recalled in his memoirs, "to the feeling that if one did not belong to a strong nation one could slide back into the statelessness I had experienced. Thus, an emotional engagement always threatened that liberalism to which I remained faithful." Mosse, moreover, later became one of the great analysts and critics of the discourse and functions of the ideology of masculinity. Yet confronted in Israel with what he half-mockingly referred to as "Muskeljuden" (Max Nordau's term), the muscular "new Jew," he confessed that this "represented a normalization, an assimilation to general middle-class ideals and stereotypes which otherwise I professed to dislike. But I could not help myself; faced with this Zionist ideal my reason and historical knowledge were overcome."[142]

The attitudes of Stern and Gay to Zionism and, indeed, their own Jewish self-identification is clearly more complicated and ambivalent. Perhaps Walter Laqueur had them in mind when he wrote:

When I met in later years some of my contemporaries, especially in the academic world, who had emigrated to the United States

or Britain or some other Western countries, I came across a syn-
drome which greatly puzzled me. That they had no interest in Israel could be explained, but it was less obvious why they should
have no interest in their own heritage—especially if they happened to be historians. Some of them were writing books about
their German problem, but I suspect what really bothered them,
not always consciously, was their Jewish problem, or to use that
overworked term, the question of their identity. When I met or
read them I often had the feeling that this, but for the grace of
God, would have been my fate too if the years in Palestine and
Israel had not provided an excellent antidote against any self-
consciousness about being Jewish."[143]

For all that, Stern and Gay have also revealed their intellectual and
emotional investment in this regard. Of his 1942 meeting with the Zionist leader and first president of the State of Israel, Chaim Weizmann,
Stern wrote thus: "I have never forgotten that moment. I felt that I was
in the presence of a great man with a great, transcending cause. . . .
Weizmann . . . was in harmony with what was best in our century, and
it was that harmony that empowered great labors to work a miracle."[144]

And Gay, perhaps the most "assimilationist" of these émigré historians ("My overriding desire was to become a good American")[145] reports
how in late November 1945, he wrote of Hitler's murder of the Jews
and the world's

"cynical disregard" for the survivors [sic] desperate plight. Surely
the solution was to adopt President Truman's proposal to have
Jews looking for a homeland admitted to Palestine. I was very severe with the obstructionists attempting to sidetrack this obvious
and humane solution: the British policy makers who turned back
ships laden with refugees had Jewish blood on their hands; the
nationalistic Arabs who disregarded the wishes of their Palestinian
brethren to bring in Jews who, after all, had "performed miracles";
and, ever evenhanded, the "rabid Zionists" who insisted on a purely
Jewish state. Though I was not a Zionsit, rabid or relaxed, I was
willing to be rather indulgent about their terrorist acts, which I
explained as an indication that "the Jews are getting fed up with
the British double-dealing."[146]

Thirty-three years later he wrote—in response to Ernst Nolte—that the latter

> has no grasp of the essentially defensive drive for Palestine; no
> sense that Zionism is an ideal born amidst pogroms and amidst
> persecutions in which Nolte's countrymen particularly distinguished
> themselves. . . . Zionism or not, securing the survival of Israel is
> a moral obligation on the Western world since that world, after all,
> made that refuge, quite literally, a matter of life and death."[147]

We must return, however, to our central focus. I hope to have shown
how and why these émigré scholars turned to certain methodologies and
foci of attention in their quest to understand the nature and traumas of
modern German and German-Jewish history. Just like their German
social-historian counterparts, their biographies, personal backgrounds,
and experiences nudged them in particular directions, biased them toward certain questions and interpretations, and rendered the "cultural"
and ideational dimensions centrally relevant and significant.[148] It is clear
that the refugee experience was a factor, that theirs was a history written beyond older geographical and conceptual borders. Nevertheless, it
is necessary to add that if personal embitterment existed at all, it did not
overwhelm historical judgment: a certain critical judiciousness, the search
for balance, is palpable. All dismissed the notion of "collective guilt"
while rejecting, as Fritz Stern put it, a widespread German conviction
that "none were guilty."[149] Still, unlike the social historians whose conceptual net was not designed to capture questions of guilt, responsibility, and personal complicity, the émigré scholars made methodological
and conceptual space for such questions—but always in differentiated
form. As Walter Laqueur put it:

> I never believed in the collective guilt of a people. I knew from
> my own experience that if it had been up to most individual
> Germans, there would not have been a Gestapo, or military at-
> tacks in every direction, or the mass killings of Jews and others.
> But I also knew with what blind enthusiasm so many had fol-
> lowed the Fuehrer while the going was good.[150]

And indeed, among these scholars, an unmistakable ongoing sympathy for German humanist, Enlightenment, and Bildung culture re-

mains. This, of course, is connected to the fact that this is the culture of their own upbringing and self-identification. Indeed, it seems to me, they belong to the school that views Nazism, not as having incarnated, but as having destroyed what was best in German culture—and that, in fact, the Jews became the carriers of Germany's most worthwhile qualities (this is emblematic of Mosse's *German Jews beyond Judaism*, and it may also constitute the driving force behind Gay's ongoing passion for Freud and his universe, Fritz Stern's study *Einstein's German World*, and Laqueur's depiction of Weimar culture as essentially a Jewish one).

I have dwelled on these historians' sympathy for German culture and their insistence on measured historical judgment, for these belie a well-documented German suspicion of "emigrant" history as in some way prompted by ressentiment, a kind of wounded, mythical victim narrative hopelessly incapable of "objectivity" and measured perspective.[151] In a brilliant (and very provocative) recent study, Nicolas Berg has argued that similar "German" and "Jewish" tensions have applied—and still do—throughout the history of Holocaust scholarship.[152] He points to the dichotomies entailed in intentionalist (purportedly "Jewish") and functionalist (purportedly "German") interpretations of the *Endlösung:* "intention" versus "structure," "deeds" versus "process," "perpetrators" versus "system," "particularity" versus "universality," "ideology" versus "cumulative radicalization."[153] Rather surprisingly, he does not remark that these "structural"-"ideological" dichotomies also closely mirrored the strategies behind the social and cultural histories of the nineteenth- and twentieth-century pre-Holocaust German experience.[154]

Yet, we should also make clear the historiographical costs that this kind of "cultural" bias entailed. For while these scholars virtually invented a cultural and intellectual history that placed the study of the varieties of "irrationalism" at its center, they, perhaps, too often clung to an unreflective, regulative notion of "rationalism." The "rational" was somehow both self-evident and valid and certainly not part of the problem. For these historians the firsthand experience of European fascism encouraged what Michael Steinberg has called a kind of "fortress rationality," one disinclined to accept the complex intertwining of the rational with the irrational. By adopting this strict posture, he argues, they were able to "abjure negotiation with cultural demons."[155] Thus, these liberal scholars remained far removed from Adorno-like proclamations—

there is very little negative or dialectical in their conceptions of, or com-
mitments to, the Enlightenment (although in his later career Mosse, at
least, considerably deepened his understanding of both the sources and
nature of "irrationality"; his later oeuvre stressed that some of the problematic, indeed pernicious, properties lurked inside the Enlightenment
fortress itself and within the constrictions of an ever less tolerant "bourgeois morality").[156]

It is also true, as Jennifer Jenkins has incisively noted, that their
common Sondwerweg lense apart, the social and cultural historians also
shared some "powerful similarities . . . which operated to exclude broader
journeys of exploration." If 1933, 1939, and 1942 constituted their focal
endpoints, other critical dates such as 1919 and 1949 were excluded
from view. Both emphasized the "political" and operated within an essentially "national" framework that virtually excluded the laboring classes,
regional developments, women, and so on from serious consideration.[157]

Yet, as this chapter has suggested, the differences are significant enough
to warrant analysis and critical commentary. This has been the burden
of analysis here. For all that, it is important to note that exposure of the
("German" or "Jewish") biographical and experiential influences upon
the conceptualization and writing of history does not resolve the question
of the respective validity of these paradigms.[158] While I have argued
that these different accounts, to a greater or lesser extent, mirror different group perceptions, interests, and memories, I would not want to reduce any of these accounts to a simplistic ethnic essentialism.[159] Indeed,
these words are animated by the hope and insistence that historians—if
they are to be worthy of their profession—need not necessarily be pris-
oners of the narratives they construct. (The fact that there is no necessary connection between national identification and historical narrative
is strikingly illustrated by a new generation of younger German historians who, in fundamental ways, are presently questioning the conventions and elisions of their fathers.) Historians are no doubt, to some degree, products and reflections of their own groups, cultures, cohorts, and
so on, yet they belong to a profession that prides itself upon its honed
capacity both for self-criticism and for empathy, entering sympathetically into the shoes of the "other." We should note too that good history
should (and implicitly if not always consciously and overtly will in-

evitably) entail both "structure" and "experience," "impersonal process" and collective and personal action, thought, and sentiment.[160] The crossing of these cognitive borders should apply to German, Jewish, and Israeli historians alike.

The contrasting epistemologies of social and cultural history similarly raise the dilemma of the relation between "understanding" and "judgment" in historical analysis. Historians seek to understand and explain events, not assign "guilt." At the same time, it would be obtuse to deny the ethical impulse that drives much of our work. The tension between dispassionate contextual analysis and moral concern and disapproval is not an easy one; the dilemma is built in. Because it cannot be ultimately resolved, it must be constantly negotiated: explanation can too easily become exculpation and apology; hunting down historical quarry and pinning accusatory labels of guilt quickly renders history a prosecutorial and puritanically didactic exercise. Finding the balance is an ongoing and delicate matter.

It is part of our profession to historicize. Historians too must undergo historicization,[161] and this is what I have attempted here, even while keeping in mind Carl Schorske's admonition that sociointellectual and philosophical critique of historical work is itself a historical product.[162] Historicization does not mean that narratives and paradigms can simply be reduced to their circumstances, or for those reasons be rendered valid or invalid, but rather that the historian must be aware of such conditioning factors and incorporate such self-reflexive criticism into the marrow of his or her work. We know that today, unlike the decades between 1960 through the 1980s, "cultural" history is on the ascendant, and social history very much on the defensive. Indeed, the social historians *have* lately been engaged in such self-criticism.[163] Wehler has thus on numerous occasions openly conceded the deficits of German social history, its ignoring of agency, perception, and experience—indeed, has acknowledged the betrayal of its own self-avowed Weberian "Verstehen" principles.[164] This, he admits—rather simply and too casually—as a "legitimate inner-scientific" critique but then proceeds to attack "the new cultural history," the "linguistic turn" and its frivolous, relativist, anti-Enlightenment impulses, devoid of social structure and political and intellectual direction.[165]

On this he may be right or wrong. But within our context, the point of the critique appears rather misdirected, for at the same time as Wehler's social history was being written, the cultural historians that we have discussed here *were* writing precisely the kinds of narratives that he admits were absent in his. Unlike the new "cultural history," these scholars *were* morally driven, *were* committed to a liberal, Enlightenment position and steeped in social and political contexts. Yet, even in the most recent reconsiderations undertaken by the social historians, these émigré cultural historians remain virtually invisible, their work and importance given short shrift. The regrettable nondialogue continues.

But we must move on. It is worth remarking that among their many contributions beyond the border, these cultural and intellectual historians brought to our attention the work and achievements of some of the Weimar Jewish thinkers who, at the turn of the twentieth century, have become iconic figures in Western culture. Indeed, their renderings of the progressive "spirit of Weimar," their portrait of this brilliant cultural and intellectual episode and its aftermath—"the exiles Hitler made," Peter Gay once hyperbolically wrote, "were the greatest collection of transplanted intellect, talent, and scholarship the world has ever seen"[166]—has become very much our own, the accepted version and, in many ways, a model for emulation. Although the cultural historians were instrumental in the making and popularization of this canon, they did not enter it themselves. (It is seldom that professional historians themselves become canonic—this is usually reserved for more daring, speculative thinkers.) We must turn now to those who did and ponder how and why these intellectuals—Theodor Adorno, Hannah Arendt, Walter Benjamin, Franz Rosenzweig, Gershom Scholem, and Leo Strauss—have became current icons of Western culture, far, indeed, beyond their borders.

3

Icons beyond the Border

Why Do We Love (Hate) Theodor Adorno, Hannah Arendt, Walter Benjamin, Franz Rosenzweig, Gershom Scholem, and Leo Strauss?

> Dwelling, in the proper sense is now impossible. The traditional resi-
> dences we grew up in have grown intolerable. . . . The house is past. . . .
> It is part of morality not to be at home in one's home.
>
> —Theodor Adorno[1]

> Great writers are either husbands or lovers. Some writers supply the solid
> virtues of a husband: reliability, intelligibility, generosity, decency. There
> are other writers in whom one prizes the gifts of a lover, gifts of tem-
> perament rather than of moral goodness. Notoriously, women tolerate
> qualities in a lover—moodiness, selfishness, unreliability, brutality—that
> they would never countenance in a husband, in return for excitement, an
> infusion of intense feeling. In the same way, readers put up with unintel-
> ligibility, obsessiveness, painful truths, lies, bad grammar—if, in com-
> pensation, the writer allows them to savor rare emotions and dangerous
> sensations. And, as in life, so in art both are necessary, husbands and
> lovers. It's a great pity when one is forced to choose between them.
>
> —Susan Sontag[2]

It would not be an exaggeration, I think, to state that at the beginning
of the twenty-first century, certain Weimar German-Jewish thinkers—
specifically, Theodor Adorno (1903–1969), Hannah Arendt (1906–1975),
Walter Benjamin (1892–1940), Franz Rosenzweig (1886–1929), Gershom Scholem (1898–1982) and Leo Strauss (1899–1973)—stand as central, virtually iconic, figures of Anglo-American, indeed, Western intel-

lectual and academic culture. All have been recognized as being, in some
way or another, "Jewish" thinkers but their thought, writings, and reception have far transcended those borders. Celebrated or castigated, canonized and critiqued, appropriated and interpreted in manifold ways, dissected
in minute (and often contested) detail, they have all achieved remarkable
prominence, well beyond the borders of their birth. With the passing of
time, it seems, their resonance has increased rather than diminished.

Some of this is truly remarkable. Thus, Leo Strauss, who by all contemporary accounts was an exceedingly shy and unworldly refugee figure,[3] is presently being celebrated or reviled (in both the popular as well
as the academic press) as perhaps the most positively or perniciously influential political thinker of our time.[4] Gordon Wood has called Straussianism the largest academic movement of the last century.[5] Whether
or not correctly, Strauss is by now widely regarded as the founder of radical American neoconservatism, characterized, as one hostile observer put
it, by its aversion to liberalism, the rejection of pluralism, its dread of nihilism, populism, dualism, and its appropriation of religiosity. There is a
lively, widespread (and often ridiculous) discussion presently under way,
in fringe, popular, and more highbrow organs alike, as to whether or not
Strauss—via his followers, many of whom currently occupy positions of
power in Washington—is the hidden power behind the present Bush
throne, even the force behind the Iraq War.[6] Of course, neither his devotees nor his many critics and adversaries will find any specific policy
recommendations or endorsement of "a Judeo-Christian crusade against
Islam" or an advocacy of a militant democratization of the world, anywhere
in his writings.[7] On the contrary, throughout his life Strauss remained
an elitist and severe critic of liberal democracy (in fact, some militantly
antiliberal, antisecular Iranian clerics currently find succor in his writings).[8]
If Strauss later endorsed liberal democracy, he did so critically and with
reformist inclinations.[9] In this respect, Arthur Schlesinger's recent assessment that Strauss was apparently not a Straussian seems accurate.[10]

Hannah Arendt, too, has been appropriated by any number of feminist, postmodernist, Jewish, and politically diverse circles.[11] There is an
internationally sponsored Hannah Arendt newsletter. In Germany, where
her presence is particularly pervasive, the Hannah Arendt express train
runs from Karlsruhe to Hannover. Her face adorns a stamp, and her
name a prize given for political thought, a research institute in Dres-

den, and a street that runs directly opposite the new Berlin Holocaust monument.[12] There is, indeed, a veritable and growing international "Arendt cult" (as a rather distressed Walter Laqueur, critical of both the cult and Arendt's political judgment, has recently noted).[13] Her "actuality" is regularly invoked as are attempts to creatively apply her post-totalitararian categories and ruminations concerning freedom to contemporary crises of politics and civilization.[14] Perhaps most surprisingly, with her putatively ideologically motivated Cold War comparison of the Soviet Union with Nazi Germany, Arendt was, until a few decades ago, viewed with some suspicion by the left. Yet, in the post-1989 climate she has become (as Slavov Zizek complains) "an untouchable authority,"[15] reinvented as the "political thinker of hope," an inspirer of the East European dissenters and their "velvet revolution" of free civil society.[16] Like our other thinkers, Arendt's politics were idiosyncratic in cutting through conventional left-right borders. Her refusal to be simply classified, no doubt, encouraged such diverse readings. "You know," she told Hans Morgenthau, "the left think I am conservative, and the conservatives sometimes think I am left or a maverick or God knows what. And I must say I couldn't care less. I don't think the real questions of this century get any kind of illumination from this kind of thing."[17]

The public and political influence of Arendt and Strauss (who, ironically, could not abide each other) is most conspicuous, but a widespread cultural and intellectual mystique also adheres to all our other figures, around whom entire academic industries have been created. It would be a mammoth task to register and analyze this in systematic fashion; indeed, it would be rather futile to render and grade their popularity in statistical or hierarchical manner. But a glance at the continuing attention—qualitative and quantitative—showered on all these thinkers (in the form of books, articles, novels, dramas, and even apparel) makes their appeal patently obvious. To be sure, a cursory search of Google gives Walter Benjamin a remarkably sizeable numerical advantage.[18] He is cited over an astonishing range of topics, disciplines, and issues; manifold ideological and political currents regard him as authoritative, and his fame has moved beyond highbrow circles (where we would expect to find him) and percolated into surprisingly diverse areas of popular culture.[19] He is the only one of these intellectuals for whom a monument has been built—by the Israeli sculptor Dani Karavan at Port Bou, the place of his

suicide—and that has become a site of pilgrimage. Noah Isenberg tells
us that:

> Not only does there now exist an International Walter Benjamin
> Association and a bilingual yearbook, but there are several web-
> pages, a so-called "Walter Benjamin Research Syndicate," a comic
> book-style [*sic*] introduction to this work, and a semi-fictional
> novel on his failed escape from Vichy France. There are widely
> produced photographic portraits and postcards, a Benjamin
> monument in Spain and a Berlin Jewish museum designed with
> a Benjaminian inspiration; there are films, paintings music
> [*sic*]—and the inventory seems to expand each year.[20]

In loose and complicated ways, Benjamin was affiliated with the Frankfurt School, especially Theodor Adorno, who, perhaps only a little less
densely than Benjamin himself, has achieved similar fame. "Should we
Adore Adorno?" Charles Rosen has recently asked.[21] For many the answer is a resoundingly positive one. Certainly, for a while he achieved
the status of an intellectual rock star in Germany and was the subject of
student "look-alike" contests.[22] Frankfurt now has an Adornoplatz. There
is even a Theodor Adorno Jazz Quartet (ironically intended, one would
like to believe, given Adorno's hostility to that form of music). He is,
above all, celebrated (and reviled)[23] as the founder of "Critical Theory."
He has been valorized by Edward Said as the quintessential thinker of
displacement, of actual and metaphorical exile, a "forbidding but endlessly fascinating man . . . the dominating intellectual conscience of the
middle twentieth century."[24]

Rosenzweig and Scholem, it is true, are best known to more limited
Jewish audiences but their presence within general intellectual culture
continues apace. Over the past few years, virtually all of Franz Rosenzweig's writings have appeared in English.[25] "In terms of his depth, his
originality, his immense learning, the power of his mind, and the com-
passion of his vision (not to mention his wide influence on non-Jewish
as well as Jewish thinkers)," Hilary Putnam comments, Franz Rosenzweig
ranks ". . . as one of the most important Jewish thinkers of the twentieth century."[26] There has been a veritable flood of Rosenzweigiana over
the past decade or so.[27] Of late, his politics and indeed erotic life and the

relationship of both to his philosophy and religious thought have aroused interest and heated debate.[28]

Scholem has been compared to Freud;[29] Arnaldo Momigliano once dubbed him "The Master of Mysticism,"[30] and, indeed, his work in that Jewish field has been so pervasively influential that it is often (mis)taken for the Kabbalah itself.[31] As a creator of what Henry Pachter describes as a "mastermyth," Scholem has been invoked by such varied figures as Jorge Luis Borges, Paul Celan, and Harold Bloom.[32] Upon his death, Hans Jonas may well have been speaking for countless leading Jewish, German, European, and American intellectuals who had come into contact (and often combat) with Scholem when he wrote (in a moving letter to Scholem's wife, Fania née Freud): "He was the focal point. Wherever, *he* was, you found the center, the active force, a generator which constantly charged itself; he was what Goethe called an *Urphänomen*."[33]

The continuing relevance and centrality of these intellectuals is a rather extraordinary phenomenon worth remarking and analyzing. Why does it pertain? To some extent, no doubt, it can be attributed to an ongoing post-Holocaust commemoration and the rather romantic valorization of German-Jewish intellectuals and their legacy in general. Portrayed, as Peter Gordon has pointed out, as "a special type, distinctive and separate in character," there is in particular "a certain kind of nostalgia . . . around the memory of Weimar's most prominent Jews, who became the belated representatives of a fascinating past."[34] But while this surely provides the general context, it tells us little about these intellectuals in particular and why, in the present cultural climate, their work appears to be especially riveting. We can begin to approach this question by examining the history and defining qualities of these figures and focusing on their common—rather than many distinguishing—features.

The successful migration of their thought, that these thinkers all became "icons beyond the border," may be related to the fact that while they began their careers in Weimar Germany, most also physically left the borders of their birth and, in various ways and places, pursued their productive lives elsewhere. Franz Rosenzweig was the exception. His tragic 1929 death in Germany from a painful and progressive paralysis—amyotrophic lateral sclerosis (otherwise known as Lou Gehrig's disease)—and his heroic comportment prior to that, has become an integral part of his legend.[35] All the others traversed the German border and—Walter

Benjamin's tragic case apart—despite the many hardships they encountered became exceedingly successful in their various continuing intellectual enterprises. Their personal odysseys have become almost as much a factor in their subsequent fame as the nature and quality of their thought.

Gershom Scholem was the first to depart Germany. He left as early as 1923 for Palestine—not as an exile or refugee but as an enthusiastic, if always idiosyncratic, Zionist. Formidable and immensely erudite, he spent the rest of his life in Jerusalem virtually inventing the academic field of Jewish mysticism, achieving international recognition, all the while subverting the conventional ideological borders of liberalism, Zionism, and normative Judaism alike.[36]

Perhaps predictably, *Benjamin's Crossing* (the name of a popular novel, filled with overheated erotic intimations, on this subject by Jay Parini)[37] turned out differently: fleeing from the Nazis in 1940 and believing himself trapped, he killed himself at Port Bou on the French-Spanish border. His suicide and person have become virtually emblematic of the Jewish intellectual who both questioned and was robbed of recognized borders: "the dialectical Jew," as Terry Eagleton dubbed him, "at a standstill, declaring the small hoarse sound of the Torah in the customs shed."[38]

The others were all, and indeed considered themselves, exiles—refugees from Nazism who found shelter in the United States. Hannah Arendt and Leo Strauss made North America their new home and continued to write and live there until their deaths.[39] Theodor Adorno's American sojourn, on the other hand, lasted from 1938 to 1953 when he returned—with little enthusiasm from the German academic community—to his native land.[40] (He was initially greeted with great fanfare by the students but as the protest movements of the late 1960s got under way, relations there also soured and the tensions became palpable.)[41] His disdain for America, the discomfort and sense of foreignness he exuded is well known. A fellow immigrant, Paul Lazarsfeld, noted of him that: "He looks as you would image a very absent-minded German professor, and he behaves so foreign that I feel like a member of the Mayflower society."[42] "Adorno's disdain for American culture bordered on the pathological," another commentator has declared, "and he was barely tolerant of other émigrés' attempts to master that culture; nobody was less inclined to assimilate."[43] (To be sure, as Martin Jay has shown, the matter was more complex than

these assertions. The American model, and its methodological preferences, did have its impact, and not an entirely negative one, on Adorno.)[44]

Whether or not these figures felt integrated, they retained a clear aura
(to use a Benjaminian expression) of foreignness. There is, surely, some
validity to Walter Laqueur's laconic observation that the views of these
refugee thinkers on American society were exceedingly narrow because
few of them could drive a car![45] This was a cohort, then, whose formative years were spent in the Weimar Republic and whose oeuvres stubbornly bore the creative and often problematic imprint of its culture,
politics, and sensibility. Indeed, it is my contention, that the perception
that they *were quintessentially Weimar thinkers* constitutes an integral
part of their charisma and canonization beyond the border. They are
feted in the way they are partly because they fit the myth of the Weimar
Republic—a double-edged myth that is half danger and warning (of
failed democracy, economic, social and moral breakdown, the rise of fascism, the consequent persecution of intellectuals and minorities) and
half an idealized picture of the daring experimental spirit, the dissenting temperament, the revolutionary burst of intellectual innovation and
artistic creativity[46] that characterized those years. In many accounts of
that republic's history, these two halves are portrayed as integrally inter-
connected. The émigré historians we discussed in the last chapter were
at the forefront of the formulation and dissemination of this version.
Much of the liberal Anglo-American image of that republic, the inter-
related nature of its flaws and greatness, derives from their writings. Here
the highly charged "myth of Weimar" stands as both the dark precondi-
tion and the ultimate antithesis of Nazism.

The cult of Weimar is also no doubt related to a general attraction to
"European" thinkers—their passionate intellectuality, critical engagement, formidable "depth"—and a certain estrangement from American
culture. Susan Sontag once dubbed Benjamin the "Last Intellectual,"[47]
and Benjamin, upon contemplating emigration to the United States
imagined himself as the "Last European."[48] To be sure, Benjamin was
acutely aware of the dangers of cultlike transmission: "But from what
can something from the past be saved? Not so much from the contempt
and disregard into which it has been handed down. The way in which it
is celebrated as our 'heritage' is more ominous than oblivion."[49] Indeed,

he wrote to Adorno in 1939 that ". . . homesickness for the Weimar Republic . . . is simply appalling."[50]

These warnings would not make much difference when it came to the later reception of these intellectuals. Indeed, for some readers, paradoxically, the very difficulty of thought, the obscurity and impenetrability of style, rendered these thinkers more attractive, apparently in possession of a certain intellectual magic, of secrets available only to initiates. Nietzsche's self-referential comments could well apply to many of the thinkers under consideration here: "Posthumous men—I, for example—are understood worse than timely ones, but *heard* better. More precisely: we are never understood—*hence* our authority."[51] Scholem put it a little more charitably of Benjamin (to a certain degree his words could be applied as much to himself and the other figures under consideration here). Benjamin's prose had an

> enormous suitability for canonization: I might almost say for quotation as a kind of Holy Writ. . . . In this respect it enjoys one advantage over the canonical texts of Marx, Engels, or Lenin so beloved by Marxists: its deep connection with theology. . . . His sentences often enough have the authoritarian stance of words of revelation. . . . [H]e would have accepted his appointment as Church father, or . . . Marxist rabbi, quite graciously, though with dialectical reservations.[52]

(To be sure, there were, and continue to be, those who resisted such work, precisely for these reasons. Thus the publisher Salman Schocken who was closely linked to these Weimar figures—he published or patronized Rosenzweig, Strauss, Scholem, and for a while employed Hannah Arendt in New York—found Benjamin's work incomprehensible and despite the imprecations of Arendt, Scholem, and Adorno was wary of putting him into print.)[53]

For American students and intellectuals, such Weimar figures, Paul Breines once noted, represented an exotic Other, foreign yet close enough to encourage identification—particularly given their own marginal status as Jews, or victims or outsiders. To be sure, this attraction in part constitutes a species of "identity politics," one in which Jewishness and critical intellectuality have come to be seen as virtually synonymous.[54] This has become a kind of credo. There is by now a large literature—

George Mosse and George Steiner are only the better-known authors in this regard—in which Central European, and especially Weimarian, Jewish intellectuality serves as a metaphor for the critical, yet always humanizing mind.[55] This was an impression that many of these figures themselves encouraged. "For me," Benjamin declared, "Jewishness is not in any sense an end in itself but the noble bearer and representative of the intellect."[56]

But, again, such a very generalized account only takes us so far. It does not really tell us why these particular Weimar German-Jewish intellectuals rather than others are currently so resonant, why they rather than other figures of their time have traveled so well. Why, for instance, do Scholem and Rosenzweig presently attract more respectful attention than, say, Martin Buber? Why is it that Arendt and Strauss are so much more audible than, say, Ernst Cassirer? Why, for that matter, do we hear far more today of Adorno and Benjamin than Ernst Bloch and even Herbert Marcuse?

To be sure, intellectual reputation, as Stefan Collini has recently reminded us, always contains a degree of indeterminacy. "Membership of the jury is heterogeneous," he writes,

> the various parts of a writer's oeuvre or achievement may receive different ratings from different categories of reader; it is almost impossible to maintain a clear distinction between questions of merit and the neigbouring territories of celebrity and utility; and at any given moment judgement is almost inevitably contaminated by hearsay, selective recall, and cultural lag.[57]

Clearly, then, no single account will suffice. Intellectual fads and fashions will always enter into the equation.[58] Yet fads and fashions usually possess some contextual and political grounding, and in this respect, our thinkers seem closely aligned to the "textual" and paradoxical sensibilities that characterize much of current academic culture. Thus Buber, who was feted especially during the 1950s, now appears (however unfairly) too pious and pontificatory, too prophetic and "Christian," insufficiently "textual" (indeed, his reputation was sullied in no small measure by Scholem, and to some degree as well by Benjamin on these grounds). Ernst Cassirer, though by no means entirely neglected, somehow seems too classically "liberal," too conventionally "bourgeois" to make his way into the current pantheon. And while Adorno and Benjamin indulged in qualified, complex ruminations, Marcuse and Bloch were unabashedly "political," prophets of clear and activist "hope." Their heyday occurred in the optimistic, heady 1960s. In our own grayer, more ambiguous times, more shaded, indeterminate approaches, seem congenial.

Thus, Walter Benjamin's vaunted messianism is celebrated precisely because it is a densely complex, qualified one. "I came into the world under the sign of Saturn," he wrote, "the star of the slowest revolution, the planet of detours and delays."[59] Benjamin's project, his attempt to salvage doomed or forgotten pasts and defeated, oppressed communities necessarily came mixed with memories and intimations of catastrophe. (As Ehud Greenberg has suggested, his very refusal to make an ultimate political commitment—either for Marxism or Zionism—has been transfigured by his devotees into an admirable internal imperative, a mark of impeccable authenticity, rather than as a sign of confusion or defeatism as some of his acquaintances believed at the time.)[60]

But the iconicity of these thinkers is surely not just limited to their determined complexity and sophistication of mind. Despite some large and obvious differences between them, their present appeal derives from a number of shared characteristics. They were all suspicious of bourgeois conventions and liberal pieties, and their thought was animated by complex but always radical impulses and heterodox sensitivities. Orthodoxy, of almost any kind, was not an option (even the apparent "return" to traditional Judaism of Rosenzweig was performed on the basis of a radical and immanent reconceptualization of its classical precepts).[61] A collective portrait of their creations (and contestations) may help us understand a little better perhaps both the nature of their concerns and our attraction to them.

Of course, their projects went in very different directions. None of them can be easily pigeonholed; indeed, it is partly in their resistance to simple ideological classification, their turn to heterodoxy, and their amenability to manifold appropriations that much of their appeal may lie. Adorno and Benjamin—each with his own literary, philosophical, political, or musicological twist—are usually regarded within the prism of a theologically inflected "negative metaphysics" of cultural critique (high and low) and, for many, with a humanistically reconceived "Western" Marxism.[62] Hannah Arendt is renowned not only as the analyst of totalitarianism but for her thinking through of its implications for the Western philosophical tradition as a whole, and her formulation of a postmetaphysical pluralist politics as the sphere of autonomous and spontaneous action.[63] Franz Rosenzweig is known for his interrogation and dismissal of idealist metaphysics and his re-aligning of traditional "religious" and transcendental categories such as creation, revelation, and redemption within a temporal frame. His "existential" understanding of immanent Jewish life insisted that it take place beyond conventional physical and political borders, as something ontologically separate from its surroundings.[64] Gershom Scholem, that "primordial" Zionist, was animated by an antinomian theologico-metaphysical dream of the regeneration of Judaism, fueled by his single-handed embrace of the study of Jewish mysticism. He integrated into his radical philosophy of history, sects and movements previously regarded as too obscure and obscurantist for serious consideration and decipherment and bestowed upon them a vitalizing function at the very heart of the Jewish historical project.[65] Leo Strauss reread classical politicophilosophical texts against the modern (and liberal) grain, privileged premodern rationalism, and sought to delineate the separate functions of (everyday, cynical) politics—he approved of Plato's "noble lies"—from (truthful though dangerous) philosophy. Not always fully convinced, he reasserted the claims of faith over Enlightenment reason but was able neither to surrender loyalty to his ancestral community nor to the claims of a transcendent philosophical tradition (perhaps, in the end, through his interpretation of the esoteric meaning of Plato, he conflated the two, and Athens and Jerusalem became, as it were, one.)[66]

Strauss is the only one of these intellectuals who can be said to occupy a right-wing position (whatever that may mean) on the political spectrum. Rosenzweig, it is true, once described himself as a monarchist, but unlike Strauss, his thought has been interpreted (correctly or not) as decidedly apolitical, even antipolitical.[67] What is relevant here, however, is the fact that Strauss's conservatism was highly idiosyncratic: he belongs to the present group of thinkers by virtue of this heterodox stance, his insistent radicalism (in the original sense of going back to and understanding texts and problems at their root), and his ongoing interrogation and suspicion of the modalities of liberal and mass modernity. Like our other thinkers, the origins and directions of his work are

to be located in Weimar. To be sure, some of Strauss's Weimar friendships and influences—such as his friendship with Carl Schmitt and the
spell cast over him by Martin Heidegger—are not particularly alluring.
There are many who will not forget Strauss's pert observation in the
1930s that Schmitt's critique of liberalism was not radical enough because it took place "within the horizon of liberalism."[68]

But before throwing ahistorical stones, it is necessary to note that in
one way or another the projects of all our thinkers were infused with—
and often directly influenced by—Heideggerian themes or, at least, a
post-Nietzschean sensibility, acutely aware after the Great War, of a
great crisis of continuity, tradition, and normative values. Their sensibilities, the nature of their preoccupations, the kinds of questions they
posed, and the answers they proffered were projects that today we take to
be quintessentially Weimarian.[69] What connects our group to other such
posthumously celebrated and inevitably problematic Weimar thinkers—
Martin Heidegger, Ernst Jünger, Carl Schmitt, and so on—is the fact
that all engaged in essentially postliberal ruminations, posited on the
ruins of, and a disbelief in, the old political and conceptual order. For all
their differences, left, right, and Jewish circles advocated a kind of "root"
rethinking that variously explored novel ways in which to comprehend
the disarray of post–World War European civilization—and to provide
radical solutions for its predicament.[70]

There were great differences among the thinkers we are considering
here, yet in many ways they constituted a kind of community of affinity.
They chose different objects of reflection and distinct modes of self-
definition and political hope—indeed they insisted upon these markers
of separateness—but the issues and dilemmas that plagued them, the
categories in which they thought were of one cloth. They were all extreme and heterodox thinkers—beyond the borders in both literal and
metaphorical ways. They naturally gravitated to issues and agendas of
displacement and sought to remap the cognitive frontiers, a source of
both their originality and ongoing attractiveness.

Radical themes and transformative sensibilities also characterized the
thought and work of Heidegger and Schmitt. But while these figures
exert an influence on contemporary intellectual culture, their overt associations with National Socialism have rendered them consistently dubious, suspect. Our thinkers, on the other hand, precisely because they

were Jewish exiles, refugees, and victims of Nazism, "outsiders as insiders" in Peter Gay's memorable phrase, could far more easily be accommodated. Moreover, all—in one way or another (Rosenzweig obviously excepted)—later became analysts and critics of the Nazi and totalitarian experience: many of their ruminations upon the Third Reich, mass murder, and the German-Jewish experience remain foundational. These analyses in tandem with their personal histories rendered their work particularly salient: it also helped to make their ongoing critiques of liberalism and bourgeois modernity more acceptable, palatable, *salonfähig*. It may indeed be that it was this status as Jews and vulnerable outsiders that defined the limits of their antiliberalism, that rendered them immune to the kind of integral and Völkisch nationalism that so attracted figures like Heidegger, Schmitt, Jünger, and so on.[71] In that sense, our thinkers can more easily serve as "ideal types" of the Weimar experience, while the Heideggers and Schmitts seem to incarnate its darker impulses.

There is, of course, another obvious difference. In the turbulent and hostile circumstances of their time, our thinkers were all explicitly confronted with—and attempted to provide creative solutions to—what Leo Strauss has called the Jewish "theologicopredicament."[72] This entailed dealing, in one way or another, with the subtle tensions and ambiguities of their own Jewish, culturally hybrid, identity. There is nothing new or surprising in this. But, given the later canonic status of these thinkers it *is* rather startling to note that (with the exception of Adorno) these figures were all either profoundly involved in or, at least, in dialogue with or intimately aware of the world of German Zionism. This is surprising because German Zionism was, after all, a fringe phenomenon.[73] The Zionist engagement of so many German-Jewish intellectuals who were later to achieve international fame, the creative energies it inspired, is rather astonishing and a tale that awaits its historian (our own figures and those discussed in chapter 1 apart, names like Erich Fromm, Leo Löwenthal, Hans Jonas, and Norbert Elias by no means exhaust the list).[74]

Perhaps its very marginal nature constitutes part of the explanation. It would be an exaggeration—but not a great one—to say that the alternatives for sensitive, dissenting, antibourgeois, postliberal, youthful Jewish intellectuals of the Weimar Republic consisted of the choice between Zionism and Marxism (and sometimes a combination of the two—even if later they moved beyond or refined both these positions). Rosenzweig was entirely exceptional for his devising a viewpoint that bypassed—and challenged—both.

Zionism, like Marxism, was a boundary phenomenon, a form of personal and intellectual displacement—and re-placement. At the time, it appeared to its proponents as a genuinely regenerative, even revolutionary, option: its attractiveness derived in no small part from its critique of bourgeois Jewish hypocrisy. In a sense joining the Zionist movement was both a déclassé and an antipatriotic statement. In this respect, the case of Gershom Scholem is exemplary. When the young Gerhard refused to sign up for service in the German army's World War I effort, his father threw him out of his house, whence, characteristically, he went to board with like-minded, relatively impoverished East European Zionist intellectuals, including the later Nobel Prize winner Shmuel Yosef Agnon (Czazckes) and a later Israeli president, Zalman Shazar (Rubashoff).[75] Likewise, Franz Kafka's impassioned, if always vicarious, flirtation with Zionism, as well as his attraction to the Ostjuden, was intimately connected to his distaste for the insipid, hypocritical, liberal, bourgeois Judaism of his Prague home (as immortalized in his classic *Letter to His Father*).

There were of course significant differences in the respective Zionism of these figures. Detailed elaboration would require an almost book-length treatment. But for all the differences, their affirmation of nationalism went together with a heterodox radicalism and the rejection of conventional Herzlian "political" Zionism whose "normalizing" impulses they regarded as essentially "assimilatory." In Weimar (and its immediate aftermath), Scholem, Strauss, and Arendt, formulated highly idiosyncratic Zionist visions—ranging from Scholem's rather apocalyptic vision of a dialectically generated "religious-mystic" regeneration of Judaism to Strauss's critique of the liberal State's inability to sustain Jewish life. "To realize that the Jewish problem is insoluble," he declared, "means ever to bear in mind the truth proclaimed by Zionism regarding the limitations of liberalism." Indeed, provocatively, in 1923 he invoked the work of a notorious anti-Semite as a model of intellectual probity for Zionists to emulate: "It is hardly an exaggeration to say," he declared, "that the level of the anti-Semitic argumentation of a man such as Paul de Lagarde . . . has yet to be reached in Zionism."[76] While Zionism

would indeed redress Jewish honor—cleanse "the Jews of their millen-
nial degradation,"[77] as he later put it—from very early on, he opposed
the "assimilatory" dimensions of Max Nordau's political Zionism: its
overtly secular nature would drain Judaism of its special ethical and
messianic content and thus render it imitatively mundane.[78] Zionism
was essential to modern Jewish life but its inherent secularity and its desire to liquidate the Galut meant that the ultimate questions of Jewish faith
and life would remain unresolved. Hannah Arendt's Zionism, unlike that
of Strauss and Scholem, was entirely uninterested in Judaism but was
passionately concerned with anti-Semitism and the reaction of the Jews
as a people, particularly under conditions of persecution. It was vital, she
wrote, to collectively and individually affirm an identity that was under
attack.[79] She formulated a bitter critique of debilitating assimilation and
pleaded, above all, for effective national and political action. (Arendt's
later turn away from Zionism has obscured the fact that apart from her
biography of *Rahel Varnhagen,* her treatment of anti-Semitism, Jewish
comportment, and the need for solidarity in *The Origins of Totalitarianism* is crucially informed by her postassimilationist Zionist perspective.)[80]

This shared sensibility and world of interests extended to our other
figures. Through his intense friendship and correspondence with Scholem, Benjamin was intimately apprised of issues that were preoccupying
Zionism and constantly expressed his opinions on them and some of
its leading personalities (especially Martin Buber).[81] Much like Kafka,
he constantly flirted with the idea of studying Hebrew and moving
to Palestine (without, of course, ever seriously considering it). Franz
Rosenzweig's depiction of the Jews as profoundly metahistorical, a nation that lived outside of history, his valorization of exile as both intrin-
sic to the Jewish cycle and a condition of redemption as an immanent
possibility—eternity as "now really there"—was, of course, profoundly
non-Zionist or even anti-Zionist.[82] But the early Rosenzweig was convinced that Jewish intellectuals had only two choices, Zionism or bap-
tism.[83] Later, as is well known, he formulated another option, yet his
understanding of the exhaustion of bourgeois liberalism—"The liberal
German-Jewish position," he wrote in 1924, "which has been the meeting ground to almost the whole of German Jewry for nearly a quarter of
a century, has obviously dwindled to the size of a pin-point"[84]—his
search for radical alternatives and the need for "a new thinking," and

above all, his configuration of the Jews as a living, separate (indeed organic) entity, made him an obvious *Gesprächspartner,* the relevant and most serious point of contestation for the Zionists with whose leading intellectuals he was close friends and in constant touch. If he remained skeptical it was sympathetically so. In 1922 he told Richard Koch: "Zionism is perhaps after all one of the nation's roads into the future. This road, too, should be kept open," and in 1927 declared to Hans Ehrenburg:

> You can get a better understanding of Zionism by considering
> the significance of socialism for the church. Just as the Social
> Democrats, even if they are not "religious socialists," even if they
> are "atheists," are more important for the establishment of the
> kingdom of God through the church than the church-minded . . .
> so the Zionists are for the synagogue.[85]

It was, indeed, to Rosenzweig that Hermann Cohen made his famous contemptuous clinching argument against Zionism—"those guys [*kerle*] want to be happy!"[86]—precisely because he found the latter too tolerant of that movement.

Weimar Jewish intellectuals in general often were linked by a dense network of relationships.[87] To be sure, at no time did the figures under consideration here form an organized or institutional "group." Still, they were more than merely an accidental "community of affinity"—their interconnections went deep and encompassed the whole spectrum of relationships ranging from close friendship to serious enmity. The tensions between Arendt and Adorno, for instance, were manifold and too well known to rehearse here. But, as so often happens in charged relations like these, they were hardly the ones to recognize the historical and ideational commonalities that later generations would increasingly emphasize.[88] In fact, to the end, these figures were each others' real interlocutors, the relevant others—even, perhaps especially, when they were engaged in intense intellectual, personal, and ideological combat.

One wonders whether or not those who have separately canonized these thinkers have any idea of the intellectually engaged and often charged personal relations that obtained between them. It is well known that Adorno, Arendt, and Scholem enthusiastically spread the word of Benjamin and in effect were instrumental in creating his aura (even though they differed passionately about the nature and meaning of his legacy and their varying roles in this popularization),[89] but few would be aware, for instance, that Leo Strauss's 1930 work on *Spinoza's Critique of Religion* was dedicated to the memory of Franz Rosenzweig. The mutual influences and fascinating interchanges between these passionate and highly opinionated intellectuals would make a rather riveting study. Although the temptation is great we will resist undertaking this here. Suffice it to say that, usually with Scholem as the connecting or central figure, these encounters were tempestuous, volatile, and complex. (Scholem's love for Benjamin, his early admiration for, and later detestation of, Arendt are familiar enough; perhaps less known is the mutual regard and suspicion in which Scholem and Rosenzweig related to each other—Rosenzweig, not entirely inaccurately labeled him "evil . . . a nihilist"—and the respectful connection that prevailed between him and Leo Strauss.)[90] I cannot resist citing, as just one small, and lesser-known, example, Adorno's initial 1938 meeting with Scholem in New York. Adorno wrote to Walter Benjamin that the "spiritual energy of the man [Scholem] is enormous, and he certainly belongs amongst those very few individuals with whom it is still worthwhile discussing such serious matters." His encounter with what he incisively called the "antinomian Maggid" produced "a certain trust—rather like that which might develop between an Ichthyosaurus and a Brontosaurus meeting for coffee, or even better, as if Leviathan should decide to drop in on Behemoth."[91]

The interconnections, then, are clear and intriguing. But the fact that these Weimar, Jewish (and often Zionist) thinkers were acquainted either with each others' works or person does not, on its own, explain why they have subsequently achieved posthumous canonic status through to the present moment.[92] The romance of personal exile, a certain marginality, and even victimhood do play a certain role in the iconicity of these figures. Their lives and thought were conducted both literally and conceptually beyond their inherited geographical and normative borders. Their confrontations with Jewishness (and Zionism), their personal plights, correspondences and critiques, indeed their projects themselves revolved around issues of displacement and replacement.[93] If they left old borders behind, they also sought to recast the boundaries. Scholem, the ardent Zionist, was surprisingly aware and affirmative of this exilic dimension of intellectual creativity. Freud, Kafka, and Benjamin, he wrote, did not fool themselves. They knew that they were German writers—but not Germans. They never cut loose from that experience and the clear awareness of being aliens, even exiles. . . . I do not know whether these men would have been at home in the land of Israel. I doubt it very much. They truly came from foreign parts and knew it.[94]

This was a generation for whom dislocation was often a constitutive personal experience and later a preferred theoretical stance. "Life among the émigrés is unbearable," Benjamin wrote in 1933 from Paris, "life alone is no more bearable, and a life among the French cannot be brought about. So only work remains, but nothing endangers it more than the recognition that it is so obviously the final inner mental resource (it is no longer an external one)."[95] In 1943 Hannah Arendt caustically complained about the refugees' "mania for refusing to keep their identity" and the reluctance of others to endure their version of the world ("how often have we been told that nobody likes to listen to all that: hell is no longer a religious belief or fantasy, but something as real as houses and stones and trees"). She concluded with a conception of refugeehood as a universal condition, one that ironically would at last provide the mode of Jewish connection to the wider world:

> [T]he outlawing of the Jewish people in Europe has been
> closely followed by the outlawing of most European nations.
> Refugees driven from country to country represent the vanguard
> of their peoples—if they keep their identity. For the first time
> Jewish history is not separate but tied up with that of all other
> nations. The comity of European peoples went to pieces when,
> and because, it allowed its weakest member to be excluded and
> persecuted.[96]

Suffering and victimization do, of course, figure as general themes in the intellectual iconicity of the twentieth century, and in this respect, some of our thinkers have become exemplary. The pain, courage, and piety of Rosenzweig, the driven desperation and suicide of Benjamin have become integral to their reception, their personal, martyred fates often indistinguishable from the ideas themselves (this may encourage commemoration but is not always conducive to an equally necessary cri-

Portrait of Gershom Scholem; 1962. Copyright
Hebrew University Jerusalem. Courtesy of the Leo
Baeck Institute, New York.

tique).[97] Moroever, displacement entered the modalities and marrow of
their thought: for Rosenzweig exile was no longer antithetical to redemption but became a condition for it; the later Strauss believed that
the liquidation of exile (Galut)—as an essential binding force—would
spell the end of genuine Jewish existence; Scholem dwelled endlessly on
the dialectic transformations Jewish mystics wrought on the notion of
Galut as a central component of Jewish political and spiritual economy.

   Indeed, not all could resist the temptation to universalize that condition of difference and marginality. Leo Strauss once commented that
"... it looks as if the Jewish people were the chosen people in the sense,
at least, that the Jewish problem is the most manifest symbol of the
human problem as a social or political problem."[98] It has even been suggested that because Adorno was of mixed German-Jewish descent, neither "fully" one nor the other (he derived his name from his non-Jewish
mother—his father's name was Wiesengrund), this "double-negative"
became incarnated in his work. Elizabeth Wilcox has recently provocatively suggested that it was because of this "that Adorno wrote *Negative*

Dialectics and the concept of negative identity is central to his work."[99] His own mixed, indeterminate background and identification is reflected in the warp of his philosophical thought and forms the basis of his attack not only on Heidegger's *Jargon of Authenticity* but also, Wilcox argues, for a critique of an intolerant, essentialist "Jewish" identity. While Wittgenstein demanded silence about that which we cannot speak, Adorno insisted: "If philosophy can be defined at all, it is an effort to speak of things one cannot speak about, to help express the nonidentical despite the fact that expressing it identifies it at the same time."

But important as this marginal Jewish (or semi-Jewish) condition may have been, this does not sufficiently account for a fame and canonicity that clearly also transcends Jewish and ethnic boundaries. An examination, for example, of Adorno's and Benjamin's reception in the fields of literary, film and art theory, political thought, musicology, philosophy, Marxism, postcolonialism, and so on, reveals that more often than not there is no mention of their Jewishness; it is simply irrelevant. Their thought and persons were and remain resonant because they included but also went beyond this particular dimension. In a clearly autobiographical remark, Hannah Arendt perceptively noted—and here she was acting not merely as the ornithologist but also as the bird—that the most clear-sighted intellectuals "were led by their personal conflicts to a much more general and radical problem, namely to questioning the relevance of the Western tradition as a whole."[100]

Little wonder, then, that Franz Kafka was seminal for most of our figures.[101] His depiction of writing as "an assault against the frontiers"[102] perfectly matches their endeavors. Displacement was not just a personal predicament; their very modes of thinking, their styles and methods reflected that condition. Rosenzweig envisioned a Judaism of national belonging and redemption that essentially nullified place. Scholem's insistence upon the dialectical role of the mystical impulse in Jewish life crucially entailed displacing the purported exclusive hegemony of Jewish normative law and was animated by an acute consciousness of "the fine line between religion and nihilism."[103] Indeed, in his youth Scholem defined Zionism as a life lived without illusions—at the boundary.[104]

The oeuvres and methods of all these figures resist classification and clear demarcation; they function "on the border of several areas."[105] "But

Theodor Adorno. Courtesy of the Leo Baeck Institute,
New York.

really," Scholem asked Benjamin, "where could your work be placed?"[106]
If this liminality in part reflected their inherited historical situation, it
also energized their creative vitality—and is an important ground for our
own intrigued responses to them.[107] Their heterodox projects were simultaneously engaged, critical, paradoxical, despairing, and salvationary. Thus,
in 1931, Benjamin justified his communism by likening himself to "a cast-

away who drifts on a wreck by climbing to the top of an already crumbling mast. But, from here he has a chance to give a signal for his rescue."[108]

Acutely sensitive to the overall crisis of tradition and authority, contemptuous of the bourgeois present, wary of easy liberal duplicity, they were aware, as Arendt put it, that there was no possibility of an unmediated "return" to either the German or European or Jewish tradition.[109] They all thus sought new and unexpected ways and sources for reconfiguring such traditions and finding renewed modes of relating to them at a time when both their message and authority had come into question. Thus, when Benjamin was asked to write a history of ideas in the modern era, Adorno advised him that a totally new approach would have to be found, "one which would be capable of abruptly grasping and simultaneously shattering the totality and the intellectual history involved . . . beyond *all* the available categories of bourgeois conformism."[110]

They all rejected historicism and despised positivism. They abjured social science for its false "value neutrality" and for a relativism that diminished both the actual and potential human condition:[111] ". . . the Social Sciences, an abominable discipline from every point of view," Arendt once declared.[112] They dismissed traditional idealism and approached their materials in antitotalizing ways;[113] many searched for cracks and fissures and the significance that could be ascribed to them; most were attracted by the fragmentary, the esoteric (Strauss even revived this as a guiding interpretive method). Most were fascinated by the subterranean and the antinomian ("by its very nature" Scholem declared, "mysticism involves the danger of an uncontrolled deviation from traditional authority").[114] In one way or another, all were propelled by, or at least interested in, what one observer has called "the heretical imperative."[115] No wonder that Scholem defined the Frankfurt School (with which Benjamin was—albeit uneasily—associated) as a kind of Jewish heresy, one "of the three remarkable 'Jewish sects' that German Jewry had produced"[116] (a comment members of the Frankfurt School would most probably not have particularly welcomed).

Given all these characteristics, it is no wonder that one important force behind the lionization of these thinkers is that identified with what, for lack of a better word, we call postmodernism. They were, after all, masters of interpretation and textuality—all virtues "privileged" by postmodernism. Moreover, precisely because their projects were multifaceted

Portrait of Walter Benjamin; 1926 (Photograph by Germaine Krull). Copyright Germaine Krull Estate, Museum Folkwang, Essen. Courtesy of the Leo Baeck Institute, New York.

and protean in nature, an assault on the frontiers, they lend themselves to manifold readings and interpretations. As early as 1919, Scholem conceived of the canonic as "pure interpretability."[117] Part of their own present canonicity flows from this aspect of their work, and it is surely no coincidence that (with the obvious exception of Strauss) they have all been annexed to, or associated with, this dominating intellectual impulse of the late twentieth century. In one way or the other, they have

Hannah Arendt. Courtesy of the Hannah Arendt Blücher
Literary Trust.

been depicted as among its forerunners, prefiguring or mirroring its
concerns, or, at least, interpreted in terms of its guiding tenets. Their
own arcane, dense, portentous, paradoxical, often oracular and (sometimes annoyingly) impenetrable mode of writing demands complex decipherment and creative exegesis, perfect grist for the endless deconstructionist mill.

There is, of course, some validity to this appropriation. The emphasis on rupture, fragmentation, and "nonidentity," the critique of positivist and historicist reason, the postmetaphysical rejection of "system" and totalities are of one piece with many postmodernist predilections. In order to make this case in a suitably differentiated fashion, one would have to undertake detailed analyses of each individual. This cannot be undertaken here. Still, all our figures do represent examples of what Hannah Arendt called "thinking without banisters." Arendt's emphases on narrative disclosure and performativity, on "stories," her resistance to homogeneity and emphasis on plurality render such an interpretation quite plausible in her own case.[118]

For all that, the differences may be more important than the commonalities and illuminate why, in my view, despite the influence some of these thinkers have had on the deconstructionist moment, they may very well outlast it. This is partly a methodological difference and partly one of sensibility—if one must classify our thinkers, they should be regarded within the prism of modernism, not postmodernism. Thus Benjamin's theory of language—"that there is no event or thing in either animate or inanimate nature that does not partake of language"—is, on the surface remarkably consonant, with the linguistic turn. But, as Susan Handelman has persuasively demonstrated, the gulf is significant, for as Benjamin insisted, "the view that the mental essence of a thing consists precisely in its language—this view, taken as a hypothesis, is the great abyss into which all linguistic theory threatens to fall, and to survive suspended precisely over this abyss is its task." Benjamin did not regard this as a mere methodological question. For him the matter was, rather, historical, ontological, even theological. The "semiotic view of language as an arbitrary system of signs," he declared, "is a result of the 'Fall' from an original pure nonsignifying language of names." Benjamin most certainly did not abandon "history" for "language" or dissolve the former into a pure form of the latter. Cultural forms were comprehensible only through time; indeed their works contained the "capacity to refer to the future as well."[119] With Benjamin, Handelman argues, "the fragments are quite different, but in running up each against each other at the broken places they 'somehow' are of a piece."[120]

Scholem's world too neatly approximates some postmodernist preferences: the emphasis on transgression, paradox, and the abyss; on the

Leo Strauss. Courtesy of Heinrich Meier.

breakdown of tradition and its transmissibility; on normative messages that have lost their significance (even if they still contain validity). Yet, despite his warnings of the messianic impulse, he was obviously drawn to and fascinated by it. The world *did* ultimately contain revelatory and redemptive possibilities. Which deconstructionist could have written, as did Scholem in 1937: "Today, my work lives in this paradox, in the hope of a true communication from the mountain, of that most invisible, smallest fluctuation of history which causes truth to break forth from the illusions of 'development'"?[121]

The same assumptions inform Adorno's dialectical method. For, while analyzing the totalizing dangers of identity thinking, he provides the conceptual tools for dealing with the postmodernist dilemma of "a blunt prioritization of particularity, diversity and non-identity" (in Peter Dews's words).[122] He resists absolutizing "difference" by insisting that non-

Franz Rosenzweig; 1926. Courtesy of the Leo Baeck
Institute, New York.

identity cannot be respected by abandoning completely the principle of
identity: "the sense of non-identity contains identity."[123] Nihilism is not
the only conclusion: the structures of meaning and rationality have not
entirely broken down.

Rosenzweig too has lately been described and appropriated as a
prophet of postmodernism. But as Peter Gordon has perceptively noted,

the differences are more significant than the putative resemblances.
While Rosenzweig certainly opposed the notion that philosophy was
able to encompass the "All" and that knowledge was "always bounded,
local and finite," he regarded this as essentially coherent, "while postmodernism sees local knowledge as inevitably prone to disruption from
the meanings beyond its frame." Moreover, Rosenzweig nowhere cele-
brates disunity and alterity: Difference does not triumph over holism.
On the contrary there is an "affirmation of the community as the specific and irreducible unit of redemptive meaning."[124] Diversity "*is not
constitutive of human experience as such*"; what counts in Rosenzweig's
"messianic theory of knowledge" is the traditional Jewish precept, "the
idea that the future will bring unity to the now-fragmented world."[125]

I am not concerned here with the relative weaknesses and strengths
of these positions but rather with situating our thinkers and their projects historically and examining in which ways they may account for their
ongoing iconicity. Like the postmodernists, these figures both reflect
and speak to our sense of a fractured, post-Nietzschean modernity, the
predicament of meaning and coherence in a world that is itself "blank,
purposeless, indifferent, chaotic."[126] But while the poststructuralists are
not consumed by this condition, but rather play with and perhaps ironically celebrate its possibilities, our modernist figures, dwell on lost or
threatened tradition and yearn for the transcendent.[127] They have a "long-
ing for ultimacy," or at least trace its putative shattering with regret.
Even the most "secular" of these thinkers, Arendt, was fond of quoting
René Char's plaint that "our inheritance was left to us by no testament"
and regretted "the lost treasures of political life," a tradition that definitively began with Plato and Aristotle and "came to a no less definite end
in the theories of Karl Marx."[128] Unlike the postmodernists, albeit in
complex, convoluted, paradoxical (and often highly problematic) ways,
they were in constant search for, and offered possible avenues of, evacuation and rescue from this condition of fractured modernity. To be
sure, no neat Hegelian progression is in sight, the tablets have been shat-
tered; but in one way or another, they present us with considered and
committed reconfigurations of the fragments,[129] signals, and directions
for reconstituted meanings (whether of the premodern, dialectical, political, or messianic variety). Like the postmoderns, their sense of displacement, of being "beyond the border" is constitutive. Yet their con-

tinuing iconicity consists perhaps in their attempt to go beyond that state. In one way or another they redefined the frontiers and provided us with new moral and intellectual maps that the postmoderns, almost by definition, would or could not do. Those maps, to be sure, are provisional and problematic. They are not definitive "Guides to the Perplexed" (although Rosenzweig's work may have been intended as such), but rather, as Benjamin put it in another context, "the jagged edges which offer a foothold to someone who wants to go beyond that work."[130]

All, each in their own way, were riveted by the question of "origins" and the recovery of lost meanings, on truth as hidden, part of a greater structure waiting to be revealed, and the possibility of redemptive moments. Some were obsessed with the messianic dimension, and all recovered the politically loaded, theological impulse—what Eric Jacobson has recently described as "the metaphysics of the profane."[131] Just as significant for our purposes, all have been interpreted in terms of this bent (even Arendt, perhaps the least theological minded has been read this way).[132] This passion for and return to—or, at least, intense engagement with—theology certainly did not involve a return to religion as traditionally conceived. The theological was now addressed in respectively idiosyncratic ways—Strauss turned to premodern rationalist esoteric readings and recoveries, Benjamin to a qualified and oblique messianism, Scholem to its apocalyptic and antinomian possibilities and dangers, Rosenzweig to a conception of the transcendent that emerged from the temporally finite, and Adorno to a theologically-laced negative dialectic.[133]

In addition, traditional boundaries of time, history, redemption, and language came under question and were remapped. Strauss and Arendt displaced Hegelian or Enlightenment notions of linear historical progress: For Strauss the accumulative "waves of modernity" constituted the problem, not the solution. "Strauss's distinctiveness—indeed, his uniqueness," Harry Jaffa has written, "lay above else in the fact that he was the first great critic of modernity whose diagnosis of the ills of modernity did not end by a solution of those ills through a radicalization of the principles of modernity."[134] Arendt, that great analyst of the post-totalitarian rupture at the heart of Western civilization put her trust (or hope) in the possibility of permanent and spontaneous "new beginnings" rendered possible by the human condition of natality.[135] All these thinkers developed a critique of the liberal Enlightenment notion of history as an inevitable and incremental story of upward development. Already in 1914, debating his Marxist brother, Scholem declared: "where in history, there are laws, history will be of no use or the laws will be valueless."[136] In their world, it is true, rifts, ruptures, and revolutions took precedence over the continuum of homogenous time. But for most this was not merely a negative critique. Redemptive alternatives were very much the order of the day, and in place of an uninterrupted progressive totality, time was now conceived in jagged terms of qualitative moments and flashes.

Scholem, Adorno, Rosenzweig, Benjamin, and even Arendt all reconceived "redemption" as a constant, immanent possibility, able to be actualized now or at any given time (*Jetztzeit*). "Time as a religious category," Scholem observed in his 1918 diary, "becomes the eternal present."[137] Rosenzweig displaced the Hegelian notion of time with the eternal Jewish cycle and linked it to Jetztzeit where redemption was possible immanently and at all times. Eternity occurs within finitude, it is "wrested from time"; indeed, as Peter Gordon shows, in Rosenzweig's world it becomes a *modification* of time, within it—yet not fully of it.[138] Arendt's emphasis on worldly new beginnings derived from the possibilities of never-ending processes of natality. Benjamin, that metaphysical Marxist, no longer conceived of revolution as the culmination of a progressive process but as the sudden eruption of a deeper truth that explodes the continuity of history (continuity represented by the victors and discontinuity by the realm of the oppressed).[139] Similarly, and strikingly, Adorno declared:

> The only philosophy which can be responsibly practiced in the face of despair is the attempt to contemplate all things as they would present themselves from the standpoint of redemption. Knowledge has no light but that shed on the world by redemption: all else is reconstruction, mere technique. Perspectives must be fashioned that displace and estrange the world, reveal it with its rifts and crevices as indigent and distorted as it will appear one day in the messianic light.[140]

I stated at the beginning of this chapter that the oeuvres of these thinkers stubbornly bore the creative and often problematic imprint of their Weimar provenance. The creative nature and content of these projects should, by now, be evident. But in what sense are they problematic? In one way or another all these thinkers consistently critiqued and at times directly attacked liberalism and mass modernity. This is especially (but not exclusively) true of their earlier thought and often most clearly expressed in their private comments.

The young Scholem, for instance, railed against his liberal father and friends, atheists schooled in "science": "Beat them dead, this band of lice . . . strangle them around the throat."[141] He poured his wrath upon bourgeois liberalism and rationalism for the role they played in the liquidation of Jewish identity. No wonder then that he adopted a Nietzschean turn to a Zionism of wager and danger—his fellow German Jews, he commented, knew nothing of the "unbourgeois nature of things"[142] (Unbürgerlichkeit der Sache). Zionism was not about the moderations and balances of an assimilationist and wishy-washy liberalism but about a Jewish and Judaic "task of life that borders on the extreme," animated by anarchic, experimental, revolutionary (spiritual rather than conventionally political) impulses.[143]

We have already noted Strauss's early antipathy to liberalism. As late as 1933, from his Roman exile, he sent the following remarks to Karl Löwith:

> From the fact that Germany, which has turned to the right, has expelled us, it simply does not follow that the principles of the right are therefore to be rejected. To the contrary, only on the basis of principles of the right—fascist, authoritarian, *imperial*— is it possible, in a dignified manner, without the ridiculous and pitiful appeal to the "droits imprescriptibles de l'Homme," to protest against the mean non-entity. I am reading Caesar's *Commentaries* with profound comprehension and think of Virgil's "in regni imperio . . . parcer subjectis et detellare superbos." There is no reason to crawl to the cross, even to the cross of liberalism, as long as anywhere in the world a spark glimmers of Roman thinking. And, moreover, better than any cross the ghetto.[144]

None of our other thinkers, of course, ever went as far as this, but the critique of liberalism and bourgeois or mass modernity with which it is associated invariably informed the nature of their projects and the political positions they adopted—conservative, Zionist, Marxist, even Rosenzweig's revisioning of Jewish life. These sentiments were very much in the mold of Weimar intellectuals.[145] When they were not hostile, they were certainly quite indifferent to the workings of constitutional and popular democracy, to questions of parliamentary representation, to the various individual "bourgeois freedoms," to the messy everyday "bread and butter" politics of barter and negotiation.[146] In their powerful critiques of liberal-bourgeois instrumentality, Benjamin and Adorno remain above such mundane affirmations. Given their distaste for the distorting, leveling nature of modern mass society, this is even more evident in the case of Arendt and Strauss (albeit each on different grounds).[147]

It is true that while Strauss's early German writings, as Eugene Sheppard points out, consisted of "a scathing assault upon the foundations of liberalism or more broadly 'liberalism as a system': liberal culture, religion and politics," in light of the Nazi experience and the Cold War, this later changed to a more ameliorative approach.[148] Liberal democracy was certainly to be preferred to totalitarianism. Yet the unease, indeed a certain hostility, remained. The major ongoing Straussian critique of liberal democracy consisted of what he regarded as the great crisis of its ethical foundations, its moral neutrality concerning choices of ways of life, its indifference to issues that matter most to people. For Strauss, this mirrored and reinforced the lack of standards, the nihilism and atomism inherent in a relativist, historicist frame.[149] He regarded pluralism as the natural bedfellow of this worldview and attacked this as itself a violation of vaunted liberal neutrality: "by asserting, if only implicitly, the rightness of pluralism, it asserts that pluralism is *the* right way: it asserts the monism of universal tolerance and respect for diversity; for by virtue of being an ism, pluralism is a monism."[150]

While Strauss's critique of liberalism sprang from an authoritarian and intellectually aristocratic suspicion of (mass) democracy, Arendt castigated the liberal (indeed, the entire Western philosophical) tradition for downgrading the very notion, the autonomous realm, of the "political" in favor of the "social" (the realm of necessity) and the "private" (downgraded very often to the realm of the household as mere "consumption"). She rather bizarrely defined the political as a sphere of virtuosity, where interests did *not* play a role.[151] The Arendtian political world revolves around ultimate existentialist moments—the dark totalitarian abyss or the ecstasy of the revolutionary moment, the spontaneous action of the councils, or the *disinterested* and high-minded decision making in the polis. There is very little here about the humdrum world of lobbying, pressure groups, and so on; the quotidian details of representative democracy hardly excite her interest.

To be sure, there are a number of mitigating factors here. With the obvious exception of Rosenzweig, all these critics of liberalism in one way or another later famously became analysts and fierce opponents of fascism, Nazism, and totalitarianism. Their experiences and status as Jewish victims, as exiles and refugees also somehow softened their critiques of liberalism and rendered them more palatable. And for all their overt rejections, their various projects conserved a certain openness and humanizing core that was at the base of the Bildungs legacy that willynilly they inherited as German Jews.

All this leads to a final, interesting question. Why do we elevate as icons thinkers that seem so critical of—or at best, indifferent to—liberalism in an intellectual and academic culture that in many ways conceives itself to be essentially a liberal one? Perhaps we can best answer this by shifting our perspective somewhat. At the beginning of this chapter I asked why it was these specific thinkers rather than others who have been canonized in our culture. Now, I want to compare them to another intellectual who *has* very much achieved that status and who presently occupies a central and remarkably iconic position within that same culture precisely because he *is* a liberal. I am referring to the celebrated Sir Isaiah Berlin.[152]

Berlin is canonic—his legendary conversational skills and capacity for friendship aside—because in his person and writings he most quintessentially incarnates an updated liberalism's positions and values. It is he who most compellingly articulates—and reflects—our culture's idealized liberal and tolerant self-image. Mark Lilla has put it thus:

> Berlin's essays in the history of ideas are not only *about* liberalism; they are also displays of the liberal temperament that inspire admiration and imitation. For Berlin believed that liberalism is not just a matter of principle of theory; it [is] an existential matter, a certain way of carrying oneself in the world and in the company of others.[153]

Berlin certainly did not regard himself as having much in common with our countericons—although, strikingly, he too expressed both a passionate interest in, and support of, Zionism. (This commitment has respectively delighted, dismayed, or perplexed Berlin's supporters, and there has been much discussion about the possible relations or tensions between his liberalism and his Zionism.)[154] Berlin, in fact, had met Arendt a number of times and knew her work. He scathingly declared that she "produces no arguments, no evidence of serious philosophical or historical thought. It is all a stream of metaphysical associations."[155] In 1958 he expressed his concern to the Israeli historian Jacob Talmon that Arendt and her *Origins of Totalitarianism* were "much praised in America and if you tell me there is something in it I will try to read it. She seems an unbearable writer to me, but I fear we may hear more of her."[156] He despised her for her recanting of Zionism, mistrusting anyone who could change one's mind on so fundamental a question. He found her Eichmann book with its summary moral judgments on Jewish behavior during the Holocaust arrogant, uncomprehending, and insensitive in the extreme.[157] Nor did he make a secret of what he thought of Adorno. "The first time I met Sir Isaiah Berlin in 1973," Martin Jay relates,

> he told me how insufferable he had found Adorno in Oxford in the 1930's; the last time I saw Berlin, a year before his death in 1997, we hadn't finished walking up the stairs to his study when he launched into the same diatribe. Clearly, Adorno's "damaged life," as he had famously called it in *Minima Moralia,* had left some destruction in its wake.[158]

(Parenthetically, some of these feelings were, perhaps less forcefully, reciprocated. Arendt described Berlin as "a serpentine dove, moralistic, familial, perhaps not very brave."[159] Instructively, although Scholem respected Berlin, he too somewhat doubted his willingness to tackle sensitive subjects. Berlin, he wrote, was one of the very few people able to write an unapologetic piece on the "the prominence of the Jews in intellectual life" but nevertheless was someone "who will never touch it."[160] Leo Strauss too knew Berlin and was one of the few who remained openly skeptical about his liberal project and his attack on the idea that the good in morals and politics was noncontradictory.[161] Berlin, in turn, although he liked and respected Strauss, found many of his ideas "wrong-headed" and "absurd.")[162]

It was in a private letter (to Jean Floud) that Berlin expressed his real opinion and gut feelings about many of these Weimar-bred exiled intellectuals and the milieu that had produced them: "the terrible twisted Mitteleuropa in which nothing is straight, simple, truthful, all human relations and all political attitudes are twisted into ghastly shapes by these awful casualties who, because *they* are crippled, recognize nothing pure and firm in the world."[163]

Damaged people, Berlin theorized, produced damaged ideas. These remarks may or may not illuminate much about the thought or psychological state of those in question but the tensions do tell us something significant not only about Berlin himself but, more pertinently perhaps, about our own perceived condition and the needs of a culture that is compelled to celebrate *both* the quintessentially liberal Berlin and these "twisted Middle Europeans." They are, so to speak, necessary mirror opposites, foils for an ongoing tension in our own self-image and life predicament. Berlin, that "amiable sage" (as Clive James has aptly described him), is an icon because he so neatly seems to fit and represent our open and liberal sensibilities. If our intellectuals are displaced "casualties," people who render "displacement" at the center of their projects, Berlin—that Riga-born Jewish refugee from the Bolshevik Revolution—is (or at least appears to be) in both literal and cognitive ways deeply at home. Ensconced and revered in his cosy, beloved Oxford he would have found Adorno's dictum—"Dwelling, in the proper sense is now impossible. The traditional residences we have grown up in have grown intolerable. . . . [T]he house is past, over. . . . It is part of morality not to be at home in one's home"—exceedingly distasteful.

The recently published collection of Berlin's early letters is entitled *Flourishing*.[164] Anyone who has read the correspondences of Adorno, Benjamin, Scholem, Arendt, Rosenzweig, and Strauss could never imagine having their letters similarly titled. Their dispatches are haunted and probing. In Berlin's youthful missives (1928–46), the contemplative life, the agonizing over ultimate issues, is largely absent. Berlin, quite unlike the icons we have studied here, was, as Simon Schama points out, "that unlikely thing, a seriously happy Jew."[165] The horrors of the twentieth century may have formed the backdrop to his liberal thought yet, strikingly, there is almost nothing in the way of a concrete analysis of Nazism and its atrocities, and, as one commentator has recently provocatively argued, his political thought does not seem adequate to the destructive

forces ranged against it.[166] Clive James has described the work of those
who felt less comfortable: "Not always sprightly but always dense with
implication, it is the unmistakable and addictive music made by those
who have felt on their own skins, even as a flash of heat from the far
horizon, the full destructive power of human history and are still wed-
ded to making sense of it."[167]

James does not mention our writers in this regard, but it applies almost uncannily to the thinkers we have analyzed here. This would certainly include Rosenzweig who although he did not live through the totalitarian experience was deeply scarred by World War I and made the
fear of death the cornerstone of his postidealist thought. The opening
line of *The Star of Redemption* reads: "All cognition of the All originates
in death, in the fear of death." Scholem's mystics, as he was determined
to show, brought back what liberal-bourgeois Judaism elided, "the reality of evil and the dark horror that is about everything living."[168] (We
should not take this picture of Germanic seriousness too far—Scholem,
after all had a deeply mischievous, impish side to him as well. Still, a
dash of some of Berlin's lightness and air would have not harmed some
of the other thinkers. Adorno, on the other hand, was said to be "such
a German; he made everything so complicated. He would translate
the simplest things into this meta-language, and sit back enjoying our
confusion.")[169]

We respond warmly to Berlin's work because it is both decent and
comforting. Ultimately, one does not read him to be challenged and perplexed but to be reassured. Even when he instructs us about cultural and
political incommensurabilities, or the virtues and deficiencies of both
Enlightenment and counter-Enlightenment, or when he advises us that
democracy's ultimate values cannot be reconciled, that there is an inherent clash between freedom and equality, individualism and collectivism,
and so on, it is somehow framed within a comfortable, privileged framework.[170] Berlin reinforces and confirms; our thinkers ruffle, perplex, and
often outrage. If there is little that is "straight and simple, pure and firm"
in their world, this is perhaps why they often are both more interesting—
and speculatively, and perhaps politically, awry.[171] Despite his confrontations with totalitarian democracy, Berlin maintained a donnish air; our
thinkers lived and thrived on the jagged edges, even as they doggedly
struggled to reach new landscapes. In Berlin's world, decisions are left to

the individual, and, indeed, part of his appeal consists in his critique of the dangers of an overarching conception of a single common good, an all-encompassing civic virtue. Our German-Jewish icons, however, maintained that belief and search, and refused to let this quest go.[172]

Viewed together these visions give voice to the two poles of an ongoing, and what may turn out to be a creative tension: between the affirmation of a decent, humane liberalism soberly aware of the limits of social and political action and the dangers of the utopian temptation and the radical impulse that expresses a continuing discontent with the compromised modalities of modern life and the search for (usually profane) splinters of transcendence. We want both to leave and to stay at home, torn between the desire to step out of our own frontiers and experiment with alternative worlds—and at the same time to cherish the familiar, to carefully chart our boundaries and feel safe within them. We iconize both, we need both and should be glad—pace Sontag—that we are not always forced to choose between them.

Yet perhaps the choice should not be put too starkly. Berlin's conception of the Age of Reason was by no means uncritical.[173] Indeed, at certain moments of his narrative, as Mark Lilla argues, the Enlightenment (quite inaccurately) appears as "an extremist movement of hedgehogs, a *Walpurgisnacht* of philosophical monism that foreshadowed the rise of a new race of despots."[174] (Here, ironically, Berlin's and Adorno's musings on the Aufklärung find distinctly common ground!) Moreover, Berlin's account of post-Enlightenment currents and the search for higher creative forms of romantic self-expression is almost as appreciative of their charms and temptations as it is critical of their dangers.[175] Berlin's rather nonideological Zionism, too, was based upon his understanding that what existentially linked Jews everywhere was: "A sense of social unease. Nowhere do Jews feel entirely at home."[176] Surely his instinctive understanding of Zionism as addressing a powerful need for Jewish belonging, though it did not entail making his own home in Israel, reflected some kind of personally experienced nagging unease—even in Oxford. He once revealingly declared that his greatest defect was his "eagerness to please."[177]

The reverse logic should also apply to the icons we have studied in this chapter. In many respects their radical-redemptive, jagged, often nervous, postliberal projects can be interpreted as attempts to rescue rather than merely critique the damaged Enlightenment inheritance and its tradition of free and critical inquiry.[178] To be sure, our figures constitute only a part of the German-Jewish intellectual adventure—and that at its end point. They certainly should not be romanticized. There was much in their ruminations that, no doubt, was overheated and obscure. The weaknesses, as well the strengths, of these driven intellectuals reflect their Weimar origins and a historical moment of crisis. Intellectuals are occupationally impelled to test, if not go entirely "beyond the borders," but this crisis rendered the quest of our figures particularly intense, and animated their diverse and volatile attempts at novel modes of prescriptive understanding. Their thought remains resonant because in sophisticated ways they respectively identified and diagnosed still current predicaments and provided guidelines toward possible personal and collective alternatives. To paraphrase Jürgen Habermas, it is a part of a German-Jewish sensibility that, had it not existed, "we would have to discover . . . for our own sakes,"[179] for the critical, searching, and humanizing sensibility that underlies it is something that in an increasingly politically conformist civilization, we should take care not to lose.

NOTES

Introduction

1. See the (1956) "Preface" to Hannah Arendt, *Rahel Varnhagen: The Life of a Jewess,* ed. Liliane Weissberg, trans. Richard and Clara Winston (Baltimore: Johns Hopkins, 1997), p. 82.

2. See, for instance, Rex W. Crawford, *The Cultural Migration: The European Scholar in America* (Philadelphia: University of Pennsylvania Press, 1953); Donald Fleming and Bernard Bailyn, eds., *The Intellectual Migration: Europe and America, 1930–1960* (Cambridge, Mass: Belknap Press of Harvard University Press, 1969); Laura Fermi, *Illustrious Immigrants: The Intellectual Migration from Europe, 1930/1941* (Chicago & London: University of Chicago Press, 1968); Anthony Heilbut, *Exiled in Paradise: German Refugee Artists and Intellectuals in America from the 1930s to the Present* (Boston: Beacon Press, 1983); Lewis A. Coser, *Refugee Scholars in America: Their Impact and Their Experiences* (New Haven: Yale University Press, 1984); and Martin Jay, *Permanent Exiles: Essays on the Intellectual Migration from Germany to America* (New York: Columbia University Press, 1986).

3. See his *Generation Exodus: The Fate of Young Refugees from Nazi Germany* (Hanover and London: Brandeis University Press, 2001).

4. Thus George Steiner has repeatedly analyzed and trumpeted the prodigal creative genius of post-Enlightenment German-speaking Jewish intellectuals and creative artists steeped in the emancipated, secular, critical humanism of Central Europe—and equated this with his own prescriptive, idealized conception of a quintessentially diasporic Judaism. See, for example, "A Kind of Survivor" in Steiner's *Language and Silence: Essays on Language, Literature and the Inhuman* (New York, 1977) as well as his autobiographical comments in *Errata: An Examined Life* (London: Weidenfeld & Nicolson, 1997). See too, for the most recent example, Amos Elon's best-selling *The Pity of It All: A History of Jews in Germany, 1743–1933* (New York: Henry Holt and Company, 2002). There, the German Jewish intellectual enterprise is incarnated in its ongoing, even if

ultimately tragically unsuccessful, attempt to tame nationalism and civilize other such exclusivisms. Another popular example of this genre would be Friedrick V. Grunfeld, *Prophets without Honor: A Background to Freud, Kafka, Einstein and Their World* (New York: McGraw-Hill, 1979).

5. The literature on this question is enormous. The following (apart from the scholars discussed in the body of this work) represent only a few such approaches and are not to be taken as necessarily authoritative: Isaiah Berlin, "Jewish Slavery and Emancipation" in Alexander Manor, ed., *The Jews and the National Question* (Tel Aviv: Habonim, n.d.), pp. 127–56; John Murray Cuddihy, *The Ordeal of Civility: Freud, Marx, Levi-Strauss and the Jewish Struggle with Modernity* (New York: Basic Books, 1974). See too my "German History and German Jewry: Junctions, Boundaries, and Interdependencies," in *In Times of Crisis: Essays on European Culture, Germans, and Jews* (Madison: University of Wisconsin Press, 2001), pp. 86–92.

6. See, most prominently, George L. Mosse's pathbreaking and celebratory (albeit mildly critical) analysis of the animating drive of German Jewish cultural and intellectual creativity in his *German Jews beyond Judaism* (Bloomington: Indiana University Press, 1985). This work is simultaneously analysis, autobiographical self-description, and credo, one in which he openly seeks to transmute this form of German Jewishness into a goal, an "inspiration for many men and women searching to humanize their society and lives" (p. 9). In one way or the other, almost all the figures featured in chapters 2 and 3 simultaneously documented, explicated, and, in some way, exalted these characteristics. This even applied to Gershom Scholem who, despite his withering indictment of the German-Jewish elites and their "bloodletting" assimilationist drive, also conceded that emancipation had ushered in a dialectic in which "the long-buried creativity of the Jews was liberated," and that the meeting between "Germans" and "Jews" was not only deceptive but also contained "great fruitfulness and the stimulus to significant developments." See his 1966 lecture "Jews and Germans," reproduced in his *On Jews and Judaism in Crisis: Selected Essays,* ed. Werner J. Dannhauser (New York: Schocken Books, 1976), pp. 78, 79.

7. These words—"*Stiefkinder müssen doppelartig artig sein*"—have been attributed to Ludwig Holländer, director of the mainstream liberal Jewish organization, the Central-verein deutscher Staatsbürger jüdischen Glaubens. See Peter Gay, *Freud, Jews and Other Germans: Masters and Victims in Modernist Culture* (New York: Oxford University Press, 1978), p. 183.

8. Benjamin to Florens Christian Rang, 18 November 1923, Letter 122, in Walter Benjamin, *The Correspondence of Walter Benjamin 1910–1940,* eds. Gershom Scholem and Theodor Adorno, trans. Manfred R. and Evelyn M. Jacobson (Chicago: University of Chicago Press, 1994), pp. 214–17. The quote appears on p. 215. Benjamin continued

that "nowadays a salutary complicity obligates those individuals of noble character among both peoples to keep silent about their ties."

9. As the Zionist leader Kurt Blumenfeld critically put it: "I knew how much the Jews in Germany had to beware of not transgressing the borders." ("*Ich wusste, wie sehr sich die Juden in Deutschland vor* Grenzüberschreitungen *zu hüten hatten.*") See his *Erlebte Judenfrage: ein Vierteljahrhundert deutscher Zionismus* (Stuttgart: Deutsche Verlags-Anstalt, 1962), p. 58.

10. Written under a pseudonym (and not published in the later collection of his writings), see Walter Hartenau, "Höre Israel," *Die Zukunft*, 18 (March 16, 1897), pp. 454–62.

11. In April 1922, just a few weeks before Rathenau's murder, Einstein (who was a close friend of Rathenau) accompanied Kurt Blumenfeld to try and persuade the minister to give up the office. For a fascinating account of this conversation, see *Erlebte Judenfrage*, ibid., pp. 138–45, especially p. 142.

12. *Neue Rundschau*, Vol. 33, Pt. 2, pp. 815–16, quoted in Ronald W. Clark, *Einstein: The Life and Times* (New York: Avon, 1971), pp. 359–60 and note 360, p. 810.

13. See Stern, *Dreams and Delusions: The Drama of German History* (New York: Alfred A. Knopf, 1987), p. 114.

14. For the most developed statement of this position, see again, "Jews and Germans," op. cit., pp. 71–92.

15. All of Gay's writings on German Jews are permeated with this thematic emphasis. Perhaps his strongest statement in this regard can be found in his "At Home in Germany . . . The Jews during the Weimar Era" in the bilingual *Die Juden im National-sozialistischen Deutschland/The Jews in Nazi Germany*, ed. Arnold Paucker (Tübingen: J.C.B. Mohr, 1986), pp. 31–43.

1. *Bildung* in Palestine

1. See Felix Weltsch, ed., *Prague and Jerusalem* (Jerusalem: Keren Hayessod, 1954 [Hebrew]), p. 201.

2. In his study of Brit Shalom, for instance, Shalom Ratzabi divides the group into an exclusively Central European radical component and a moderate circle. Although the latter was indeed headed by Arthur Ruppin (very much a German-speaking Posen Jew), he points out that most of its members—such as Hayim Margalit Kalvarisky, Yehoshua Radler-Feldman Ha-Talmi (known as Rabbi Binjamin), Ya'akov Tahon, and Yitzchak Epstein—were from Eastern Europe and adhered more closely to normative "practical" and "political" Zionist positions and to a theoretical rather than concrete engagement with the "Arab problem." See Ratzabi, *Between Zionism and Judaism: The Radical Circle*

in Brith Shalom 1925–1933 (Leiden: Brill, 2002), p. xii. See too the pioneering study (in Hebrew) by Aharon Kedar, "*Le-toldoteia shel 'Brith Shalom' ba-shanim 1925–1928*," in Y. Bauer, M. Davis, I. Kolatt, *Pirkei mehkar be-toldot ha-tsionut* (Jerusalem, 1976), pp. 224–85. The organization appears at times under the spelling *Brith Shalom* or *Brit Shalom*. I have decided upon the latter except when quoting others who spell it as in the former use.

3. Hans Kohn—in a late essay (1958) composed many years after he left Brit Shalom and, indeed, the entire Zionist movement—depicted Ahad Ha'am as a highly Enlightened Zionist, acutely sensitive to the moral and political issue of the Arabs. See his "Zion and the Jewish National Idea," reproduced in Michael Selzer, ed., *Zionism Reconsidered: The Rejection of Jewish Normalcy* (London: Macmillan Company, 1970), especially pp. 192–212. For a far more skeptical view arguing that Ahad Ha'am "failed to say much about the moral ambiguity of Zionism's stance toward the Arabs. . . . [T]he absence of any discussion of [the Arab problem] by him in ethical terms is jarring," see the important biography by Steven J. Zipperstein, *Elusive Prophet: Ahad Ha'am and the Origins of Zionism* (Berkeley: University of California Press, 1993), p. 309. See too pp. 200–201, pp. 306ff.

4. For a short biography on, and a collection of documents by Magnes, see Arthur A. Goren, *Dissenter in Zion: From the Writings of Judah L. Magnes* (Cambridge, Mass.: Harvard University Press, 1982). On the German connection, see particularly pp. 5, 8–9. Perhaps a caveat is necessary here. Paul Mendes-Flohr has argued that while most of Magnes's comrades-in-arms were these Central European intellectuals, they were suspicious of his heavy moralism and more complex and nuanced in their dialectical thinking: "Moreover, one suspects that Magnes remained in their eyes an American. . . . Despite his Heidelberg Ph.D. and fluent, albeit faulty, German, it seems that Magnes never quite passed as a yekke, a German Jew, in Israeli parlance." See "The Appeal of the Incorrigible Idealist: Judah L. Magnes and the Mandarins of Jerusalem" in Mendes-Flohr, *Divided Passions: Jewish Intellectuals and the Experience of Modernity* (Detroit: Wayne State University Press, 1991), pp. 390–409. The quote appears on p. 391. A comprehensive study of Magnes and his political activities has recently appeared in Hebrew. See Joseph Heller, *Mi "Brit Shalom" le "Ichud": Yehuda Leib Magnes Ve'ha'maavak le'medina duleumit* (*From* Brit Shalom *to* Ichud: *Judah Leib Magnes and the Struggle for a Binational State in Palestine)*, (Jerusalem: Hebrew University, Magnes Press, 2003).

5. See Walter Laqueur, *A History of Zionism* (London: Weidenfeld and Nicolson, 1972), p. 251.

6. It should also be mentioned that a (failed) political party made up of Central Eu-

ropean immigrants, the Aliya Hadasha, took up many points of Brit Shalom's program. See *Aliya Hadasha Statement of Policy* (Tel Aviv, 1946), n.p.

7. The fact that these groups were composed of highly literate intellectuals renders the quantity of both their political publications and individual writings (public and private) rather self-evident. These include their official Hebrew journals, "She'ifotenu" ("Our Aspirations") and "Ba'yot" (Problems). For an English-language publication outlining Brit Shalom's major policy positions and the Statutes of their Society, see *Jewish-Arab Affairs: Occasional Papers Published by the "Brit-Shalom" Society* (Jerusalem, June 1931).

8. In this essay I deal with the binationalists as a more or less coherent group. It goes without saying that there were many, sometimes crucial personal and intellectual differences between and among them. A study of this kind would be illuminating—especially given the independent importance of many of these thinkers and personalities—but this cannot be our present concern.

9. On Arendt's changing and critical views on Zionism as well as her involvement with Judah Magnes and the Ichud, see her *The Jew as Pariah: Jewish Identity and Politics in the Modern Age*, ed. Ron H. Feldman (New York: Grove Press, 1978), and *Vor Antisemitismus ist man nur noch auf dem Monde sicher. Beiträge für die deutsch-jüdische Emigrantenzeitung "Aufbau" 1941–1945*, ed. Marie Luise Knott (München: Piper, 2000).

10. On these issues and Einstein's sustained correspondence with Hugo Bergman, see the [Hebrew] article by Jochanan Flusser, "Symbiosis Is the Real Goal," *Ha'aretz* (17 December 2004), p. H3.

11. This neglect has now been corrected by a chapter entitled "Gabriel Stern and the Bi-National State" in Walter Laqueur's book *Dying for Jerusalem: The Past, Present, and Future of the Holiest City* (New York: Sourcebooks, 2006). Tom Segev has also written movingly of Stern. During the War of Independence, Segev relates, Stern found himself "facing a man with a rifle. An enemy. Stern lifted his rifle, the man opposite lifted his. Stern knew: The first to pull the trigger would live, the other would die. Stern fired. During the following seconds, he was covered with a hail of glass fragments. It was a big mirror. Stern had fired at himself. He never fired again." Stern's story also illustrates some of the paradoxes generated by the results of the 1967 war. As Segev comments:

When East Jerusalem was captured, Gabriel Stern was blissfully happy; for a long time I did not properly understand that. Why did the occupation make him so happy, this good man of peace, who loved God and people, I wondered. Stern was caught up in the illusion that eliminating the border between Jews and Arabs would lead them to live with one another in peace, as he had believed before the War of Independence. A cruel paradox has brought about a situation in which the Israeli peace movement was forced to adopt the principle of separation, including the fence, whereas the people who want to remove the Arabs from the country settled among the Arabs.

See Segev's insightful review of Joseph Heller's *From Brit Shalom to the Ihud*, "A Binational Byway," *Haaretz* (20 August 2004), p. B9.

12. On this paradox, see Hagit Lavsky (Hebrew), "*Chidat Chotama shel 'Brit Shalom' al ha'pulmus ha'Zioni B'zmana o'l'achar z'mana*," *Hazionut* (Maasef, Yud Tet), 1995, pp. 167–81. Lavsky sees the development of the Zionist binational idea as one possible outgrowth of Achad Ha'am's "cultural" emphasis and Chaim Weizmann's policy positions. In this view, binationalism was thus not a "foreign" phenomenon but rather an organic part of pre-State Zionism, albeit its most extreme edge.

13. See Michael Walzer, "The Practice of Social Criticism" in his *Interpretation and Social Criticism* (Cambridge, Mass.: Harvard University Press, 1987), pp. 35–66. See especially p. 59. See too p. 61 where he writes: The critic

is not a detached observer, even when he looks at the society he inhabits with a fresh and skeptical eye. He is not an enemy, even when he is fiercely opposed to this or that prevailing institutional arrangement. His criticism does not require either detachment or enmity, because he finds a warrant for critical engagement in the idealism, even if it is a hypocritical idealism, of the actually existing moral world.

14. The binationalists were thus quite different, for instance, from the group of disaffected left-wing socialists émigrés such as Arnold Zweig and the circle around their journal, *Der Orient*, who found themselves in Palestine during the 1930s and 1940s. "Arnold Zweig visited me today in the library," Bergman reported in March 1934. "It is uncanny how he lives here as an *emigrant*. He exists on the '*Tagebuch*.'" See Bergman's *Tagebücher und Briefe: Band I 1901–1948*, ed. Miriam Sambursky, with an introduction by Natan Rotenstreich (Königstein: Jüdischer Verlag bei Athenäum, 1985). Entry for 6.3.1934, p. 353. For an excellent analysis of this circle and its journal, see the (Hebrew) study by Adi Gordon, "*In Palestine. In A Foreign Land." The Orient: A German-Language Weekly between German Exile and Aliyah* (Jerusalem: Magnes Press, 2004).

15. Apart from the works indicated in other footnotes of this chapter, see especially the general studies by Susan Lee Hattis, *The Bi-National Idea in Palestine during Mandatory Times* (Haifa: Shikmona Publishing Company, 1970) and Aharon Kedar (Hebrew), "*Agudat 'Brit Shalom': ha-ma'avar Me-agudat mehkar ve-Iyun le'aguda politit*" in *Devar Ha-Kongres Ha-Olami* Ha-6 Le-Mdaei Ha-Yahadut, Vol. 2 (1976), pp. 365–70 and

"Le-hashkafoteia shel 'Brit Shalom'" in Yehoshua Ben-Zion and Aharon Kedar, eds., *Ideologia u-mediniyut tsionut* (Jerusalem, 1990), pp. 97–114. See too Hagit Lavsky, "German Zionists and the Emergence of Brith Shalom" in Jehuda Reinharz and Anita Shapira, eds., *Essential Papers on Zionism* (New York: New York University Press, 1996), pp. 648–70.

16. This does not mean that German nationalism was "essentially" integral and intolerant. Even if it was ultimately unsuccessful, there was another earlier, more "progressive" strain. On this, see Christoph Prignitz, *Vaterlandsliebe und Freiheit. Deutscher Patriotismus von 1750 bis 1850* (Wiesbaden: Franz Steiner Verlag, 1981).

17. This is a remarkably original piece that, with its carefully modulated distinctions and specific political analyses, will force scholars to rethink many old platitudes and deepen their own approaches. See Yfaat Weiss, "Central European Ethnonationalism and Zionist Binationalism," *Jewish Social Studies*, Vol. 11, no. 1 (Fall 2004), pp. 93–117.

18. Arthur Ruppin, *Tagebücher, Briefe, Erinnerungen*, ed. Schlomo Krolik (Königstein: Jüdischer Verlag bei Athenäum, 1985). Entry for 7 November 1933, p. 448.

19. Indeed, he reports without comment in his 1933 diary that he had traveled to Jena to talk with Hans K. Guenther, "who created the national socialist race theory. The conversation lasted two hours. He was very kind, denied authorship of the Aryan concept and agreed with me that the Jews were not inferior but different [*andersartig*] and that the Jewish question should be dealt with in respectable manner." See the entry of 16 August 1933, *Tagebücher*, op. cit., p. 446.

20. Ibid. Entry for 13 April 1923, pp. 347–48.

21. See Ruppin, *"Das Verhältnis der Juden zu den Arabern,"* *Der Jude*, no. 10 (1918–19), pp. 453–57. The quote appears on p. 445. Ruppin substantiated these statements thus:

> If we estimate the useable agricultural surface of Palestine as half the overall area, that is 15,000 square kilometers, about 17,000,000 dunam, the amount of agricultural concerns in Palestine at 80,000–100,000 and the surface of most concerns at 100 dunam, 7,000,000 to 9,000,000 remains over. That is double what is needed for Jewish colonization over the next years. (p. 455)

Ruppin's calculations could not, of course, take into account the rise of Nazi Germany.

22. Weiss observes that when Kohn later argued that "Zionist nationalism went the way of most Central and East European national movements," it became lumped into his antithesis of "bad" Eastern, exclusive nationalism as opposed to "good" Western, inclusive nationalism. This model became famous when Kohn outlined it in his influential *The Idea of Nationalism.* Weiss points out (pp. 28–29), that this dichotomous model, which was normative to the study of nationalism for decades, is shot through with anti-

historical and essentialist assumptions. Contemporary scholarship, she argues, demonstrates that Western European state nationalism proceeded on the basis of ethnic unification, which took place in these territories in the centuries prior to the rise of nationalism. Thus, she asserts, Kohn was unable to use Western models, such as England and France, for his binationalist quest. Western liberal nationalism did not have the ability to recognize hybridity or ethnic diversity and was no more able to accommodate it than Eastern European countries. She concludes that (p. 30): "Even the most progressive Zionists were not able to articulate effectively binationalism, a fact, which should make the historian more modest in his or her judgment." The point is well made. Nevertheless, a few mitigating features need to be mentioned. When seeking possible examples of binationalism Kohn most regularly turned to the Swiss and Belgian (as well as to some extent Finnish) examples. This was so also for other members of the group. Thus, see Joseph Luria, "National Rights in Switzerland, Finland and Eretz Israel" [Hebrew], *Shi'ifoteinu*, III (1929), pp. 10–29. These are, surely, "Western" models (however we may want to understand that term). Moreover, as their internal discussions and admissions of confusion and contradiction show, these binationalists were themselves acutely aware of the practical problems entailed in their project—but also pointed out the pitfalls of exclusive and majority rule. As this essay argues, they based their argument less on the availability of either Eastern or Western models but on a moral position that combined, in their view, a uniquely Jewish politicomoral stance with a commitment to universal Enlightenment principles. If their own views have been found to be impractical, it would not be unfair to suggest that majoritarian nationalism in Palestine-Israel has produced its own set of virtually insoluble problems.

23. On this issue, see my *Scholem, Arendt, Klemperer: Intimate Chronicles in Turbulent Times* (Bloomington: Indiana University Press, 2001), especially p. 26.

24. This is a substantial topic, worthy of independent consideration. As this is not my central concern, I feel exempted from elaborating upon it here, especially as the subject is presently being thoroughly researched by Adi Gordon in a doctoral dissertation entitled, "The German-Jewish 'Generation of 1914' in the Weltbühne and Brit Shalom."

25. See Hans Kohn, "Nationalism" (an article dedicated to Martin Buber), which appears in *The Jew: Essays from Martin Buber's Journal, Der Jude, 1916–1918*, ed. Arthur A. Cohen, trans. Joachim Neugroschel (Alabama: University of Alabama Press, 1980), pp. 20–30. The quotes appear on p. 27. The article appeared originally in *Der Jude* VI (1921–22), pp. 674–86.

26. See Carole Fink, *Defending the Rights of Others: The Great Powers, the Jews and International Minority Protection, 1878–1938* (Cambridge: Cambridge University Press, 2004).

27. See Dimitry Shumsky, "Historiography, Nationalism and Bi-Nationalism: Czech-German Jewry, the Prague Zionists, and the Origins of the Bi-National Approach of Hugo Bergman" [Hebrew] in *Zion* Vol. LXIX (no. 1, 2004), pp. 45–80. There is also an English abstract of this important piece that seeks to reconceive the nature of Czech-German-Jewish identity as a kind of fluid hybrid rather than in terms of set dichotomies.

28. Shumsky's emphasis on bridging and mediation in everyday life as well as his attempt to ground the notions of Bergman and others in prosaic reality, represents a counternarrative to the rather utopian, deterritorialized project presented in Scott Spector's, *Prague Territories: National Conflict and Cultural Innovation in Franz Kafka's Fin-de-Siècle* (Berkeley: University of California Press, 2000). This is a useful and original interpretation but one should not be overdeterministic about all this. For instance, while Bergman did indeed stress the possibility of intertwined Arab-Jewish coexistence, there were moments when he explicitly regarded separation as the only possibility. Thus—in response to the watershed 1929 riots—he wrote to Weltsch (25.8.29):

> How anyone can imagine that we in Palestine can progress as long as the two peoples live jointly together [*miteinander*] is a mystery to me. We are absolutely easily delivered. I think, for example, with shock how easy it would be to set the library which, in its greater portion lies on Mount Scopus, on fire at night. It is simply impossible to defend us, even if the English had the best intentions. We are a small number, easily sacrificed to a wild horde . . . as long as the peoples live together. (*Tagebücher* I, op. cit., p. 288)

Shumsky's emphasis on formative background is surely important but so too is the effect of lived and changing reality on the ground. Moreover, while his insistence on the animating place of the Czech language and culture constitutes a valuable corrective to older conceptions of Czech-German-Jewish identity, it may seriously underestimate the ongoing and central influence of, and commitment to, German language and culture in the lives of these circles. Bergman's adherence to German and his belief in its cultivating powers, as this chapter demonstrates, remained exceedingly strong even in the post-Holocaust period.

29. See Bergman's letter to Dr. Kurt Wehle, 22 January 1974, in Bergman's *Tagebücher und Briefe II, 1948–1975,* ed. Miriam Sambursky, with an introduction by Natan Rotenstreich (Königstein: Jüdischer Verlag bei Athenäum, 1985), p. 698.

30. Weiss refers to this explanation when she writes: "Rather than the liberal spirit of Central Europe it is the liberal criticism of the illiberal turn to ethno-nationalist practices in that geo-political sphere which, through a dialectical process, gave rise to a

synthesis in the spirit of conciliatory Zionism," but labels it "so simple as to be suspect" (p. 8). Her presentation of Kohn seems to reinforce rather than undermine this argument and while she does indeed demonstrate nonliberal strains and influences in Ruppin's thought and policies, his sensitivity to the wrongdoings done to the Arabs, his early writings on the desire to join in a greater Arab Union (thus emphasizing ultimate integration rather than separation), and his ongoing critique of, and hope for overcoming, Jewish chauvinism do indeed fit this explanation and the broader cultural model and sensibility outlined below.

31. See George L. Mosse, *German Jews beyond Judaism* (Bloomington: Indiana University Press, 1985). See, too, my appreciation, "George Mosse at Eighty: A Critical Laudatio" in my *In Times of Crisis: Essays on European Culture, Germans, and Jews* (Madison: University of Wisconsin Press, 2001), pp. 155–70. Mosse's text has become rather authoritative although parts of the thesis have been challenged. See, especially, the essay by Shulamit Volkov, "The Ambivalence of *Bildung:* Jews and Other Germans" in Klaus L. Berghahn, *The German-Jewish Dialogue Reconsidered: A Symposium in Honor of George L. Mosse* (New York: Peter Lang, 1996), pp. 81–97. See too the review of this book by Paul Mendes-Flohr in *Studies in Contemporary Jewry*, Vol. V (1989), pps. 377–79 and my essay, "German Jews beyond Bildung and Liberalism: The Radical Jewish Revival in the Weimar Republic" in *Culture and Catastrophe: German and Jewish Confrontations with National Socialism and Other Crises* (New York: New York University Press, 1996), pp. 31–44 (notes pp. 150–62).

32. In my "German Jews beyond Bildung," ibid., I stressed the dissent of many of these intellectuals from the hyper-rationalist, progressive and "evolutionary" emphases of the Bildungs idea. Yet, clearly, they hung on to other aspects of that tradition.

33. I owe this formulation to David N. Myers (in a communication of 11 October 2005).

34. Thus, as someone who most resisted being seen and defined as a "German Jew," Gershom Scholem put it: "Here [in Palestine] the Jews, whose great majority are Ostjuden, regard the German Jews as foreign. They see more things German than Jewish in them." See Scholem's letter to his mother (no. 185) of 26.4.1933 in Betty Scholem, Gershom Scholem, *Mutter und Sohn im Briefwechsel 1917–1946*, ed. Itta Shedletzky in cooperation with Thomas Sparr (München: C. H. Beck, 1989), p. 297.

35. This is of course a stereotypical characterization—which, like many stereotypes, possesses a grain of truth. The "Yekkes," it was said, were hopelessly formal. Thus, after an acquaintance and close relationship of almost four decades Ernst Simon would still address Martin Buber as *"verehrter Professor Buber."* See Letter 72, 11.10.1954, in Ernst A. Simon, *Sechzig Jahre gegen den Strom. Briefe von 1917–1984* (Tübingen: Mohr Siebeck,

1998), p. 144. The traditional stereotype was largely, if at times affectionately, negative. Over the past few years, however, there has been a striking public reevaluation in which the term itself and the achievements of the German Jews have been celebrated. In May 2004 an International Conference on the traditions of The Yekkes and Their Influence upon the Yishuv and Israeli Society" was held in Jerusalem and attended by over-whelmingly large audiences. For all that, we need to point out that although all these figures were deeply imprinted with the German Kulturbereich, the Jews from, say, Prague or Vienna were hardly "Yekkes," and in mannerisms, comportment, and formality rather different from, say, their "Prussian" cousins.

36. Many of Agnon's satirically named protagonists—Dr. Taglicht, Ernst Welt-fremdt, Manfred Herbst, Professor Neu, and so on—are explicitly or implicitly associated with these binationalists. As Agnon portrays them, beneath their professorial and European exteriors, lurked rather fervent erotic desires. This novel, unfinished at the time of Agnon's death in 1970, has been superbly translated into English by Zeva Shapiro (with an informative afterword by Robert Alter). See S. Y. Agnon, *Shira* (New York: Schocken Books, 1989).

37. See this citation from *Jüdische Rundschau*, 22 October 1929, as quoted in Antony David, *The Patron: A Life of Salman Schocken 1877–1959* (New York: Metropolitan Books, 2003), p. 236.

38. See the entry for 19 March 1930, Arthur Ruppin, *Tagebücher, Briefe, Erinnerungen*, op. cit., p. 422. Ussischkin later apologized for this outburst although there is little reason to believe he did not say what he thought.

39. Many years ago I wrote a study about the dynamics of this conflict within its original modern historical context. See *Brothers and Strangers: The East European Jew in German and German-Jewish Consciousness, 1800–1923* (Madison: University of Wisconsin Press, 1982; paperback, with a new introduction, 1999). The degree to which these dynamics were reproduced and seen as significant within Palestine among Zionists whose commonalities were supposed to transcend the differences remained surprisingly great. There was something simultaneously comic and nasty in the way these tensions manifested themselves. In 1908 Arthur Ruppin recalled:

The xenophobia directed against me as a "foreign" Jew by the population of the Yishuv that consisted overwhelmingly of *Ostjuden* created any numbers of ru-mors and jokes about my Jewish ignorance. This could have been forgivable, for in this lay a core of truth. What was unforgivable, is that these rumors ended in defamations, such as the following case: my wife invited some of our acquain-tances for Sylvester-evening 1908/09 and sang them some Lieder. Shortly thereafter there appeared in the "Press" a notice that I had celebrated Christmas and lighted a Christmas tree. This notice reappeared over the years many times in various newspapers.

See Ruppin, *Tagebücher,* op. cit., "Der 'Weihnachtsbaum,'" p. 171. This was only ultimately exposed when Leib Jaffe published a disclaimer.

40. See the letter to Robert Weltsch of 17.7.1928 by Schmuel Hugo Bergman, *Tagebücher und Briefe,* op. cit., p. 245. Actually, as time passed, members of the circle, notably Gershom Scholem and Hugo Bergman, became increasingly fluent and literate in the Hebrew language. Moreover, both studied and were reasonably literate in Arabic.

41. Ruppin, *Tagebücher,* op. cit. See entry for 31 December 1924, pp. 362–63. Even more extremely, Hans Kohn wrote in his diary (7.1.1927)—immediately after noting that his beloved Rilke had died without a homeland and open to the world (presumably an autobiographic remark): ". . . noteworthy, since I am in Palestine from the end of October 1925, I have the feeling of the proximity of death." See the Hans Kohn Collection, Leo Baeck Institute, New York (Box 18, Folder 2, Reel 12). I thank Adi Gordon for this reference.

42. Bergman, *Tagebücher und Briefe II, 1948–1975,* ed. Miriam Sambursky with an introduction by Nathan Rotenstreich (Königstein: Jüdischer Verlag bei Athenäum, 1985). Entry for 9.1.1964, p. 448.

43. On this tension, see George L. Mosse, "Jewish Emancipation: Between *Bildung* and Respectability" in Jehuda Reinharz and Walter Schatzberg, eds., *The Jewish Response to German Culture: From the Enlightenment to the Second World War* (Hanover and London: University Press of New England, 1985), pp. 1–16.

44. See Segev "A Binational Byway," *Haaretz,* op. cit., p. B9.

45. In his memoirs George L. Mosse recounts both the conventional and intellectual moments in this atmosphere and his fascination with what he calls "Weimar in Jerusalem":

Gershom Scholem and his wife were at the center of German Jewish intellectual life. On their "Saturdays" and at their dinner parties, one met many other members of this circle: not refugees from Hitler's Germany, but usually committed Zionists who had come to Palestine in the 1920s. This circle was like a floating discussion group, always in deadly earnest about intellectual questions, while maintaining the lifestyle these people had known in Germany. I was fascinated by this aspect of that circle as well, since both at boarding school and in my fragmented yet luxurious family life I had largely missed the gemütlich side

of the cultivated German bourgeoisie. The birthday celebrations, with their po-
etry readings, are particularly vivid in my memory, but also the love of recitation
in general, combined with a devotion to the German classics. Here one met a
veritable hunger for culture so largely absent in outside society.

See Mosse's *Confronting History: A Memoir* (Madison: University of Wisconsin Press,
2000), pp. 193–94.

46. This even applied to the more practical and moderate Arthur Ruppin (albeit in
a different way), who was older than the other figures discussed here and thus genera-
tionally closer to the founding fathers of the movement. Zionism, he noted in 1923, was
actually

only a springboard for a greater task, the renewal of the culture of the near East. I
was always against "political Zionism." My entry into the Zionist Movement,
occurred under the slogan, "against political Zionism (that is, the Charter Idea
of Herzl), and for practical work in Palestine." I wanted to base the rights of the
Jews to come to Palestine not on some political "contracts" and concessions but
rather on their historical and racial affinities with Palestine and wanted them to
acquire as many rights as they could earn through their work.

See his *Tagebücher*, op. cit. Entry for 29 April 1923, p. 349.

47. The secular, humanist Bildung dimension apart, Zohar Ma'or has recently, in-
terestingly and provocatively, emphasized a rather neglected aspect of the Brit Shalom
worldview: its Jewish mystical, redemptive-prophetic sensibilities. This approach thus
locates this movement far more firmly (and internally) within a certain line of religious
Zionism, one that ironically finds a certain affinity with its apparent political opposite,
the post-1967 settler project of Gush Emunim and their messianic redemptive project.
See his (as yet unpublished) paper, "The Mystical Roots of 'Brit-Shalom': Berlin and
Prague after the First World War," presented at a conference on Brit Shalom's Central
European Context at the Hebrew University, Jerusalem (2 August 2005).

48. Letter of 21.10.1933 in Bergman, *Tagebücher* I, op. cit., p. 345. This extremely
personal and revealing letter, here somewhat freely translated, sought to address the
painful rift between the two men:

I have not written to you for a long time, for I lacked the courage to address a
really decisive letter to you. We have become estranged over the last one or two
years, and as much as I regret this, neither you nor I can change this, not so
much because of your convictions as the way in which you express them in

small circles. There is no one who will not humanly understand your hate or *ressentiment* against Jewish Palestine; one has done much bad against you and you were too internally bound to the matter. Yours is ultimately nothing but disappointed love. Still, it hurts that you (in your speeches, not your writings) see only the one side of the Palestine issue and not the other.

49. Simon, Letter 58 to Walter Falk, 8.2.43 in *Sechzig Jahre Gegen den Strom,* op. cit., p. 120.

50. Ernst Simon, "*Prushim lo isim*" [Hebrew], *Davar* (11.11.1932). Quoted in Ratzabi, *Between Zionism and Judaism,* op. cit., pp. 267–68.

51. See Kohn's letter of resignation from the Zionist movement (to Dr. Berthold Feiwel), 21 November 1929 in Paul Mendes-Flohr, ed., *A Land of Two Peoples: Martin Buber on Jews and Arabs* (New York: Oxford University Press, 1983), p. 97. The whole letter can be read on pp. 97–100.

52. *Tagebücher* I, op. cit., 20.7.1927, p. 221.

53. See, for instance, Ze'ev Stern, "How Do We Approach Getting Closer to Our National Neighbor?" [Hebrew], *Ba'ayot* (July 1947), pp. 268–70.

54. "*Das Verhältnis der Juden,*" op. cit., p. 457.

55. See the entry for 31 December 1925 in Ruppin, *Tagebücher,* op. cit., p. 375.

56. See *Tagebuecher,* op. cit., Entry for 26 May 1928, p. 400.

57. Bergman, *Tagebücher,* Vol. I, op. cit., Letter to Leo Herrmann, 19.7.1922, p. 175.

58. Ibid. Letter to Robert Weltsch, 6.9.28, p. 255. Bergman does not mention his name, which was Shlomo Mordecai Zalman. Zipperstein, *Elusive Prophet,* op. cit., does not shed further light on the man relative to these views.

59. Ruppin, *Tagebücher,* op. cit. Entry for 23 February 1929, p. 412.

60. Entry for 9.1.18, *Tagebücher* I, op. cit., p. 106.

61. Entry for 2.22.1959, *Tagebücher* II, op. cit., p. 321.

62. Ibid. Letter to Luise Herrmann, 2.12.1954, p. 183.

63. Ibid. Diary entry for 8.5.1938, p. 468.

64. *Tagebücher* II, op. cit., Entry for 9.11.1971, pp. 644–45. It is noteworthy that Bergman clearly subsumed Czech and Hungarian Jewish productions under the label of German culture.

65. Bergman, *Tagebücher* I, op. cit. Letter of 16.10.1928, p. 260. To be sure, the overall relationship to "Western" culture constituted a complicated question for these Zionists. As Zionists they were bound to adopt a critical attitude, at least to some aspects of their European inheritance. Although, as I argue here, their Bildungs predilections were constitutive, they often combined these with an attraction toward other cultural fash-

ions and options. Thus Bergman in a diary entry for 3.4.1930 (op. cit., p. 307) mused upon the negative attitudes of Russian and Polish Jews to Russian culture: "I do not understand their attitude to Russia. For me, Russia is always the land of Tolstoy and Solovjev and Dostojevsky and would only wish that my Volk would be more influenced by the spirit of Russia. There is more truth in the Russian spirit than in western civilization." In this East-West dichotomy, Bergman pointedly maintained the charged German distinction between *Kultur* and *Zivilisation.*

66. Bergman, *Tagebücher* I, op. cit. See 27.10.26, pp. 206–07.

67. Ibid. Bergman, letter to his wife Escha, 17.5.1936, p. 422.

68. Hans Kohn, "*Bemerkungen: Zur Araberfrage,*" *Der Jude* (Heft 8–9), 1920–21, pp. 513–14. The quote appears on p. 514.

69. See "*Unser Nationalismus*" in Hans Kohn, Robert Weltsch, *Zionistische Politik: Eine Aufsatzreihe* (Maehrisch-Ostrau: Verlag Dr. R. Farber, 1927), pp. 141–50. The quote appears on p. 143. The piece was originally published on 11./XII.1925.

70. Letter 19 to Harry Heymann, 12 November 1916, in Gershom Scholem, *Briefe I, 1914–1947,* ed. Itta Shedletzky (München: C. H. Beck, 1994), p. 58.

71. Thus, in a conversation with Edwin Samuel as reported in a letter of 6.9.28 to Robert Weltsch. See *Tagebücher* I, op. cit., p. 255. Theodor Herzl's *Altneuland* also contains intimations of this sort.

72. Documenting this multidirectional complex in detail would be a book-length project. Bergman, for instance, was throughout his life interested in parapsychology, mysticism and life after death—see the as yet unpublished dissertation by Zohar Maʿor on these predilections among members of the Prague Bar-Kochba Circle (Bergman, Max Brod, Franz Kafa, Felix Weltsch, etc.), "Mysticism, Regeneration and Jewish Birth: The Prague Circle in the Beginning of the Twentieth Century." Buber's role in mediating myth and legend as part of a Jewish fin de siècle "irrationalist" revival is too familiar to rehearse here, but see especially Paul Mendes-Flohr, "Fin-de-Siecle Orientalism, the *Ostjuden,* and the Aesthetics of Jewish Self-Affirmation" in *Divided Passions,* op. cit., pp. 77–109, and chapter 6, "From Rationalism to Myth: Martin Buber and the Reception of Hasidism," in *Brothers and Strangers,* op. cit., pp. 121–38; the early Hans Kohn's neoromantic, but always spiritually autonomous and culturally inner-directed, cosmopolitan inclinations are clearly reflected in his biography of Martin Buber, *Martin Buber. Sein Werk und seine Zeit—Ein Beitrag zur Geistesgeschichte Mitteleuropas 1880–1930* (Cologne: Joseph Melzer Verlag, 1961, 2nd edition; the original was published in 1930) and his essays outlining his ideas on nationalism. See, for instance, his 1921–22 essay *Nationalism,* reproduced in Arthur A. Cohen, *The Jews: Essays from Martin Buber's Journal Der Jude, 1916–1928,* trans. Joachim Neugroschel (Alabama: University of Alabama Press, 1980), pp. 20–30:

At the beginning of the twenties in our century, one can see this reformation of
nationalism everywhere. It is the sense of a new, powerful, connected life, the
certainty of standing in tradition and yet being touched by totally new winds,
the yearning for a new, strong faith. . . . At the same time there is a conscious
seeking for an ethical anchoring of nationalism . . . trying to shift it from its involvement in the realm of being to the moral level of duty. . . . They are giving
it Messianic hues. Nationalism is becoming a question of personal ethics, personal shaping of life (pp. 27–28). . . . The nation bound up with territorial and
economic politics and its forced formation will be replaced by the freedom and
personal responsibility of national tradition and life (p. 30).

Even though Scholem caustically labeled Kohn, as an "Ober-Quatscher" (in letter 123
to Adoph S. Oko, *Briefe* I, op. cit., p. 292), he too—apart from his immersion in the
academic study of mysticism—cannot be understood outside of these dynamics. See,
for instance, the excellent exposition by David Biale, *Gershom Scholem: Kabbalah and
Counter-History* (Cambridge, Mass: Harvard University Press, 1979) and my essays,
"German Jews beyond Bildung and Liberalism: The Radical Jewish Revival in the
Weimar Republic" in *Culture and Catastrophe: German and Jewish Confrontations with
National Socialism and Other Crises* (New York: New York University Press, 1996),
pp. 31–44; notes 150–62) and "The Metaphysical Psychologist: The Life and Letters
of Gershom Scholem," *Journal of Modern History* 76 (December 2004), pp. 903–33. The
cultivated businessman Salman Schocken (a relatively marginal associate of the leaders
of Brit Shalom) was intent on discovering or inventing a Jewish equivalent to the German Niebelung myth. See Anthony David, *The Patron, A Life of Salman Schocken, 1877–
1959* (New York: Metropolitan Books, 2003), especially chapter 11.

73. The classic statement here, again, is Mosse's "The Influence of the Volkish Idea
on German Jewry" in his *Germans and Jews: The Right, the Left, and the Search for a 'Third
Force' in Pre-Nazi Germany* (London: Orbach & Chambers, 1971), pp. 77–115. Such
influences, Mosse argues, ran deep. Nevertheless, he insists upon a crucial distinction:

[F]or Jewish youth the acceptance of this ideology never quite obliterated that
belief in humanity which their liberal parents held so ardently. Those who
played an important role in the Zionist aspect of this ideology, like Buber and
Weltsch, became the principal spokesmen for a binational, Jewish-Arab state of
Israel. Fichte and Volk were part of a specifically German culture which was assimilated, but mankind as a whole was never lost from sight. Racial ideas had
no place here. (p. 111)

74. This was already noted by Ernst Simon in 1926 when Siegfried Kracauer accused Buber of such Völkisch tendencies. "In truth," he wrote,

> Buber is even the champion against such nationalism in the Zionist movement; he and he alone is to be thanked not just for the 12th Congress in Carlsbad rejecting Jabotinsky's Legion proposal but also an explicit resolution that advocates fraternal co-operation with the Arabs. Also in all particular questions of a . . . spiritual nature Buber has always been on the side and at the head of those who have regarded the self-consciousness of the Jewish People as unique and universal and completely in contrast to a nationalist assimilatory position or a nationalist concept of European militarism.

See Letter 22 to Siegfried Kracauer, 7 May 1926 in Ernst E.Simon, *Sechzig Jahre gegen den Strom,* op. cit., pp. 50−54, but especially p. 52. On this issue, see Martin Jay, "Politics of Translation: Siegfried Kracauer and Walter Benjamin on the Buber-Rosenzweig Bible" in his *Permanent Exiles: Essays on the Intellectual Migration from Germany to America* (New York: Columbia University Press, 1986), pp. 198−216. In his autobiography, Hans Kohn writes that

> Buber's intellectual breadth preserved our Zionism from cultural narrowness and made our nationalism compatible with a broad humanitarian and cosmopolitan outlook. At the same time, official nationalism throughout Central Europe was characterized by a narrow, militant patriotism which regarded the destiny and power of the nation-state as the most important premise of political life and as the spiritual fulfillment of the individual's own life.

See Kohn's, *Living in a World Revolution: My Encounters with History* (New York: Simon and Schuster, 1964), p. 69.

75. Hans Kohn, "Der Araberfrage," *Der Jude,* 4 (1919−20), pp. 566−57. See the translation of this article, "The Arab Question" in Wilma Abeles Iggers, *The Jews of Bohemia and Moravia: A Historical Reader* (Detroit: Wayne State University Press, 1992), pp. 239−42. (This piece was written in Irkutsk, Russia, in the summer of 1919). Kohn wrote extensively about this problem.

76. Ibid. Just as the Palestine of Arabs and Jews would later become a Palestine of Jews and Arabs—the limit, at that time, of Kohn's liberalism?—so too he combined linguistic reciprocity with a similar shift. Hebrew, he proclaimed, could be the exclusive language of Jewish colonies and autonomous areas "but once there will be a Palestinian state, it will have two languages for many decades: at first Arabic and Hebrew, later Hebrew and Arabic" (p. 240).

77. Ibid. The quotes appear on pp. 240, 241, and 242 respectively.

78. This is comprehensively documented in Mendes-Flohr, *A Land of Two Peoples*, op. cit.

79. Ibid. "Instead of Polemics" (November 1956), pp. 269–72. The quote appears on p. 271.

80. Ibid. "Politics and Morality" (April 1945), pp. 169–73. The quote appears on pp. 170–71.

81. "Introduction," *A Land of Two Peoples*, op. cit., pp. 6–7. There is an excellent précis and bibliography here of general Zionist attitudes to the Arab presence. See, too, Anita Shapira, *Land and Power: The Zionist Resort to Force*, trans. William Templer (New York: Oxford University Press, 1992).

82. Letter to Feiwel, op. cit., p. 98.

83. See my essay, "The Metaphysical Psychologist," op. cit.

84. In a remarkable (complex and almost incomprehensible) letter to Walter Benjamin—reporting on what he regarded as the crisis and bankrupting of Zionism and the attacks on Brit Shalom's position—Scholem characterized his Zionism as "a religious-mystic quest for a regeneration of Judaism" and not as an empirical "political" attempt to solve the "Jewish Question." See the letter of 1 August 1931, reproduced in *Walter Benjamin: The Story of a Friendship*, trans. from the German by Harry Zohn (Philadelphia: Jewish Publication Society of America, 1981), pp. 169–74. The quote appears on p. 171.

85. See "With Gershom Scholem: An Interview," in Gershom Scholem, *On Jews and Judaism in Crisis: Selected Essays*, ed. Werner J. Dannhauser (New York, Schocken Books, 1976), p. 43.

86. Thus Ernst Simon declared that after what had transpired in the 1948 war, all Jews and Zionists were "complicit in deep guilt . . . for the 400,000 new homeless, the plundering of Katamon, of Abu Tor, the destruction of villages and fields." See his Letter 66 to Martin Buber, 30.VII. 48, *Sechzig Jahre*, op. cit., pp. 134–35.

87. As reported by Bergman in a letter to Weltsch, *Tagebücher* I, op. cit., Entry for 8.4.27, p. 216.

88. Bergman, *Tagebücher* II, op. cit., Entry for 27.9.1950, pp. 65–66.

89. I owe this insight to a conversation with John Landau, Jerusalem, 25.6.2004.

90. Letter to Feiwel, op. cit., p. 98.

91. Bergman, *Tagebücher* I, op. cit. Entry for 3.11.1938, p. 482.

92. *"Feiern, Propaganda und Politik,"* op. cit. Part II, originally 31./III.1925, pp. 227–28.

93. Bergman, *"Die Ereignisse in Palaestina,"* *Selbstwehr*, 30.5.1921. Quoted in Bergman, *Tagebücher*, op. cit., p. 159.

94. Ibid. In the entry for 19.9.1929, p. 28, Bergman wrote: "Brith Shalom finds it-

self extremely active." The most active is Scholem, who has become quite the politician and more extreme in his outlook than before." On 25.9.1929 he wrote to Weltsch (p. 291): "Brith Shalom is more active than it ever was. The soul of this activity is Scholem, who in this respect is completely transformed."

95. See Betty Scholem, Gershom Scholem, *Mutter und Sohn im Briefwechsel*, op. cit., Letter 127, 12.9.1929, pp. 203–205.

96. Bergman, *Tagebücher* I, op. cit. Entry for 4.7.1925, p. 192. Early on, this view was shared by the two extremes of Brit Shalom—Ruppin and Kohn. Men like Rabbi Binyamin (Radler) based such schemes upon the notion that the Jews were themselves essentially an Eastern Volk, indigestible to the West. Bergman on the other hand warned of the exaggerated romanticism entailed in such visions. The rise of Arab nationalism was a product of Western capitalism and modernization not Eastern thought. The role of Zionism was thus to act as a bridge between East and West.

97. Ibid. See Bergman's 7.12.1929 report of a Brit Shalom meeting, pp. 297–98.

98. Ibid. See Bergman's report of this meeting in his letter of 27.5.1941 to Luise Herrmann, p. 555.

99. Ibid. Entry for 18.9.1950, p. 63. At other times, there was some relief, even if the cause related to this discrimination: the decidedly aged Bergman reported his satisfaction in 1972 when he joined a demonstration concerning the evacuation of the Arab villages Ikrit and Biram and his joy of demonstrating together with Arabs under the Israeli flag. See the entry for 23.8.1972, p. 666.

100. See Anthony David, *The Patron*, op. cit. See pp. 158 and 269 for the respective quotes.

101. See Simon's essay, "*Erziehung zum Frieden in Kriegszeiten. Dargelegt am Beispiel Israel*" (1971) in his *Entscheidung zum Judentum: Essays und Vorträge* (Frankfurt am Main: Suhrkamp Verlag, 1979), pp. 365–66.

102. This was most palpable when Buber and Magnes submitted testimony to the 1946 Anglo-American Commission of Inquiry. There they argued that as both Arabs and Jews had legitimate claims to Palestine, the future State should neither be an "Arab" nor a "Jewish" entity; they also rejected the option of partition as both impractical and a moral defeat for all concerned.

103. Bergman, *Tagebücher* I, op. cit. Entry for 6.5.1929, p. 285.

104. Ibid. Entry for "*Kongress für Wissenschaft des Judentums*" (1928), pp. 231–34. The quote appears on p. 233. These were the words of Yechiel Halpern, and in this particular case, the issue was one of the creation of a Yiddish chair.

105. Ibid. See Bergman's approving account of Magnes's words in the entry for 5.1.1929, p. 279.

106. Ibid. Entry for 25.6.1931, pp. 330–31. See, too, Weltsch's *"Feiern Propaganda und Politik (Zur Eröffnung der Universität Jerusalem)"* (originally published 17./2.1925) in *Zionistische Politik*, op. cit., pp. 219–23.

107. This is part of the July 1945 issue of the underground monthly *Herut* (Freedom)—distributed illegally as a wall poster—in which the Irgun attacked the Ichud. It is reproduced in Paul R. Mendes-Flohr, *A Land of Two Peoples*, op. cit., pp. 173–75.

108. Yoram Hazony, *The Jewish State: The Struggle for Israel's Soul* (New York: Basic Books, 2000).

109. Walter Laqueur has summed up this position well:

Jabotinsky had early on reached the conclusion that Zionism did not make sense without a Jewish majority in Palestine. . . . Other Zionist leaders, he argued, also knew this, but preferred not to talk about it openly, on the mistaken assumption that the Arabs could be fooled by a more moderate formulation of Zionist aims. But the Arabs loved their country as much as the Jews did. Instinctively they understood Zionist aspirations very well, and their decision to resist them was only natural. Every people fought immigration and foreigners, however high-minded the motives for settlement. There was no misunderstanding between Jews and Arabs but a natural conflict. No agreement was possible with the Palestinian Arabs, they would accept Zionism only when they found themselves up against an "iron wall," when they realized they had no alternative but to accept Jewish settlement. . . . Zionism, Jabotinsky argued, was either *ab initio* moral or immoral. If the basic principle was moral, it was bound to remain so even if some people opposed it. There were no empty spaces in the world. . . . He thought that it was impossible to expel the Arabs and that Palestine would always remain a multinational state. . . . In their transfer to Palestine Jabotinsky's views lost much of their sophistication and moderation, and served as the ideological justification for primitive and chauvinistic slogans which helped to poison Arab-Jewish relations during the 1930s and 1940s.

See his *A History of Zionism*, op. cit., pp. 256–57.

110. See the *"Politische Debatte und Beschlüsse des Jenaer Delegiertentages, 29–30 Dezember 1929,"* which appeared in the *Jüdische Rundschau* XXX Jg., Nr. 2, 7 January 1930, pp. 11–16; Nr. 1, 3 January 1930, pp. 1–3, and reproduced as document 191 in Jehuda Reinharz, *Dokumente zur Geschichte des deutschen Zionismus 1882–1933* (Tübingen: J.C.B. Mohr, 1981), p. 463.

111. See the (as yet unpublished) paper by Adi Gordon, "Hans Kohn's departure

from 'Zion' (1929–1934): From Jewish Nationalist to American Scholar of Nationalism," which notes that already in 1921, Kohn had toyed theoretically with leaving the
Zionist movement (p. 3) and that, given his public utterances and publications, rather
than voluntarily resigning, was actually forced to do so (pp. 4–5).

112. See the detailed letter outlining his position and analysis to Hans Kohn, 30 May
1928 in *Tagebücher,* op. cit., pp. 400–404.

113. Ibid. Entry for 31 December 1931, p. 435.

114. Ibid. Letter of 3 December 1931, p. 434.

115. Letter to Dr. Berthold Feiwel, 21 November 1929 in Mendes-Flohr, *A Land of
Two Peoples,* op. cit., pp. 97–100.

116. Gordon, "Hans Kohn's departure . . ." op. cit., p. 5.

117. See Letter 96 to Robert Weltsch, 22 September 1929 in *Scholem, Briefe* I, op.
cit., pp. 240–42. The quote appears on p. 242.

118. Letter 94, 10 July 1937 in Gershom Scholem, ed., *The Correspondence of Walter
Benjamin and Gershom Scholem 1932–1940,* op. cit., pp. 199–201. The quote appears on
p. 200.

119. For a good selection of her various proposals in this spirit—and her support of
and shifting relationship to Judah Magnes—during this period, see, especially Part III
of Hannah Arendt, *Vor Antisemitismus ist man nur nich auf dem Monde sicher,* op. cit.

120. Letter 131, 28 January 1946, *Briefe* I, op. cit., pp. 309–14. The quotes appear
on pp. 310–11. This letter consisted of a long and angry refutation of Arendt's critical article "Zionism Reconsidered," which appeared in *The Menorah Journal* 33 (no. 2, October–December 1945), pp. 162–96. A shorter version in translation appears in Anthony
David Skinner, ed., *Gershom Scholem, A Life in Letters, 1914–1982* (Boston: Harvard
University Press, 2001), pp. 330–33. I have analyzed aspects of the Arendt-Scholem relationship in my "Hannah Arendt in Jerusalem" in *In Times of Crisis,* op. cit.

121. It is worth providing the precise context and quote here. This was part of a 1961
exchange Scholem conducted with Geʿulah Cohen (a right-wing activist who had been
part of the militant *Lehi* underground). There he wrote:

I was never a *fundamental* pacifist (only in certain concrete cases was I a pacifist
in regard to our relations with the Arabs). I cannot deny, that there are circumstances in which a war or a struggle of an underground movement could be
justified. . . . We all have dreamed but not the same dream. And still when I
dream, I can find nothing in the kingship and heroism that so enthused you
and your friends. But how horrible the thought that history has equally mocked
both your dreams and mine [his italics].

See Letter 55 (in Hebrew), 15 December 1961, in Gershom Scholem, *Briefe II: 1948–1970*, hrsg. Thomas Sparr (München: C. H. Beck, 1995), pp. 84–85. Scholem may have been a little less complacent about the failure of Cohen's dream after the 1967 war. In Israel today, many view the (undesirable) realities on the ground of an undivided Palestine as something approaching a binationalist nightmare.

122. See Simon to Scholem, Letter 67, posted from New York and dated 30.7.48, *Sechzig Jahre,* op. cit., pp. 135–38, where Simon painfully replies to these accusations. He justified his actions by arguing that this particular war was not a justified one. "An unnecessary war is a Moloch—and you know that I hold this war to have been avoidable. . . . *For me* to throw my own child to the Moloch in revenge, appears to me, no: it is religiously and morally forbidden" [his italics]. The quote appears on p. 137.

123. See, for instance, Scholem's letter, No. 50, to Victor Gollancz, 13 June 1961 in *Briefe* II, op. cit., p. 80. See, too, the Notes, No. 50, p. 263, and, in the same volume, his exchange with Erich Kahler, Letters 122 and 122a, pp. 186–88. In the letter quoted above, Scholem wrote to Arendt: "I am a nationalist and fully unmoved by apparently progressive declarations against a view that since my earliest childhood has been repeatedly declared as superseded" (p. 310).

124. See Georg Landauer, *Der Zionismus im Wandel der Zeiten* (Tel Aviv, 1957), pp. 241 and 451. On these personalities, see too Mosse's "Gershom Scholem as a German Jew," op. cit., p. 189.

125. On Buber's copious writings on these topics, see Mendes-Flohr, *A Land of Two Peoples,* op. cit., pp. 228–305. Bergman, too, was concerned with these problems. At times, there was some relief, even if the cause related to such discrimination. Thus, the decidedly aged Bergman reported his satisfaction in 1972 when he joined a demonstration concerning the evacuation of the Arab villages Ikrit and Biram and his joy of demonstrating together with Arabs under the Israeli flag. See the entry for 23.8.1972 in *Tagebücher* II, op. cit., p. 666.

126. See *A Land of Two Peoples,* op. cit., pp. 245–53.

127. Hans Kohn, of course, is the exception here. Already on December 22, 1929, he declared in his diary: "Zionism is founded on the link between politics and violence. Our raison d'être was to combine Zionism with ethical demands. A vain [attempt] for this is a contradiction in terms. We must withdraw and as much as we are active, combat Zionism." See the Hans Kohn Collection, Leo Baeck Institute, New York (Box 18, Folder 4, Reel 17). My thanks to Adi Gordon for this quote. Yet, as late as 1958, while engaging in a virulent critique of the power-political and Herzlian versions of Zionism, he could still positively defend his Achad Ha'amian vision, to "rekindle the spiritual

heritage and ethical tradition of Judaism." See his "Zion and the Jewish National Idea," op. cit. The quote appears on p. 210.

128. In a later letter, the political contents of which may well have been a function of its addressee (the minister-president of Niedersachsen, Hannover), Simon placed the Holocaust, Germany, and the Arab-Israeli conflict within a somewhat unexpected Brit Shalom light: "No one," he told the German official,

> can bring the murdered, amongst whom was also my blessed mother, back again
> but we all can and must do our part to make sure that such a thing never occurs
> again. Germany's role in this must be to undertake a constructive part in the
> creation of Israeli-Jewish-Arab understanding. The State of Israel is not only
> the organically developed result of the Zionist movement; it is, no less impor-
> tantly, the revolutionary answer to the catastrophic events, that goes under the
> horrifying name of "Bergen-Belsen." Had we had the possibility of slowly
> building up the Jewish community, perhaps then Arab enmity would not have
> been as vehement as it is today. For that Hitler's Germany has at least an indi-
> rect part, the historical weight of which is no less than the direct co-operation
> with the earlier Mufti of Jerusalem.

Simon, *Sechzig Jahre,* op. cit. Letter 83 to Georg Diederichs, 24.3.1965, pp. 165–66.

129. See Ernst Simon, "The Costs of Arab-Jewish Cold War: Ihud's Experiment in Moral Politics," *Commentary,* Vol. 10, No. 3 (September 1950), pp. 256–62. The quote appears on p. 258. Though Simon described the underestimation of such desires as an Ichud error, he nevertheless regarded them as somewhat irrational. Because Jewish history in the Diaspora was "anachronistic," it

> caused emotions that had been late in developing to manifest themselves in more
> intense and violent forms than otherwise—like a case of delayed puberty in an
> individual. Passions long damned and forcibly repressed burst forth all at once;
> a messianic longing was fulfilled, however much the reality now achieved has
> fallen short of the messianic ideal. (pp. 258–59)

130. Ibid., p. 262.

131. See his comments to P. Pitter in *Tagebücher* II, op. cit. Entry for 19.10.1964, p. 469. These comments also somewhat temper Shumsky's analysis of Bergman's politics.

132. To be sure, given the drastic contextual changes, the renewed debate on bi-nationalism in contemporary Israeli politics is quite different from that which we have reviewed here. More often than not, "binationalism" is transformed into a frightening

slogan indicating the changed demographic realities in light of Israel's continued hold over territories conquered in 1967. It points to the belief that the Palestinian Arabs will soon constitute a majority and thus threaten either or both the Jewish and democratic nature of the State. Binationalism has thus become a specter not only of, and to the right but also to much of Israel's moderate left, which proposes a two-state solution. There are those (very few) who, like Meron Benvenisti, regard this binational situation both as a reality and as a possible shared political solution. See his superb study, *Sacred Landscape: The Buried History of the Holy Land since 1948* (Berkeley: University of California Press, 2000), trans. Maxine Kaufman-Lacusta.

133. The rush of new and invigorating research—much of which has been discussed in this chapter—is clearly related to present dilemmas. This is to be welcomed. However, a relevant and influential article by Tony Judt on the subject, while clearly responding to the present Middle East deadlock, is decidedly ahistorical. It proposes a binationalist solution without giving the slightest indication that this is not his own invention but, instead has a rather long and tortuous history of achievements and failures, and without any consideration of the problems this proposed solution may provide. "The time has come to think the unthinkable," he writes, and then advocates "a single, integrated, binational state of Jews and Arabs, Israelis and Palestinians," with nary a word about those who, long before him, proposed and considered the details of such an idea. Judt is, of course, quite right that the present state of affairs is exceedingly problematic but his article provides little intellectual or existential evidence that he has wrestled and struggled with the dilemmas entailed in any of these proposed solutions. In this, the disturbing (though, of course, highly controversial) reflections made on the ground by Benvenisti, stand as exemplary. Judt's dismissal of the "Jewish State" as "anachronistic" is facile (we have seen how Gershom Scholem replied to such accusations) and presumes a knowledge of the "progressive" nature and direction of the historical process that I thought few historians would today venture to propound. See his "Israel: The Alternative," *New York Review of Books* (23 October 2003), pp. 8–10.

134. See Lavsky, "*Chidat Chatoma . . .*" op. cit., especially pp. 168–69.

135. Mosse writes:

That this nationalism did not prevail does not make it any less relevant. As nationalism refuses to go away, as every minority continues to search for its national identity, the task of giving nationalism a human face becomes all the more pressing. Nothing in this book is meant to deny the necessity of nationality; not only has it been dangerous in the past to have been a people without a nation, but the national community rightly conceived can be a source of strength and pride, humanizing rather than brutalizing its members. . . . To be sure, this seems a utopia expressed only by a few pioneers in the past, for it was easier simply to denounce all nationalism. But if nationalism with a human face is not realized, we might once more abandon the world to oppression and war.

See the Introduction to *Masses and Man: Nationalist and Fascist Perceptions of Reality* (New York; Howard Fertig, 1980), pp. 17–18.

136. See his essay "German Jews and Liberalism in Retrospect" in his *Confronting the Nation,* op. cit., pp. 146–60. The quote appears on p. 149.

2. The Tensions of Historical *Wissenschaft*

1. Reinhart Koselleck, "*Wozu noch Historie? Vortrag auf dem deutschen Historikertag in Köln am 4 April 1970,*" reproduced as "*Über das Studium der Geschichte,*" in Wolfgang Hardtwig, *Geschichtskultur und Wissenschaft* (Munich, 1990), p. 361.

2. See 13, "Protection, Help and Counsel," in Theodor Adorno, *Minima Moralia: Reflections from Damaged Life,* trans. E.F.N. Jephcott (London, 1974), p. 33.

3. I have no idea whether or not these historians would concur with my admittedly rather idiosyncratic interpretation of their projects. George Mosse, to whom I was most close, is no longer with us and I have not shown the other historians this work. For the record, I consider myself a friend of Walter Laqueur but am acquainted only fleetingly with Fritz Stern and Peter Gay.

4. See Gay's preface to his to *Freud, Jews and Other Germans: Masters and Victims in Modernist Culture* (New York: Oxford University Press, 1978), p. ix. The literature on this theme is large. See, too, Saul Friedlander, "Trauma and Transference," in his *Memory, History, and the Extermination of the Jews of Europe* (Bloomington: Indiana University Press), pp. 117–37. Dominick LaCapra has analyzed many of these issues in his *Representing the Holocaust: History, Theory, Trauma (*Ithaca: Cornell University Press, 1994). Of course, with regard to the German-Jewish cultural historians, acknowledged emotional engagement will differ in intensity. We will later analyze this in detail, but compare Peter Gay's highly charged attitude with that of Walter Laqueur as presented in his memoir: "My attitude to Germany has remained markedly unemotional; I have been interested in German affairs since the war, but much of the time I've been even more interested in other countries and cultures." See his *Thursday's Child Has Far to Go: A Memoir of the Journeying Years* (New York: Charles Scribner's Sons, 1992), p. 105.

5. Sebastian Conrad characterizes historicism thus: (1) a belief in the "objectivity" of the study of the past that is, however, facilitated by the historian's present standpoint,

(2) an idealist conception of history in which ideas are seen as the carrier of historical events, (3) a method in which past events are seen as part of a hidden continuity, (4) an epic form of narrative, (5) whose goal is the construction of a national identity. See his *Auf der Suche nach der verlorenen Nation. Geschichtsschreibung im Westdeutschland und Japan 1945–1960* (Göttingen: Vandenhoeck und Ruprecht, 1999), p. 38.

6. See his *The German Catastrophe* (Boston: Harvard University Press, 1950). To be sure, the case of Meinecke is more complex than stated here. His account did include a critique of certain aspects of the Prussian tradition and the German *Bürgertum*. Still, it rested upon the assumption of the superiority of the high humanist German cultural tradition—Nazism was a symptom of its collapse. The reconstitution of Germany depended upon renewing its Goethean cultural splendor. Nevertheless, the German catastrophe derived mainly from external sources. The victims of the catastrophe were Germans rather than those singled out by Nazism. Indeed, the Jews are here pictured as naggingly complicit in the resentment they evoked. There is no discussion of the "Final Solution" (*Endlösung*) as such.

7. See *The German Problem* (Columbus: Ohio State University Press, 1965). See, too, the massive study by Christoph Cornelissen, *Gerhard Ritter. Geschichtswissenschaft und Politik im 20 Jarhhundert* (Düsseldorf, 2001).

8. *The Origins of Totalitarianism* (New York: Harcourt, Brace and Company, 1951).

9. Since the pioneering work by David Blackbourn and Geoff Eley, *The Peculiarities of German History: Bourgeois Society and Politics in Nineteenth-Century Germany* (Oxford: Oxford University Press, 1984), it has become necessary to argue and substantiate such a Sonderweg rather than simply assert it.

10. The literature on the constitutive conditions for the writing of history in general has recently mushroomed. The same applies to the issue of German history. Separate disciplines constitute and reproduce cultural fields with their own interpretive strategies, selection of questions and issues, categories of analysis, exclusions, etc. To some degree these will also reflect broader social and consensual realities. These issues are well explored in Sebastian Conrad, op. cit.

11. There is one such, insufficiently known study by Heinz Wolf, *Deutsch-jüdische Emigrationshistoriker in den USA und der Nationalsozialismus* (Peter Lang: Bern, 1988). See, too, David Sorkin, "'Historian of Fate.' Fritz Stern on the History of German Jewry: An Appreciation" in *Fritz Stern at Seventy*, ed. Marion F. Deshmukh, Jerry Z. Muller (Washington, D.C: German Historical Institute, 1997). See, too, Stanley G. Payne, David J. Sorkin, John S. Tortorice, eds., *What History Tells: George L. Mosse and the Culture of Modern Europe* (Madison: University of Wisconsin Press, 2004).

12. The emergence of, and catalyst for much of the new history (especially German

social history) was in many ways related to the controversy around the Fritz Fischer affair and Fischer's (at the time) highly revisionist thesis placing the onus of responsibility for World War I unambiguously at Germany's feet and attributing it to the machinations of Germany's conservative elites. The oppositional lines in this debate were clearly generational with the younger historians focusing upon the problematic nature of the German past and insisting that its responsibilities could not be deflected outward. Fritz Stern played a major role in this controversy. The social and cultural historians were at one with regard to these emphases. Yet, despite the apparent affinity, there was a subtle lack of reciprocity, not in terms of personal relations or scholarly contact but regarding incorporation into the works themselves.

13. I should note here that my approach differs slightly from that of Hartmut Lehmann—one of the few German observers who, it must be said, is perceptively sensitive to the issue at hand. He argues that it was only with the generation under examination that German and émigré historians became serious dialogical partners. I would claim that while personal and professional contacts were, indeed, created, this was not reflected particularly in the works themselves. See *"Kooperation und Distanz: Beobachtungen zu den Beziehungen zwischen der deutschen und der amerikanischen Geschichtwissenschaft im 19. und 20. Jahrhundert"* in Hartmut Lehmann, *Alt und Neue Welt in wechselseitiger Sicht. Studien zu den transatlantischen Beziehungen im 19. und 20. Jahrhundert* (Göttingen: Vandenhoeck und Ruprecht, 1995), pp. 150–65. See especially p. 153. It should also be apparent here that my concern differs—and, in part, dissents—from Theodor Hamerow's rather naive assessment of social history. His identification of the phase of a highly critical "social history" as that of a reflection of German "guilt" does not get to the interesting nuances, ambiguities, and defensive postures that have revealed themselves over the last few years and are explored here. See his otherwise perceptive review essay, "Guilt, Redemption, and Writing German History," *American Historical Review* 88 (1983), pp. 53–72.

14. Perhaps the most representative of these is Hans-Ulrich Wehler's 1973, *Das Deutsche Kaiserreich*. See *The German Empire 1871–1918*, trans. Kim Traynor (Leamington Spa: Berg Publishers, 1985).

15. Jürgen Kocka has correctly argued that the Sonderweg approach is helpful in explaining why there were so few barriers to fascism in Germany but less so when accounting for Nazism's unique radical impulse. He does not, however, inquire as to *why* this should be so. See his "German History before Hitler: The Debate about the German Sonderweg," *Journal of Contemporary History* 23 (1988), pp. 3–16.

16. Despite Peter Gay's insistence "that I have deliberately refused to dwell on the mass murder of Europe's Jews," as both his memoir (from which this quote is taken) and

his work (including several quotes reproduced in this chapter) indicate, his experience under Nazism is central to his life and thought. His *My German Question: Growing Up in Nazi Berlin* (New Haven and London: Yale University Press, 1998) tells the tortured tale of his attempts to "work through" this problem.

17. Peter Gay, "The German-Jewish Legacy—and I: Some Personal Reflections" in *The German-Jewish Legacy in America, 1938–1988 A Symposium, American Jewish Archives,* Number 2 (November 1988), p. 203. This later appeared as a volume, edited by Abraham J. Peck, *The German-Jewish Legacy in America 1938–1988: From* Bildung *to the Bill of Rights (*Detroit: Wayne State University Press, 1989).

18. *My German Question,* op. cit., p. 48.

19. See Laqueur, *Thursday's Child,* op. cit. (pp. 100–106). Still, Laqueur adds: "It would not have occurred to me to deny that I was Jewish." Given Nazi policy, he writes, there was not so much an "identity" but rather a common bond arising from past and present persecution. Finding oneself in the same boat "was quite sufficient for me at a time when introspection had not the highest order of priority."

20. There is a growing literature on this. See Dirk Moses, "The Forty-Fivers: A Generation between Fascism and Democracy," *German Politics and Society* 17 (1999), pp. 94–126. See too Ulrich Herbert, "*Liberalisierung als Lernprozesse. Die Bundesrepublik in der deutschen Geschichte—eine Skizze,*" in the important volume he edited, *Wandlungsprozesse in Westdeutschland. Belastung, Integration, Liberalisierung 1945–1980* (Göttingen: Wallstein Verlag, 2002).

21. See the fascinating piece by Michael Jeismann, "*Im Schatten alter Männer Blüte: Über die Nicht Vererbare Vernunft der Vater,*" *Kursbuch* 135, March 1999, pp. 172–80. See especially pp. 172–73. I thank Till van Rahden for this reference.

22. This hegemony has by now been extremely well documented (and this chapter will include such references). Many of the personalities discussed here were actively involved in German-Israeli historical exchanges. Here we are dealing only with social history and the relation to cultural history but others too have noticed a disinclination to suffer kindly dissenting opinions and methods. See Michael Stürmer, for instance, on this monopoly (of positions, method, and Fragestellung) in Rudiger Hohls, Konrad H. Jarausch, *Versäumte Fragen: Deutsche Historiker im Schatten des Nationalsozialismus* (Stuttgart München: Deutsche Verlags-Anstalt, 2000), p. 367.

23. As they begin to lose their influence, a new cadre of younger German scholars— no doubt as part of a conflictual generational shift of power and perspective—is presently undertaking an intensive and fascinating critical appreciation and assessment of the scientific work, motives, and political engagement of this generation in general, and of the social historians in particular. Indeed, Wehler himself has called for a collective examination of the spirit of his "Generation 1945" and its "long-standing influence" in his

Historisches Denken am Ende des 20.Jahrhunderts 1945–2000 (Göttingen: Wallstein Verlag, 2001), p. 60. Wolfram Fischer (in *Versäumte Fragen,* op. cit. (p. 87) claims that the new debate constitutes a youthful reckoning with the Bielefeld School, especially with Wehler, and that it smacks of schadenfreude; Helga Grebing has described this attack as "parricidal" in nature, the counterattack of the "täter" generation's great-grandsons (*Versäumte Fragen,* p. 161).

24. See Herbert, *Wandlungsprozesse,* op. cit., p. 47, for a slightly different but related point. See, too, Gerhard A. Ritter: "We intensively and consciously engaged the question of what led to a totalitarian State and a dictatorship and the presupposition and conditions necessary for the functioning of a democracy," in *Versäumte Fragen,* op. cit., p. 137.

25. Apart from the aforementioned piece by Jeismann, see the excellent article by Paul Nolte, *"Die Historiker der Bundesrepublik: Rückblick auf eine 'lange Generation,'" Merkur* 53 (no. 5, May 1999). Jürgen Kocka was born in 1941—later than the rest of this group. He must, however, considered a member less by dint of birth and circumstance than choice and sensibility.

26. I say "fathers" here advisedly. Virtually no women (both on the side of the social and the cultural historians) played a role in the histories explored here.

27. This is graphically illustrated in the superb volume of interviews *Versäumte Fragen,* op. cit.

28. See the insightful piece by William H. Sewell Jr., "The Political Unconscious of Social and Cultural History, or, Confessions of a Former Quantitative Historian" in his *Logics of History: Social Theory and Social Transformation* (Chicago: University of Chicago Press, 2005). This is a superb analysis of the achievements and drawbacks of both social and the "new cultural" history and their (usually unconscious) relation to the dynamics of capitalism. My approach is more limited and emphasizes the role of biography and generational and national experience in the construction of divergent "disciplinary epistemic practices" (Sewell's phrase, p. 24). But, again, Sewell entirely bypasses the cultural historians (and their rather different methods and assumptions) who were writing at the time that social history achieved hegemony and only addresses those influenced by the later "linguistic" turn. It is precisely this ongoing omission that this chapter addresses and tries to correct. I thank Michael Silber for drawing my attention to Sewell's work.

29. Fernand Braudel, *"Die Suche nach einer Sprache der Geschichte. Wie ich Historiker wurde"* in *Der Historiker als Menschenfresser. Über den Beruf des Geschichtsschreibers* (Berlin: Verlag Klaus Wagenbach, 1990), pp. 7–13. See especially pp. 12–13. I thank Nicolas Berg for this reference. And as Braudel put it in a 1965 afterword to one of his major works: "So when I think of the individual, I am always inclined to see him imprisoned

in a destiny in which he has little hand. . . . In historical analysis . . . the long run always wins in the end. Annihilating innumerable events . . . it indubitably limits both the freedom of the individual and even the role of chance." See Fernand Braudel, *The Mediterranean and the Mediterranean World in the Age of Phillip II* (New York: Harper and Row, 1972), pp. 1242–44.

30. As Sewell, "The Political Unconscious," op. cit., demonstrates, its commonalities apart, social history assumed slightly different forms in different countries according to their special circumstances. This chapter seeks to investigate the particularly strong national and generational weight of the German past upon its particular variant of social history.

31. See his *"Nationalsozialismus und Historiker"* essay in *Umbruch und Kontinuität. Essays zu 20.Jahrhundert* (C.H.Beck: München, 2000), p. 41.

32. Long before these revelations about the "fathers" became known, Heinz Wolf, *Deutsch-jüdische*, op. cit, p. 420, perceptively noted that this kind of history-writing was perfect for avoiding "a genuine confrontation with National Socialism." It constituted, he wrote, a kind of "refuge" historiography.

33. A certain lip service is paid to ideational and ideological factors, but these tend to be either relegated to the margins or to disappear entirely as explanatory factors of analysis. Thus "intentions" and "convictions" are effectively displaced as factors of historical action.

34. Winkler in *Versäumte Fragen*, op. cit., (p. 381) writes that Hermann Lübbe's 1983 "communicative silence [beschweigen]" also demonstrated that one could have a scientific and public political confrontation with National Socialism that went together with a silent acceptance of individual burdens. In the same volume, Kocka (p. 393) correctly points out that there is a difference between examining paradigms and methods of a school—and investigating their political enterprises and biographical guilt. This is certainly so but does not exempt us from nevertheless tracing the extra-scholarly, generational connections and inquiring as to how these impinge upon scholarly concerns.

35. See his piece in *Felix Gilbert as Scholar and Teacher*, ed. Hartmut Lehmann (Washington, D.C.: German Historical Institute, 1992). Occasional Paper No. 6, p. 6.

36. Most accounts of the rise of the new social history claimed both emigrants and "outsiders" such as Hans Rosenberg and Eckart Kehr respectively as legitimizing pedigree. More recent "counter"-versions hold that deep Zunft insiders, such as Werner Conze and Theodor Schieder, constituted the more relevant paternity.

37. The links between these three leading scholars of the Bundesrepublik Zunft and the younger historians are deep and manifold. Some are discussed in this chapter. On

"literal" fathers, Wolfgang is the son of Theodor Schieder, and the Mommsen brothers, Hans and Wolfgang, the sons of Wilhelm Mommsen (Wolfgang Mommsen passed away in August 2004). All these links are discussed by the relevant "sons" in the volume *Versäumte Fragen,* op. cit.

38. This story deserves separate, detailed treatment. It has been well documented by Robert G. Moeller, *War Stories: The Search for a Useable Past in the Federal Republic of Germany* (Berkeley: University of California Press, 2001), especially chapter 3, and Conrad, *Auf der Suche,* op. cit. Ten volumes documenting the expulsions—commissioned by the *Bundesministerium für Vertriebene*—were published between 1953 and 1957. Including legal texts and commentary, its heart was the over seven hundred personal testimonies and eyewitness accounts. As Hans Rothfels (p. 60) put it: "the task of historical understanding, is to put oneself in place of the actors as well as the sufferers." Eyewitnesses were granted a privileged position. The authors, Moeller claims, respected silence and selective memory and asked no difficult questions of their sources. They never commented on ways in which testimony was solicited—through expellee interest groups—and offered no reflections on how memories of the past might be blurred by the present. Some of the editors who were themselves expellees never suggested how their own experiences might influence their relationship to the project. This was clearly considered the most calamitous event of the war—the Shoah was ignored except as a foil for comparison.

39. The most comprehensive discussion of these issues is to be found in Winfried Schulze and Otto Gerhard Oexle, *Deutsche Historiker im Nationalsozialismus* (Frankfurt am Main: Fischer Taschenbuch Verlag, 1999).

40. The origins of German "social history" are clearly diverse and include both overseas strands and work done in the Weimar Republic. See the excellent pieces by Jerry Z. Muller, "'Historical Social Science' and Political Myth: Hans Freyer (1887–1969) and the Genealogy of Social History in West Germany," and James Van Horn Melton, "From Folk History to Structural History: Otto Brunner (1898–1982) and the Radical-Conservative Roots of German Social History," in Hartmut Lehmann and James Van Horn Melton (eds.), *Paths of Continuity: Central European Historiography from the 1930s to the 1950s* (Washington, D.C.: German Historical Institute, 1994). Well before these links became a major controversy, Winfried Schulze had uncovered them in his *Deutsche Geschichtswissenschaft nach 1945* (München, 1989).

41. Thus the philosophically inclined historian Reinhart Koselleck reports similarly in an interesting interview with Manfred Hettling and Bernd Ulrich, "Formen der Bürgerlichkeit" in *Mittelweg* 36 12 (April/May, 2003), pp. 62–82. See especially p. 72.

Koselleck, too, like so many other young historians of the time, served as Werner Conze's assistant (p. 80).

42. See the pieces by Wehler, Kocka, Hans Mommsen, and Wolfgang Schieder in *Deutsche Historiker,* op. cit. and virtually all the interviews in *Versäumte Fragen,* op. cit. As Wolfram Fischer puts it (in the latter volume, p. 87): "And I believe that none of us were inclined to poke around the past of our teachers." Or Hans Mommsen (p. 176): "There was no awareness in the 60s to question historians like Conze and Schieder, who endeavored to extricate themselves from the trodden tracks of relativist historicism and a history of political ideas that had become meaningless, about their own past."

43. Ibid. Lothar Gall (p. 305): In the atmosphere of the 1950s one could not pose such questions to and of one's elders—the authoritarian distance between generations was too great for that.

44. Ibid. As Hans Mommsen writes regarding his father, the historian Wilhelm (p. 164): "Regrettably it seems to me that most young historians are no more in the position to judiciously analyze writings that were composed under totalitarian circumstances and who do not take the context into account."

45. No longer does one speak of the historian's independence and special responsibilities. "The historian is not essentially distinct as a social group from the rest of society so that the notion of 'going off the rails' is a misleading one as it assumes a normal attitude of the majority" ["*Die Historiker unterscheiden sich als soziale Gruppe nicht wesentlich von der übrigen Gesellschaft, so dass der Begriff der "Entgleisung" ein irreführendes Bild ist, da es ein majoritäres Normalverhalten voraussetzt*"]. See *Versäumte Fragen,* p. 182. The social historians began their careers as outspoken opponents of historicist relativization. Within this context, however, the argument is made that those implicated in Nazism underwent a gradual democratization, a kind of redemptive learning process, and that an understanding of this necessarily must render moral judgment less harsh. "Is there really no way," Wehler asks, "to nevertheless create a superior counter-weight to that great burden that arises out of the 'Third Reich'? How many years must one live an honorable life not to make up for but to relativize these years?" See his *"Nationalsozialismus and Historiker"* essay (*Umbruch,* p. 33):["*Gibt es aber wirklich Keinen Weg, von trotzdem ein überlegenes Gegengewicht zu jener grossen Belastung zu schaffen, die aus den Jahren des 'Dritten Reiches' stammt? Wie viele Jahrzehnte muss man ein honoriges Leben führen, um dies Jarhre zwar nicht wettzumachen, aber doch zu relativieren?*"].

46. "The Political Unconscious of Social History," op. cit., p. 28.

47. I owe this insight to Atina Grossmann, who made this comment at a symposium on "The Politics of Social and Cultural History, 1945–2000" at Schloss Elmau, 12 July

2004. See, too, Stefan Collini, "Moralist at Work: E. P. Thompson Reappraised," *Times Literary Supplement* (18 February 2005), pp. 13–15. I later came across Sewell, ibid., who writes: "Thompson was profoundly hostile, almost allergic, to quantification, which he regarded as a violent abstraction from the textures of lived experience. His own work probed the thoughts, feelings, and experiences of the English poor, attempting, as Thompson put it, to rescue them from 'the enormous condescension of poverty'" (p. 31).

48. This has been well documented by George Iggers, who, it seems, very much accepts the social historians' progressive "Whiggish" account of their own history. He does not, however, realize that in its larger rejection of the role of ideas, ideology, and culture—the cultural historians, after all, were also critical of the idealist tradition— the social historians have thrown the baby out with the bathwater. Any account, especially of this object of investigation, that leaves out culture, rational and irrational, will omit crucial dimensions of the object under study. See his *The German Conception of History: The National Tradition of Historical Thought from Herder to the Present* (Middletown: Wesleyan University Press, 1968; 1983), and Wolf, *Deutsch-jüdische Historiker,* op. cit., p. 87.

49. Thus Peter Gay: "For the historian, the study of past politics entails more than tracking the pursuit of power under specified rules; showing classes in action, it points directly at fundamental self-appraisals, at expectations and anxieties." See his *Schnitzler's Century: The Making of Middle-Class Culture 1815–1914* (New York: W. W. Norton, 2002), p. 12. This was certainly not the idea of German historians even before the new emphasis on social history. Thus the highly conservative returned Jewish émigré Hans Rothfels—whose contested and baneful influence on postwar German historiography is increasingly coming under scrutiny—remarked in 1962 to Mosse when the latter told him he was working on an article on the "occult origins of National Socialism": "Leave that topic alone" ("*Lassen Sie die Hände davon*"). See George L. Mosse, *Confronting History: A Memoir (*Madison: University of Wisconsin Press, 2000), p. 170. See too Wolf, *Deutsch-jüdische,* op. cit., p. 526.

50. Jürgen Kocka puts it thus in *Versäumte Fragen,* op. cit., pp. 388–89. Fritz Stern has described his programmatic vision in a rather different way:

Of course there are "the broad, anonymous forces" that characterize the setting or structure of an age, but it is the interplay between these forces and actual people that allows us to recapture something of the spirit of an age. In this fashion one can hope to detect not only the rational political motives of particular actors, but perhaps something of their less conscious, more spontaneous responses as well.

See Stern's introduction to his *Dreams and Delusions: The Drama of German History* (New York: Alfred A.Knopf, 1987), pp. 5–6.

51. Wolf, op. cit., p. 420.

52. The very name was coined by Wehler as a conscious oppositional concept to historicism.

53. Wolf, op. cit., distinguishes the cultural historians "from the occasionally lifeless . . . stiff German of contemporary social scientists" (p. 332). The social historians claim Max Weber as their model, yet, as Till van Rahden has pointed out to me, they have appropriated the Parsonian systemic guise of Weber rather than the *"Verstehend"* ("understanding") version. In various places, Wehler has admitted to not living up to his own Weberian precepts. Of much of the writing produced by the Munich Institute of Contemporary History, Nicolas Berg, p. 278, op. cit., writes that it reads like "a sedative for one's own personal and collective conscience."

54. See the introduction to Wehler's *The German Empire 1871–1918*, trans. Kim Traynor (Leamington Spa: Berg Publishers, 1985), p. 7. It is interesting to note that in the 1973 German original, Wehler's formulation was far less specific and spoke only of "the road to the catastrophe of German Fascism." See the *Einleitung* to his *Das Deutsche Kaiserreich 1871–1918* (Göttingen: Vandenhoeck und Ruprecht, 1973), p. 12.

55. The term is Dan Diner's. See the symposium between German and Israeli historians, "The End of Social History," in the Hebrew journal *Historia* (2004), pp. 93–112, but especially pp. 101–4.

56. Indeed, as Wolf argues, the very evasion of intentionality derives from a strategic, defensive intention of the historian. See his, *Deutsch-jüdische Historiker*, op. cit., p. 421.

57. Nolte, *"Die Historiker der Bundesrepublik,"* op. cit., p. 426. Gerhard Paul has noted that a similar pattern applies to German functionalist accounts of the "Final Solution," which operates as an "automaton without people, above all without perpetrators, conducted by abstract structures and institutions bereft of history." Quoted in Conrad, *Auf der Suche,* op. cit., pp. 256ff.

58. Personal conversation, Berlin, 16 September 2003.

59. I have already mentioned Laqueur's *Thursday's Child*, op. cit. He has also recently published a work that contains some memoirlike material entitled *Dying for Jerusalem*, op. cit. For the rest of the group, see Peter Gay, *My German Question*, op. cit.; George L. Mosse, *Confronting History*, op. cit.; and (fragmentarily—there are reports that a full memoir will be published shortly) Fritz Stern, *Five Germanies That I Have Known* (Wassenaar: NIAS, 1998) and *Reden über das eigene Land 1996* (München: C.Bertelsmann, 1997). I thank Jerry Muller for providing me with these latter refer-

ences. See too the LBI Occasional Paper #5, on the occasion of Stern receiving the medal of the New York Leo Baeck Institute on 14 November 2004 (New York: Leo Baeck Institute, 2004).

60. Would it be too far out to suggest that this venture acted as a (conscious or unconscious) kind of émigré counternarrative to the Institute and Journal of Contemporary History (*Institut für Zeitgeschichte*) founded in Munich in 1956 by this cohort of German social historians? Both emphasized politics but the German side was heavily structural, the London-based version more (though not exclusively) cultural and intellectual.

61. The following is a suggestive rather than comprehensive list of Laqueur's works—which have also been translated into numerous languages—in these multiple fields: *Communism and Nationalism in the Middle East* (Westport, Conn.: Praeger, 1956); *Nasser's Egypt* (London: Weidenfeld and Nicolson, 1956); *The Middle East in Transition* (Westport, Conn.: Praeger, 1958); *Young Germany: A History of the German Youth Movement* (London: Routledge and Kegan Paul, 1962); *Russia and Germany: A Century of Conflict* (London: Weidenfeld and Nicolson, 1965); *The Fate of the Revolution: Interpretations of Soviet History* (London: Weidenfeld and Nicolson, 1967); *The Road to War: The Origins of the Arab-Israel Conflict* (London: Weidenfeld and Nicolson 1968); *Europe since Hitler* (London: Weidenfeld and Nicolson, 1970); *A History of Zionism* (London: Weidenfeld and Nicolson, 1972); *Weimar: A Cultural History, 1918–1933* (London: Weidenfeld and Nicolson, 1974); *Guerilla: A Historical and Critical Study* (London: Weidenfeld and Nicolson, 1977); *Terrorism* (Boston: Little Brown, 1997); *The Terrible Secret: An Investigation into the Suppression of Information about Hitler's "Final Solution"* (London: Weidenfeld and Nicolson, 1980); *A World of Secrets: The Uses and Limits of Intelligence* (New York: Basic Books, 1985); *The Age of Terrorism* (Boston: Little Brown, 1987); *The Long Road to Freedom: Russia and Glasnost* (New York: Scribner's Sons, 1989); *The Dream That Failed: Reflections on the Soviet Union* (New York: Oxford University Press, 1994); *The New Terrorism: Fanaticism and the Arms of Mass Destruction* (New York: Oxford University Press, 1999). Laqueur has also published numerous collections of his own essays, edited countless volumes on various topics and even authored a novel. He has also taught at Brandeis University (1967–70) and Tel Aviv University (1970–80). From 1965 to 1992 he served as the director of the Wiener Library and the Institute of Contemporary History in London and chaired the Research Council of the Center for Strategic and International Studies in Washington, D.C.

62. Fritz Stern's personal status and self-identification are sometimes the source of confusion. In his memoir *Five Germanies*, upon relating the impact of Nazism, he clarifies the question:

I was barely seven when all this happened; it was then that I first learned that our family, immediate and extended—who had always so normally, so cheerfully celebrated Christmas and Easter—were in the eyes of the new regime non-Aryan. That is, my grandparents were Jewish; the paternal ones had converted to Lutheranism; my parents, my sister and I had been baptized at birth; in the eyes of the regime and in my own, I was a full-blooded non-Aryan.

See *Five Germanies,* op. cit., p. 7.

63. Ibid., Stern, p. 7; Gay, *My German Question,* op. cit., p. ix.

64. Laqueur, *Thursday's Child,* op. cit., p. 105.

65. See Mosse's "*Politisches Erwachen. Berlin, das Exil und die antifaschistiche Bewegung*" in Wolfgang Benz and Marion Neiss, *Die Erfahrung des Exils. Exemplarische Reflexionen* (Berlin: Metropol Verlag, 1997), pp. 67–80 (see p. 72). See, too, chapter 5, "Experiencing Exile" in *Confronting History,* op. cit., especially p. 75 where Mosse states that "exile energized me and challenged me as nothing had ever challenged me before."

66. *My German Question,* op. cit., p. 21.

67. See Mosse, *Confronting History,* op. cit., p. 5.

68. See *Confronting History,* op. cit., p. 219. Mosse put it thus elsewhere: "all my books in one way or another have dealt with the Jewish catastrophe of my time which I regarded as no accident, structural fault or continuity of bureaucratic habits, but seemingly built into our society and attitudes towards life. Nothing in European history is a stranger to the holocaust" See *George Mosse: On the Occasion of His Retirement* (Jerusalem: Hebrew University, 1986), p. xxviii. This statement, to be sure, is hyperbolic. I have dealt with accusations that such thinking is teleological (and other issues) in "George Mosse at Eighty: A Critical Laudatio" in *In Times of Crisis,* op. cit., pp. 155–70.

69. See Jerry Z. Muller, "American Views of German History since 1945," in *Whose Brain Drain: Immigrant Scholar and American Views of Germany,* ed. Peter Uwe Hohendahl (AICGS Humanities Vol. 9, February 2001).

70. There is a good generational analysis of this in Wolf, *Deutsch-jüdische,* op. cit., pp. 18. He also includes Erich Eyck, Gerhard Masur, Hans Kohn, Paul Oskar Kristeller, and Golo Mann. In my study I have emphasized the cultural historians but of course there were others too in this age cohort of emigrants: Hans W.Gatzke, Andreas Dorpalen, George Iggers, Walter Simon, Fritz Ringer, Dietrich Orlow, Peter Merkl, Peter Paret, Werner Mosse, Herbert Strauss, Gerhard Weinberger, Raul Hilberg, Klemens von Klemperer (Austria); Arno Mayer (Luxembourg), T. Hamerow (Poland), as Wolf lists them. The exception here, in many ways, is Walter Laqueur whose education was never formal but whose prominence needs no demonstration. The complicated story of Hans Rothfels

has lately become the object of much controversy in Germany. Most of this is in German. For a convenient, extremely critical, English-language treatment, see Nicolas Berg, "Hidden Memory and Unspoken History: Hans Rothfels and the Postwar Restoration of Contemporary German History," *Leo Baeck Institute Yearbook* XLIX (2004), pp. 195–220.

71. *My German Question,* op. cit., pp. 4–5; "At Home in America," *The American Scholar* 46, no.1 (Winter 1976–77).

72. Irene Runge, Uwe Stelbrink, "*Ich Bleibe Emigrant.*" *Gespräche mit George L. Mosse* (Berlin: Dietz Verlag, 1991).

73. *My German Question,* op. cit., pp. 4–5.

74. *Thursday's Child,* op. cit., p. 367.

75. Hajo Holborn, from an earlier émigré generation, wrote: "There are actually great advantages for the historian to master a new environment and with it a new intellectual environment. One is able to reach a higher peak, one can observe things comparatively and free oneself from what one call[s] the provincial. All national feeling is provincial. I believe that through my emigration I became a better historian." Quoted in Wolf, *Deutsch-Jüdische,* op. cit., p. 237.

76. See Laqueur's *Generation Exodus,* op. cit., p. 8.

77. See "*Politisches Erwachen,*" op. cit., p. 80.

78. *Five Germanies,* op. cit., p. 14

79. Mosse's drive to critique respectability—and often to do so in hilarious ways—is well known. "I like to provoke," he writes, "to break taboos, but purely theoretically . . . to get people to think—not in the practice of daily life." See *Confronting History,* op. cit., pp. 180–81.

80. Ibid. Subjects that were "far removed from my own origins," Mosse wrote later, "may have played an unconscious role as I tried to dive into my new Anglo-Saxon environment," p. 142.

81. For a graphic account of this resistance, see Raul Hilberg, *The Politics of Memory: The Journey of a Holocaust Historian* (Chicago: Ivan R. Dee, 1996).

82. *The Varieties of History: From Voltaire to the Present* (New York: Meridian Books, 1956).

83. See *The Struggle for Sovereignty in England from the Reign of Queen Elizabeth to the Petition of Right* (Oxford: Basil Blackwell, 1950); *The Reformation* (New York: Henry Holt, 1953); *The Holy Pretence: A Study in Christianity and Reason of State from William Perkins to John Winthrop* (Oxford: Basil Blackwell, 1957).

84. See note 61 of the present chapter.

85. *Voltaire's Politics: The Poet as Realist* (Princeton: Princeton University, 1959); *The Party of Humanity: Essays in the French Enlightenment* (New York: Knopf, 1964); *A Loss of*

Mastery: Puritan Historians in Colonial America (Berkeley: University of California Press, 1966).

86. See *My German Question,* op. cit., p. 191. The dissertation, completed in 1951, was published as *The Dilemma of Democratic Socialism: Eduard Bernstein's Challenge to Marx* (New York: Columbia University Press, 1952).

87. *Confronting History,* op. cit., p. 142.

88. *Reden,* op. cit., p. 80.

89. For a spirited, passionately argued, and highly entertaining example of Gay's Enlightenment attitudes, see his *The Bridge of Criticism: Dialogues among Lucian, Erasmus and Voltaire on the Enlightenment—On History and Hope, Imagination and Reason, Constraint and Freedom—And on Its Meaning for Our Time* (New York: Harper and Row, 1970).

90. *My German Question,* op. cit., p. 200.

91. See Mosse's *German Jews beyond Judaism,* op. cit. Both Mosse's and Stern's classic works (*The Crisis of German Ideology* and *The Politics of Cultural Despair*) are, among other things, studies in the projects of disaffected intellectuals. For Mosse's evaluations of other aspects of the (non-Jewish) German intelligentsia, its qualities and weaknesses, see especially chapters 5–7 ("The Corporate State and the Conservative Revolution in Weimar Germany," "Fascism and the Intellectuals," and "Left-Wing Intellectuals in the Weimar Republic," respectively) in his *Germans and Jews,* op. cit.; "Fascism and the Avant-Garde" and "German Socialists and the Jewish Question in the Weimar Republic" in his *Masses and Man,* op. cit.; and "Bookburning and Betrayal by the German Intellectuals" in his *Confronting the Nation,* op. cit. Fritz Stern has written extensively on the connections between scientists and politics. See especially Part I of his *Dreams and Delusions,* op. cit., and *Einstein's German World,* chapters 1–3 (Princeton: Princeton University Press, 1999).

92. Thus Gay, *Weimar Culture: The Outsider as Insider* (New York: Harper & Row, 1968) and Laqueur, *Weimar: A Cultural History 1918–1933* (New York: G. P. Putnam's Sons, 1974).

93. This theme is pursued in the insightful article by Paul Breines, "Germans, Journals and Jews/Madison, Men, Marxism and Mosse: A Tale of Jewish-Leftist Identity Confusion in America," *New German Critique,* Number 20 (Spring/Summer 1980), pp. 81–103.

94. *Weimar Culture,* op. cit., pp. 30–31.

95. See Fritz Stern, *The Politics of Cultural Despair: A Study in the Rise of Germanic Ideology* (Berkeley: University of California Press, 1961) and George L. Mosse, *The Crisis of German Ideology: Intellectual Origins of the Third Reich* (New York: Grosset and Dunlap, 1964). These two works are often correctly grouped together. Yet their differ-

ences may be as significant as their similarities. Stern examines in detail three Völkish intellectuals (Paul de Lagarde, Julius Langbehn, and Moeller van den Bruck) while Mosse's canvas is much wider, taking in a panoply of political, educational, cultural, and recreational institutions and organizations and examining the diffusion and variations of this ideology therein.

96. For a comprehensive bibliography of Mosse's work, see *What History Tells: George L. Mosse and the Culture of Modern Europe,* eds. Stanley G. Payne, David J. Jorkin, John S. Tortorice (Madison: University of Wisconsin Press, 2004), pp. 254–78. See Laqueur, *Young Germany,* Gay, *Weimar Culture,* op. cit., and Stern, "The Political Consequences of the Unpolitical German" in his *The Failure of Illiberalism: Essays on the Political Culture of Modern Germany* (Chicago: University of Chiacago Press, 1975; originally published in 1971).

97. See his *The Culture of Western Europe: The Nineteenth and Twentieth Centuries* (Boulder and London: Westview Press, 1988), p. 2. The work was originally published in 1961.

98. In all this, it seems clear, Mosse was really the pioneer, forging paths of research that were later followed by other scholars. See my "George Mosse at Eighty," op. cit. and, especially, Shulamit Volkov's sensitive critical appreciation, "German Jewish History: Back to *Bildung* and Culture?" in *What History Tells,* op. cit., pp. 223–38.

99. In this earlier period, the cultural historians, too, viewed matters in this Sonderweg light. The analyses of the social historians would have received confirmation and deepened their anlaysis by referring to this dimension. They were reluctant to do so for reasons elucidated in this chapter, and relegated such matters basically to epiphenomena. For a critique of the reductive social-historical view in terms of its understanding of anti-Semitism, see Till van Rahden, "Words and Actions: Rethinking the Social History of German Antisemitism, Breslau, 1870–1914," *German History,* Vol. 18 (no. 4, 2000), pp. 413–18.

100. See Stern's *Um eine deutsche Vergangenheit* (Konstanzer Universitätsreden, 57, Konstanz, 1972), p. 181. Stern also wrote thus in his *Politics of Cultural Despair,* op. cit., p. x: "Specific studies . . . have shown that cultural, spiritual and psychic factors must be taken into account if we are to understand the triumphs of irrationality that marked fascism." Mosse's attention to this factor is legendary. As I have discussed this elsewhere at length I will not dwell upon it here. See my "George Mosse at Eighty," op. cit.

101. See, among others, *Freud: A Life for Our Time* (London: J. M. Dent, 1988); *Reading Freud: Explorations and Entertainments* (New Haven: Yale University Press, 1990); *A Godless Jew: Freud, Atheism and the Making of Psychoanalysis* (New Haven: Yale University Press, 1987); *Freud for Historians* (New York: Oxford University Press, 1985).

102. See *German Jews beyond Judaism*, op. cit., p. 47. This whole work illustrates the point.

103. I owe this suggestion, which places a slightly different, more benign light upon the motivations of the social historians, to Anson Rabinbach.

104. Mosse, *Confronting History*, op. cit., p. 70.

105. George L. Mosse, "*Ich bleibe Emigrant,*" op. cit. Quoted in Emilio Gentile, "A Provisional Dwelling: The Origin and Development of the Concept of Fascism in Mosse's Historiography," in *What History Tells*, op. cit., p. 44.

106. See Stern, *Five Germanies*, op. cit., p. 9.

107. See *Thursday's Child*, op. cit., p. 6.

108. See his *Party of Humanity*, p. x. Some have argued that Gay does not sufficiently practice what he preaches but that is a different matter.

109. Elsewhere I have analyzed how much attention of these schools to each other would have enriched the outcome. See "Nazism, Normalcy and the German Sonderweg," in *In Times of Crisis*, op. cit.

110. This has been well analyzed by Wolf, *Deutsch-jüdische*, op. cit. See p. 362. He also points out (pp. 413ff.) that while Wehler's reception of the first generation of émigré historians (Rosenberg, Holborn, Kehr, Meyer, etc.) was warm and elaborated upon in various texts, there is little place for the second. It is less painful to deal with them, Wolf writes, "than to be confronted with a method that scientifically integrates personal complicity, the personal relationship to the theme, into the material itself." As one indication, George Mosse's classic *The Crisis of German Ideology* (1964) was translated only in 1979, and the first review in German (by Bernd Faulenbach), as reported by Wolf, in 1981! See, too, Moshe Zimmermann, "Mosse and German Historiography," in *George Mosse*, op. cit., pp. 19-21. Even important works by non-émigré historians, such as Leonard Krieger's *The Idea of German Freedom*, went untranslated. Walter Laqueur says in *Thursday Child*, op. cit., pp. 367-68, without any apparent bitterness: "With a few exceptions, my books have been more widely read in Italy or in Japan than in the country of my origin." In Wolf Jobst Siedler's laudatio to him upon receiving the Inter Nationes Preis 1984 (see *Walter Laqueur* [Bonn, 1984], pp. 9-15), he comments that Laqueur's writings "came too early." (I would argue that this applies to the works of the group as a whole). This is a testament to the innovativeness and insight of these scholars but also does not probe into the reasons for the inability to respond earlier. Given all this, and despite the prestige Stern has acquired over the last two decades in Germany, it is strange and suprising that he does not even hint at these elisions or possible tensions in his unqualified praise for the liberating role of these social historians. See Stern, *Reden*, op. cit., pp. 85-86. It is also noteworthy that the one work of cultural history written in

Germany by Kurt Sontheimer—not a member of the *Zunft* but a political scientist (*Antidemokratisches Denken in der Weimarer Republik. Die politischen Ideen des deutschen Nationalismus zwischen 1918 und 1933* [Munich, 1962])—was refused publication by the Munich Institute of Contemporary History on the grounds that this would make heros out of scribblers who did not deserve to be remembered! See Berg, op. cit., p. 287.

111. See, for instance, the various contributions to B. Martin and E. Schulin, eds., *Die Juden als Minderheit in der Geschichte* (München, 1981) and Werner Jochmann, "Die Ausbreitung des Antisemitismus" in *Deutsches Judentum in Krieg und Revolution 1916–1923*, hrsg. Werner Mosse with Arnold Paucker (Tübingen, 1971).

112. These have been usefully collected in a volume, *Emanzipation und Antisemitismus* (Göttingen, 1975).

113. Hans Ulrich Wehler, *Deutsche Gesellschaftsgeschichte*, Vol. 3 (München: C. H. Beck, 1995), especially p. 933, 1065ff.

114. See Volkov's insightful essay (chapter 3), "*Nationalismus, Antisemitismus und die deutsche Geschichtsschreibung*" in her *Das jüdische Projekt der Moderne. Zehn Essays* (München: C. H. Beck, 2001), pp. 49–61. See especially p. 54.

115. See Mosse's classic *The Crisis of German Ideology*, op. cit., especially chapter 16, "A German Revolution," and chapter 17, "The Anti-Jewish Revolution."

116. See the book-length interview with Michael A. Ledeen, *Nazism: A Historical and Comparative Analysis of National Socialism* (New Brunswick: Transaction Books, 1978), p. 43.

117. See *Nationalism and Sexuality: Respectability and Abnormal Sexuality in Modern Europe* (New York: H. Fertig, 1985).

118. See Mosse's interview with David Strassler, *Jerusalem Post*, 17 September 1991, p. 8.

119. I have done this extensively in my "George Mosse at Eighty," op. cit.

120. Stern, more perhaps than the other cultural historians, has paid serious attention to the economic realm. It should be stressed, however, that he always relates this back to its cultural and personal dimensions. See his classic *Gold and Iron: Bismarck, Bleichröder and the Building of the German Empire* (New York: Random House, 1979). The quote appears on p. xv. The work was originally published in 1977.

121. Stern, "Introduction," *Einstein's German World*, op. cit., p. 7.

122. This is, quite clearly, a crucial distinguishing mark between these historians and Daniel Jonah Goldhagen. See Fritz Stern's critique "The Past Distorted: The Goldhagen Controversy" in *Einstein's German World*, op. cit., pp. 272–88. My own assessment can be found in chapters 9, 12, and 13 of *In Times of Crisis*, op. cit. I should add here that while—like many other historians—I dismiss his highly one-dimensional account of

modern German history and culture as monolithically anti-Semitic, Goldhagen's critique of "structural" and "functional-systemic" accounts of the Holocaust as lacking "agency" and "willing executioners" is a necessary and salutary corrective.

123. See Gay, *Freud, Jews*, op. cit., p. 9.

124. See my "George Mosse . . ." op. cit.

125. See Stern, *Dreams and Delusions*, op. cit., p. 114.

126. See *Generation Exodus*, op. cit., p. xii.

127. See, respectively, Mosse, "The Influence of the Volkish Idea on German Jewry" in *Germans and Jews*, op. cit.; Stern's *Dreams and Delusions*, op. cit., especially Section I; Gay's *Freud, Jews and Other Germans*, op. cit.; Walter Laqueur, "The Tucholsky Complaint" in his *Out of the Ruins of Europe* (New York: The Library Press, 1971), pp. 445–54.

128. See Dan Diner, "Hannah Arendt Reconsidered: On the Banal and the Evil in Her Holocaust Narrative," *New German Critique* 71 (Spring–Summer 1997), pp. 177–90.

129. See his *Freud, Jews and Other Germans*, op. cit., p. ix.

130. See his "Jews and Germans," reproduced in Gershom Scholem, *On Jews and Judaism in Crisis: Selected Essays*, ed. Werner J. Dannhauser (New York: Schocken Books, 1976). I have examined these views in greater detail in *Scholem, Arendt, Klemperer*, op. cit., and "The Metaphysical Psychologist," op. cit.

131. *Dreams and Delusions*, op. cit., p. 114.

132. *German Jews beyond Judaism*, op. cit., pp. 1–2.

133. *Weimar: A Cultural History*, op. cit., p. 73. Characteristically, Laqueur added, "to this extent the claims of the antisemites, who detested that culture were justified. They were in the forefront of every new, daring, revolutionary movement."

134. See Gay, "*In Deutschland zu Hause*" in *Die Juden im nationalsozialistischen Deutschland / The Jews in Nazi Germany, 1933–1943*, ed. Arnold Paucker (Tübingen: J.C.B. Mohr, 1986), p. 33.

135. Gay, *My Jewish Question*, op. cit., p. 49. I have discussed this debate in greater detail in my *Scholem, Arendt, Klemperer*, op. cit., especially pp. 37–40.

136. This may partly account for Mosse's insistence on recovering and emphasizing the essentially liberal, humanist, and Bildung side of German Zionism, one that may have nudged his work in this field into something of an apologetic direction. As I have written elsewhere:

> I sometimes would playfully nudge him to go beyond these assertions and examine in his scholarship—as apart from private conversation or journalistic comment—some of the darker faces of Jewish nationalism, but this (perhaps given his status as a refugee and his first-hand experience of Nazism) he was

always loathe to do. With all of George's delight in outraging his listeners and readers, here, I think, was a threshold he would not cross.

See my "George Mosse and Jewish History" in *German Politics and Society* 18 (no. 4, Winter 2000), pp. 46–57. The quote appears on p. 54. See too Volkov, "German Jewish History," op. cit., pp. 226ff.

137. See *Thursday's Child*, op. cit., p. 105.

138. *A History of Zionism* (London: Weidenfeld and Nicolson, 1972).

139. *Jerusalem beyond Zionism*, op. cit.

140. Laqueur writes:

I was from the beginning almost as much interested in the Arabs as in the Jews. Berl Katznelson, one of the spiritual gurus of Labor Zionism, had some bitter words to say about the pioneers from Central Europe, who having just arrived, were already more preoccupied with the rights of Arabs than of the Jews. There was a grain of truth in this observation, and I was certainly among those castigated. There was an element of curiosity on our part in an exotic people, but there was also the realization that it was absolutely crucial to attain a modus vivendi with the other people residing in Palestine—who also happened to be the majority. Thus, a few months after my arrival, I began to study the Arabic language; I never really mastered it, though I could eventually read a newspaper, and after mingling with Arab villagers (and Bedouins) during the war years and living in an Arab village for a year, I acquired a working knowledge of Arabic. . . . I became friendly with some of the leading figures in the field of Arab-Jewish cooperation and contributed frequently to their journal (*Be'ayot*). It was an uphill struggle [filled with] setbacks and disappointments suffered by the pioneers of reconciliation between the two peoples.

See *Thursday's Child*, op. cit., pp. 176–77.

141. It was a tragic conflict between the rights of two peoples, one fighting for its physical survival, the other for its historical rights, its land, its dignity. It never occurred to me to belittle or deny the Palestinian Arab case; had I been born a Palestinian Arab, my place would have been with them. But I was not born a Palestinian Arab, and thus found myself on the other side of an increasingly wider divide. (Ibid., p. 179)

142. The respective quotes appear in *Confronting History*, op. cit., pp. 190–91. I have also analyzed in greater depth and detail Mosse's relationship to Zionism and the State of Israel in "George Mosse at Eighty," op. cit. and "George Mosse and Jewish History" in *German Politics and Society*, op. cit.

143. See Laqueur's *Dying for Jerusalem*, op. cit., p. 11. This passage contains a hint, perhaps, of some of the tensions that pertain between the historians whom, for purposes of this chapter, I have placed in one camp.

144. See Stern's "Chaim Weizmann and Liberal Nationalism" in his *Einstein's German World*, op. cit., pp. 223 and 252.

145. *My German Question*, op. cit., p. 170.

146. Ibid., p. 190.

147. See Gay's "Preface" to *Freud, Jews*, op. cit., pp. xiii–xiv.

148. It is worth remarking that the positions adopted by these cultural historians are remarkably similar to the émigré literary *Germanisten*, as Mark Anderson has characterized them: All shared

> the commitment to Germany's Enlightenment tradition; the interest in modernist, exile and Jewish culture; a political and historical consciousness that resists purely formalist readings; an insistence on differentiating positive and negative forces in German culture; and an aversion to generalizations about "the Germans."

See his "The Silent Generation? Jewish Refugee Students, Germanistik, and Columbia University," *The Germanic Review* 78 (no. 1, Winter 2003), pp. 20–38. The quote appears on p. 32. Anderson is excellent on this generation. His assertions and generalizations about the anti-German, almost chauvinistically Jewish attitudes of the following generation (he singles out Sander Gilman here) are in need of more cautious analysis and far greater qualification (especially when it comes to historians.)

149. See Stern, *Reden*, op. cit., p. 83. Wolf, *Deutsch-jüdische*, op. cit., p. 140, puts it thus:

> *Besser kann eigentlich nicht ausgedrückt werden, was für all Emigrationshistoriker gilt: dass sie die Auffassung von der relativen Determiniertheit der Geschichte vertreten. Dass sie als Opfer einer historischen Entwicklung der Versuchung widerstehen, an dieser Entwicklung durch einen falschen Determinismus wissenschaftliche Vergeltung zu ueben, ist eine grösse persönliche Leistung, die uneingeschränktes Lob verdient.*

150. See *Thursday's Child*, op. cit., p. 366.

151. The most recent version of this is contained in Martin Brozsat's comments to Saul Friedlander in their famous correspondence, "A Controversy about the Historicization of National Socialism," *Yad Vashem Studies* 19 (1988), pp. 1–47. The quote appears on p. 7. Lately, and most crucially in the work of Nicolas Berg (to which we shall refer shortly) Brozsat's work and biography have come into serious question. Robert

Moeller, *German War Stories,* op. cit. (p. 192), comments on Brozsat's previous partici-
pation in the *Vertreibung* project (he wrote on Romania) and later his call for "historicization" that he "did not reflect on his own work of compiling expellee memories from
Romania thirty years earlier had been motivated by the same intentions and represented
another form of the 'historicization' of the war's end." This hostility to émigré historians
was very often a veiled form of "anti-Semitism" and was also aimed at general émigré
historians of modern Germany. See Volker Berghahn, *"Deutschlandbilder 1945–1965. An-
gloamerkianische Historiker und moderne deutsche Geschichte"* in Ernst Schulin, ed., *Deutsche
Geschichtswissenschaft nach dem Zweiten Weltkrieg (1945–1965)* (Munich: R. Oldenbourg,
1989) where he documents the resistance to versions of Prussian and Bismarckian history propounded by Francis Carsten and Werner Mosse, p. 241.

Gerhard Ritter put it thus: "The writings of German emigrants on the German problem in America and England has produced more confusion than enlightenment. Ressentiment, where it reigns without control, provides no fertile soil for sober objective
historiography and many years of estrangement from German soil leads easily to a dis-
tortion of reality." [*"Das Schrifttum deutscher Emigranten in Amerika und England über das
deutsche Problem hat vielfach mehr Verwirrung als Aufklärung gestiftet. Das Ressentiment is,
wo es hemmungslos waltet, kein günstiger Nahrboden nüchtern objektiver Geschichtsschreibung, und langjährige Entfremdung vom deutschen Boden fuerht leicht zu verzerrter Sicht der
Wirklichkeit."*] See Berg, *Der Holocaust und die westdeutschen Historiker. Erforschung und
Erinnerung* (Göttingen: Wallstein Verlag, 2003), p. 167.

152. Berg, ibid., especially pp. 511ff. This is an important work and, among other
things, reflects a change in generational perspectives of German historians. Berg's challenge to the older generation of respected and established scholars has been greeted both
with approval and dismissal (for its essentially noncontextual, ahistorical, and moralistic point of view). For the most trenchant criticism, see Ian Kershaw, "Beware the Moral
High Ground," *Times Literary Supplement* (10 October 2003), pp. 10–11. For dissenting German reviews, see Hans Mommsen, *"Täter und Opfer—ein Streit um die Historiker,"* *Die Welt,* 13 September 2003; Norbert Frei, *"Hitler-Junge, Jahrgang 1926. Hat
der Historiker Martin Brozsat seine NSDAP-Mitgliedschaft verschwiegen—oder hat er
nichts davon gewusst?"* *Die Zeit,* 3.8.2003.

153. Elsewhere, Dan Diner has argued that such intentionalism and its macro-
perspective is a particularly "Jewish" narrative of the Holocaust for it is animated by the
question "why us," whereas structural history with its painstaking microperspective,
which tends to dissolve the total picture into seemingly discrete constituent parts, and
is an answer to the question "how did it happen," is strikingly suited to a "German" nar-

rative. See Diner's, "Varieties of Narration: The Holocaust in Historical Memory" in his *Beyond the Conceivable: Studies on Germany, Nazism, and the Holocaust* (Berkeley: University of California Press, 2000), pp. 173–86. See especially p. 186.

154. We have already discussed the disinclination of the social historians with regard to the "personalization" of history. For the later period, Berg provides a fascinating analysis of the importance of persons and, literally, their "names" in the great (and hitherto unknown) controversy between Brozsat and the undeservedly neglected Jewish scholar Joseph Wulf. Brozsat vehemently opposed Wulf's attempt to render Dr. Wilhelm Hagen's ugly role in the Warsaw Ghetto a matter of public record. Naming complicit names, especially of living people, was the taboo of the time, whereas for Wulf, analysis "without names would have made the whole undertaking senseless." See Berg, op. cit., p. 359. Apart from his book, Berg has conveniently summarized this disagreement (as well as Brozsat's unacknowledged late membership in the Nazi party—this from someone who regarded Jewish historians' involvement in Holocaust research as "mythical" and unscientific!) in his *"Die Lebenslüge vom Pathos der Nüchternheit"* in *Süddeutsche Zeitung*, No. 163 (17 July 2002), p. 14.

155. See Michael P. Steinberg, "Aby Warburg's Kreuzlingen Lecture: A Reading" in Aby M. Warburg, *Images from the Region of Pueblo Indians of North America* (Ithaca: N.Y.: Cornell University Press, 1995), especially p. 73, n. 27, and p. 111.

156. I have discussed these developments in detail in my "George Mosse at Eighty," op. cit.

157. See Jennifer Jenkin's trenchant, unpublished response to an oral presentation of a version of this chapter, presented at the Wolfe Symposium at Toronto University, "Tensions of Interpretation: The Holocaust in Poland, France, Germany and the Yishuv" (26 September 2005). For a related criticism of similar omissions in the field of German-Jewish history (although it does not deal specifically with the subjects of this chapter), see the review article by David Sorkin, "The Émigré Synthesis: German-Jewish History in Modern Times," *Central European History*, Vol. 34, No. 4 (2001), pp. 531–59.

158. On this point, see the useful essay by Thomas Nipperdey (one of the German historians who, exceptionally, was indeed sensitive to cultural dimensions), *"Kann Geschichte objektiv sein?"* in his *Nachdenken über die deutsche Geschichte. Essays* (München: C. H. Beck, 1986).

159. One must always beware of identifying any intellectual strategy with a particular group or with only one ideological deployment. This is equally so for "intentionalist" arguments. Ironically, early West German historians had used a Hitlercentric (and thus "intentionalist") approach and were thus able to filter out of their work long-range pro-

cesses in which responsibility for the war could be taken off the shoulders of the German nation. It is to the credit of the social historians that they broadened the vision to include large (and usually elite) segments in the story.

160. Sewell, "The Political Unconscious . . ." op. cit., argues that both a more sophisticated and self-reflexive social and cultural history could render "the compatibility of structural thinking with an emphasis on culture, contingency, and agency . . . by providing a theoretical language transcending the antinomy of social and cultural history" (p. 80). See, too, the comments by Gabriel Motzkin in the (Hebrew) symposium, "The End of Social History," op. cit., pp. 110–12.

161. This is exactly what Wehler himself understands and even calls for in a charming piece that also resists too quick an overcoming of his work. See his *"Rückblick und Ausblick—oder: arbeiten, um überholt zu werden?"* in Paul Nolte, Manfred Hettling, Frank-Michael Kuhlemann, Hans-Walter Schmuhl, *Perspektiven der Gesellschaftsgeschichte* (Munich: Beck, 2000).

162. See his "The Refugee Scholar as Intellectual Educator: A Student's Recollections" in Hartmut Lehmann and James J.Sheehan, eds., *An Interrupted Past: German-Speaking Refugee Historians in the United States after 1933* (Cambridge: Cambridge University Press, 1991; 2002), p. 143.

163. In his latest, the fourth, volume of German social history, *Deutsche Gesellschaftsgeschichte 1914–1949* (München: C. H. Beck, 2003), Wehler has taken some of the criticisms to heart and paid more attention to these previously "epiphenomenal" factors (while retaining his structural and developmental framework).

164. He writes thus of the criticism leveled against

das *"kalte" Denken in Strukturen und Prozessen die Handlungsfaehigkeit individueller Akteure, ihre lebensweltliche Erfahrung, kurz: das Moment der "Agency" zur Geltung gebracht. Diese Kritik zielte auf ein unleugbares Defizit der westdeutschen Sozialgeschichte, welche die doppelte Konstituierung von Wirklichkeit: einerseits durch "real-historische" Bedingungen, andererseits aber auch durch Perzeption und Sinndeutung, trotz aller Beschwörung Webers ignoriert hatte.*

See his *Historisches Denken*, op. cit., p. 63. Jürgen Kocka also admits that early social history ignored to its detriment the cultural and symbolic aspect of historical reality but also attributes this to the "new" cultural history, the linguistic turn, and ignores the émigré cultural historians who were doing exactly this at the same time that these social histories were being produced. See his *"Historische Sozialwissenschaft heute,"* in Nolte, *Perspektiven*, op. cit., especially p. 13.

165. *Historisches Denken,* chapters 5−8. See, too, Wehler's critique and his understanding of—and resistance to—the fact that everyone's work is eventually overtaken in "*Rückblick,*" ibid.

166. See the preface to *Weimar Culture,* op. cit., p. xiv.

3. Icons beyond the Border

1. Part I, 18, *Minima Moralia: Reflections from Damaged Life,* trans. E.F.N. Jephcott (London: NLB, 1974), pp. 38−39. The work was first published in 1951.

2. See the essay "Camus' *Notebooks*" in *Against Interpretation and Other Essays* (New York: Delta, 1964), p. 52. I thank Martin Jay for drawing my attention to this reference.

3. For a revealing contemporary portrait of Strauss's personal religio-philosophical conflicts, his shyness, and his early support of Mussolini (in the latter's pre-anti-Semitic phase), see Hans Jonas, *Erinnerungen,* ed. Christian Wiese (Frankfurt am Main: Insel Verlag, 2003), pp. 94ff and especially pp. 261ff.

4. The sectarian, cultlike atmosphere promoted by Strauss's followers is legendary. For an admittedly tendentious view, see Shadia B. Drury, *Leo Strauss and the American Right* (New York: St. Martin's Press, 1997). Drury puts it thus (p. xi): "[T]he political ideas of this very influential man are shrouded in mystery, partly because he was preoccupied with secrecy and esotericism, and partly because his students treat his work as sacred texts rather than as objects of critical analysis and debate." Yet the description of the master by one of his students, Michael Platt, tends to reinforce Drury's statement:

> And when one follows the manly path of his sentences, his steady ascents, his
> sudden dashes to a peak, or his equally sudden descents to some depth, when a
> single remark goes to the very heart of a matter that has long puzzled one, or when
> he makes something simple remarkable as well, when reading Strauss makes one
> get up and walk about the room, when all cares vanish in the bliss of thinking,
> and one is attached only to detachment, then one is inclined only to ask the Questions and forget the quarrels, remember Man and forget all cities, men, and meals.

See his essay "Leo Strauss: Three Quarrels, Three Questions, One Life" in *The Crisis of Liberal Democracy: A Straussian Perspective,* ed. Kenneth L. Deutsch, Walter Sofer, foreword by Joseph Cropsey (Albany: State University of New York Press, 1987), p. 24.

5. Gordon S. Wood, "The Fundamentalists and the Constitution," *New York Review of Books* (February 1968), pp. 33−40. Allan Bloom declared "I believe our generation will be judged by the next generation according to how we judged Leo Strauss." Quoted

in Susan Orr, "Strauss, Reason, and Revelation: Unraveling the Essential Question" in *Leo Strauss and Judaism: Jerusalem and Athens Critically Revisited*, ed. David Novak (Lanham: Rowman and Littlefield, 1996), pp. 25–53. The quote appears on p. 25.

6. See, for instance, William Pfaff, "The Long Reach of Leo Strauss," *International Herald Tribune* (15 May 2003); Nicolas Xenos, "Leo Strauss and the Rhetoric of the War on Terror," *Logos* (Spring 2004); see, for instance, Jeffrey Steinberg, "Profile: Leo Strauss, Fascist Godfather of the Neo-Cons," *Executive Intelligence Review* (21 March 2003). Jenny Strauss Clay, Strauss's daughter, a professor of classics at the University of Virginia, sought to stem this tide in an Op-Ed page of the *New York Times* (2 June 2003), where she wrote:

> My father was a teacher, not a right-wing guru. . . . Recent news articles have
> portrayed my father, Leo Strauss, as the mastermind behind the neoconservative
> ideologues who control United States foreign policy. He reaches out from his
> 30-year old grave, we are told, to direct a "cabal" (a word with distinct anti-Semitic
> overtones) of Bush administration figures hoping to subject the American
> people to rule by a ruthless elite. I do not recognize the Leo Strauss presented
> in these articles.

And, as Mark Lilla has noted: "Journalists who had never read him trawled his dense commentaries on ancient, medieval, and modern political thought looking for incriminating evidence. Finding none, they then suggested that his secret antidemocratic doctrines were passed on to adepts who subsequently infiltrated government." See "Leo Strauss: The European," *New York Review of Books* (21 October 2004), pp. 58–60. The quote appears on p. 55. For some excellent examples of the distortions and partisan uses made by interested American commentators, see Lilla's follow-up article, "The Closing of the Straussian Mind," *New York Review of Books* (4 November 2004), pp. 55–59.

7. See Anne Norton, *Leo Strauss and the Politics of American Empire* (New Haven: Yale University Press, 2004). See also Kenneth L. Deutsch and John A. Murley, eds., *Leo Strauss, the Straussians and the Study of the American Regime* (Lanham, Md.: Rowman and Littlefield, 1999).

8. Thus, as Timothy Garton Ash explains, the young mullah-philosopher Mohsen Rezvani, has written admiringly of Strauss and his "insistence that there is a single truth in a classic text and that the intentions of the author (e.g., God, in the case of the Koran) are best interpreted by a neo-Platonic intellectual vanguard (for the Koran, the Islamic jurists whose ranks Rezvani aspires to join)." See Ash, "Soldiers of the Hidden Imam,"

New York Review of Books (Vol. LII, No. 17, 3 November 2005), pp. 4-8. The quote appears on p. 5.

9. See, for instance, the collection of essays (written many years before the present Bush administration came to power) *The Crisis of Liberal Democracy: A Straussian Perspective,* op. cit.

10. Arthur Schlesinger, "The Making of a Mess," *New York Review of Books* (23 September 2004), pp. 40-43. See especially p. 40. When Strauss was asked how much he was responsible for the transcripts of his classes, he replied: "About as much as God is said to be responsible for evil or a world of evil." See Michael Platt, "Leo Strauss: Three Quarrels, Three Questions, One Life" in *The Crisis of Liberal Democracy,* op. cit., pp. 17-28. The quote appears on p. 24.

11. For sources and references, see "Hannah Arendt in Jerusalem," in *In Times of Crisis,* op. cit.

12. See Alexander Kluy, *"Das Wissen um die Fehlbarkeit,"* in the *"Album," Der Standard* (3 December 2005), p. A6.

13. See his essay "The Arendt Cult: Hannah Arendt as Political Commentator" in Steven E. Aschheim, ed., *Hannah Arendt in Jerusalem,* op. cit., pp. 47-64. See especially pp. 56-57. The books that were apparently most useful in this East European context were *The Origins of Totalitarianism, On Violence,* and *On Revolution.* In the latter two she argued that "true" power was generated not through violence but (voluntary and spontaneous) human action in concert.

14. See, for instance, Waltraud Meints, Katherine Klinger, eds., *Politik und Verantwortung. Zur Aktualität von Hannah Arendt* (Hannover: Offizin Verlag, 2004). For an example of one such creative attempt to apply her thought to current world crises, see in that volume, Nancy Fraser, "Hannah Arendt im 21. Jahrhundert," pp. 73-86. For other recent German applications, see Stefan Ahrens, *Die Gründung der Freiheit. Hannah Arendts politisches Denken über die Legitimität demokratischer Ordnungen* (Frankfurt am Main: Peter Lang, 2005) and Kurt Sontheimer, *Hannah Arendt. Der Weg einer grossen Denkerin* (München: Piper Verlag, 2005). Amnon Raz-Krakotzin has attempted an Arendtian reading of the present Israel-Palestine conflict in his, "Binationalism and Jewish Identity: Hannah Arendt and the Question of Jewish Palestine" in *Hannah Arendt in Jerusalem,* op. cit.

15. Zizek writes that in the last decade we have seen "the elevation of Hannah Arendt into an untouchable authority, a point of transference." See his *Did Somebody Say Totalitarianism? Five Interventions in the (Mis)use of a Notion* (London: Verso, 2001), pp. 2-3. "Even academics whose basic orientation might seem to push them up against Arendt . . . engage in the impossible task of reconciling her with their fundamental the-

oretical commitment." But that surely is a sign not only of Arendt's canonic enthrone-ment but also of the nature of interested interpretive reception.

16. As a result of seminars held on the subject of democracy at the New School for Social Research in New York in 1984, Arendtian notions of antitotalitarianism and civil society took hold and people like Adam Michnik in Warsaw, and Jerzy Szacki and Györgi Bence in Budapest, organized dissenting seminars on these topics. See Wolf-gang Heuer's informative *"Ich selber wirken?,' Eine Synopse der deutschen und inter-nationalen, akademischen und nicht-akademischen Wirkungsgeschichte Hannah Arendts"* in the special issue devoted to Arendt in *Text + Kritik,* 166/167 (September 2005), pp. 174–82. See especially p. 180. I thank Marie Luise Knott for drawing my attention to this issue of the journal. See, too, Richard J. Bernstein, *Hannah Arendt and the Jewish Question* (Cambridge, Mass.: The MIT Press, 1996), p. 2.

17. Quoted in Elisabeth Young-Bruehl, *Hannah Arendt: For Love of the World* (New Haven: Yale University Press, 1882), p. 451.

18. To be sure, such searches are notoriously unreliable. "Walter Benjamin" is bound to be confused with numerous other figures with a combination of these names. Still, under Benjamin (on 20 February 2005) there were an astonishing 3,280,000 entries, way outstripping the others! The other entries roughly follow the political and then intel-lectual order as I have listed them here: Strauss, 451,000; Arendt, 326,000; Adorno, 223,000; Rosenzweig, 57,400; Scholem, 43,900.

19. The examples of this popular percolation are numerous. A full study of Ben-jamin's *Rezeptionsgeschichte* would be valuable. A beginning has been made in Ehud Greenberg's excellent Hebrew M.A. thesis on the subject. Thus, Julia Eisenberg's 2001 pop record "Trilectic," based, of all things, upon Benjamin's diary entries of his 1927 trip to Moscow, and his love affair with Asja Lacis, sold hundreds of thousands of copies, not through any massive publicity by the mass media but rather through word of mouth and the Internet. See Greenberg's unpublished paper "'A Hero of Our Time'?—Walter Ben-jamin and Historical Research," p. 1.

20. See the useful reception survey by Noah Isenberg, "The Work of Walter Ben-jamin in the Age of Information," *New German Critique* 83 (Spring/Summer 2001), pp. 119–50. The quote appears on pp. 120–21. I thank Andreas Huyssen and Anson Rabinbach for this reference.

21. Charles Rosen, "Should We Adore Adorno?" *New York Review of Books,* 24 Oc-tober 2002, pp. 59–66.

22. Personal communication with Paul Breines, August 2004.

23. This paper concentrates on the "positive" reception of these thinkers. The dis-senting, critical literature, however, is also considerable—and should be taken as a mea-

sure of their relevance. See, for instance, the treatments of Western Marxism in general and of the Frankfurt School in particular by Leszek Kolakowski, especially chapters 7–12 in his *Main Currents of Marxism: Its Origins, Growth and Dissolution.* Vol. 3. *The Breakdown,* translated from the Polish by P. S. Falla (New York: Oxford University Press, 1978) and J. G. Merquior, *Western Marxism* (London: Paladin, 1986), especially III.I.

24. Edward Said, *Representations of the Intellectual* (London: Vintage, 1994), pp. 40–43.

25. For a list of these works, as well as a review of recent literature, see the illuminating article by Mark Lilla, "A Battle for Religion," *New York Review of Books* (5 December 2002), pp. 60–65.

26. Hilary Putnam, "Introduction to Franz Rosenzweig," *Understanding of the Sick and the Healthy: A View of World, Man, and God,* edited with an introduction by Nahum Glatzer (Cambridge, Mass.: Harvard University Press, 1999), p. 1. For a comprehensive survey of the remarkable volume of writings on that thinker and the modes and problems of Rosenzweig's reception, see Peter Eli Gordon, "Rosenzweig Redux: The Reception of German-Jewish Thought," *Jewish Social Studies,* 8, 1 (Fall 2001), pp. 1–57.

27. See, above all, Peter Eli Gordon, *Rosenzweig and Heidegger: Between Judaism and German Philosophy* (Berkeley: University of California Press, 2003). See, too, Leora Batnitzky, *Idolatry and Representation: The Philosophy of Franz Rosenzweig Reconsidered* (Princeton: Princeton University Press, 2000); Eric Santner, *On the Psychotheology of Everyday Life: Reflections on Freud and Rosenzweig* (Chicago: University of Chicago Press, 2001); Richard Cohen, *Elevations: The Height of the Good in Rosenzweig and Levinas* (Chicago: Chicago University Press, 1994); Robert Gibbs, *Correlations in Rosenzweig and Levinas* (Princeton: Princeton University Press, 1992).

28. See Stefan Meinecke, "A Life of Contradiction: The Philosophy of Franz Rosenzweig and his Relationship to History and Politics," *Leo Baeck Institute Yearbook* (1991), pp. 461–89, and Benjamin Pollock, "From Nation to Empire: Franz Rosenzweig's Redemptive Imperialism," *Jewish Studies Quarterly,* Vol. 11 (2004), No. 4, pp. 332–53. On Rosenzweig's affair with (the wife of a close friend) Margrit Rosenstock-Huessy, an affair consummated one month before Rosenzweig's own wedding in March 1920, and its relationship to Rosenzweig's overall theology of love, see Samuel Moyn, "Divine and Human Love: Franz Rosenzweig's History of the Song of Songs," *Jewish Studies Quarterly,* Vol. 12 (2005), No. 2, pp. 194–212. See, too, Inken Ruhle and Reinhold Mayer, eds., *Die "Gritli"—Briefe an Margrit Rosenstock-Huessy* (Tübingen, 2002).

29. See Cynthia Ozick "The Mystic Explorer," *New York Times Book Review* (21 September 1980), p. 1. I have provided a far larger list of this kind of adulation in "The Metaphysical Psychologist, " op. cit.

30. Arnaldo Momigliano, "The Master of Mysticism," *New York Review of Books* (18 December 1980), pp. 37–39.

31. Thus Moshe Idel in his *Kabbalah: New Perspectives* (New Haven: Yale University Press, 1988), p. 17.

32. See Henry Pachter, "Gershom Scholem: Towards a Mastermyth," *Salmagundi* (No. 40, Winter 1978). See, too, Susan Handelman, *Fragments of Redemption: Jewish Thought and Literary Theory in Benjamin, Scholem and Levinas* (Bloomington: Indiana University Press, 1991).

33. See Jonas's letter of 24 February in Gershom Scholem, *A Life in Letters 1914–1982*, ed. and trans. Anthony David Skinner (Cambridge, Mass.: Harvard University Press, 2001), pp. 494–95.

34. Peter Eli Gordon, *Rosenzweig and Heidegger,* op. cit., p. 8.

35. For a critical discussion of this connection, see both works by Peter Eli Gordon, op. cit.

36. See chapter 1 of this work as well as chapter 1 of *Scholem, Arendt, Klemperer,* op. cit., and "The Metaphysical Psychologist," op. cit. On the unconventionality of Scholem's "religious" thought, see Steven M. Wasserstrom, *Religion after Religion: Gershom Scholem, Mircea Eliade, and Henry Corbin at Eranos* (Princeton: Princeton University Press, 1999).

37. Jay Parini, *Benjamin's Crossing* (New York: Henry Holt, 1997).

38. See his "Homage to Benjamin" in his *Walter Benjamin; or, Towards a Revolutionary Criticism* (London and New York: Verso, 1981), p. 183. See too, Irving Wohlfarth's brilliant "'Männer aus der Fremde': Walter Benjamin and the 'German-Jewish Parnassus,'" *New German Critique,* no. 70 (Winter 1997), pp. 3–85.

39. The volume, edited by Peter Graf-Kielmannsegg et. al., *Hannah Arendt and Leo Strauss: German Emigres and American Political Thought after World War II* (Washington, D.C.: German Historical Institute and Cambridge University Press, 1995) disappointingly tells one virtually nothing about the interrelationships of these two thinkers or the importance of migration upon their thought. George Kateb's useful contribution, to which we shall return, "The Questionable Influence of Arendt (and Strauss)," is an exception.

40. On the cool reception of Adorno's academic colleagues, see Lars Rensmann, "Returning from Forced Exile: Some Observations on Theodor W. Adorno's and Hannah Arendt's Experience of Postwar Germany and Their Political Theories of Totalitarianism," *Leo Baeck Institute Yearbook* XLIX (2004), pp. 171–93. See especially pp. 183–84.

41. For a meticulous, detailed documentation of the tumultuous relationship between the Frankfurt School and the German student movement, see Wolfgang Kraushaar, ed.,

Frankfurter Schule und Studentenbewegung: Von der Flaschenpost zum Molotowcocktail 1946–1955, Vol. 1, *Chronik*, Vol. 2, Dokumete, Vol. 3, *Aufsätze und Kommentare* (Hamburg: Rogner and Bernhard, 1998).

42. Quoted in Martin Jay, "Adorno in America," in his *Permanent Exiles: Essays on the Intellectual Migration from Germany to America* (New York: Columbia University Press, 1986), p. 120.

43. See Anthony Heilbut, *Exiled in Paradise*, op. cit., p. 160.

44. Jay, "Adorno in America," op. cit., pp. 120–37. See, too, in the same volume, the essay "The Frankfurt School in Exile," pp. 28–61.

45. See his "Hannah Arendt as Political Commentator," in *Hannah Arendt in Jerusalem*, op. cit., pp. 56–57.

46. David Biale has called these various projects counterhistories. See his interesting essay "Leo Strauss: The Philosopher as Weimar Jew," in Alan Udoff, ed., *Leo Strauss's Thought: Toward A Critical Engagement* (Boulder: Lynne Rienner Publications, 1991), pp. 31–40.

47. See her essay "Under the Sign of Saturn" in the book of the same title (New York: Farrar Strauss Giroux, 1980), p. 133.

48. Isenberg, op. cit., p. 124, and note 21.

49. Quoted in Irving Wohlfarth, "The Measure of the Possible, the Weight of the Real and the Heat of the Moment: Benjamin's Actuality Today," in Laura Marcus and Lynda Nead, *The Actuality of Walter Benjamin* (London: Lawrence and Wishart, 1998), pp. 14–15.

50. Letter 113 to Adorno, 23.2.39 in Walter Benjamin and Theodor W. Adorno, *The Complete Correspondence 1928–1940*, ed. Henri Lonitz, trans. Nicholas Walker (Cambridge: Polity Press, 2003), p. 311.

51. See "Maxims and Arrows," 15, *Twilight of the Idols*, in Walter Kaufmann, ed., *The Portable Nietzsche* (New York: The Viking Press, 1954 [1968]), p. 468.

52. See his "Walter Benjamin and His Angel," in his *On Jews and Judaism in Crisis*, op. cit., pp. 198–236. The quotes appear on pp. 198–99.

53. See Letter No. 47, Scholem to Benjamin, 11 April 1934, in *The Correspondence of Walter Benjamin and Gershom Scholem 1932–1940*, op. cit., p. 103. These letters contain details of the many frustrated attempts to interest Schocken. Later, apparently, he voiced a more positive interest in publishing Benjamin but again let it slide. For details, see Anthony David, *The Patron*, op. cit., especially pp. 348 and 376.

54. See Paul Breines, "Germans, Journals and Jews/Madison, Men, Marxism and Mosse," op. cit., pp. 81–103. As Mark Lilla has written about Leo Strauss after his appointment to the University of Chicago in 1949:

The universities were expanding, both in size and reach, by admitting people who had been previously excluded. In such a context one can imagine students' excitement when a short, unassuming foreigner with a high-pitched voice voice entered the classroom and began analyzing the great books, line by line, claiming that they treated the most urgent existential and political questions—and that they might contain the truth. The effect would have been intensified for Jewish-American students, who, at a time when cultural assimilation still seemed the wisest course, found themselves before a teacher who treated Judaism and the philosophical tradition with equal seriousness and dignity.

See his "The Closing of the Straussian Mind," op. cit., pp. 55–59. The quote appears on p. 55.

55. See George L. Mosse, *German Jews beyond Judaism*, op. cit. In his autobiography, *Confronting History*, op. cit., Mosse writes that this work "is certainly my most personal book, almost a confession of faith" (p. 184). See, too, George Steiner, especially "A Kind of Survivor" in his *Language and Silence*, op. cit. See, too, his autobiographical comments in *Errata*, op. cit.

56. Benjamin to Ludwig Strauss, 21 November 1912, *Gesammelte Schriften* 2.3., eds. Rolf Tiedmann and Hermann Schweppenhäuser (Frankfurt am Main: Suhrkamp Verlag, 1977), p. 839.

57. Stefan Collini, "Moralist at Work: E. P. Thompson Reappraised," *Times Literary Supplement* (18 February 2005), pp. 13–15.

58. What could be more currently fashionable than the work of Giorgio Agamben? With the (very) surprising omission of Theodor Adorno, all our other thinkers are featured in his *Homo Sacer: Sovereign Power and Bare Life*, trans. Daniel Heller-Roazen (Stanford: Stanford University Press, 1998). The Italian original appeared in 1985. I thank Eugene Sheppard for pointing this out to me.

59. "Under the Sign of Saturn," op. cit., p. 111.

60. See the chapter on "The Myth of Weimar: Walter Benjamin in Cultural Historical Research" in his (thus far) unpublished M.A. thesis on "The Reception of Walter Benjamin." As Susan Sontag put it in "Under the Sign of Saturn," op. cit., p. 133: "Benjamin placed himself at the crossroad. It was important for him to keep his many 'positions' open: the theological, the Surealist/aesthetic, the communist. One position corrects the other; he needed them all. Decisions, of course, tend to spoil the balance of these positions, vacillations kept everything in place."

61. Thus David Biale:

> If Strauss's interpretation of Maimonides reveals something of his own esoteric
> project, his call for a return to orthodoxy in the preface must mean a return to
> the esoteric Maimonides, and not to the Maimonides of the *Mishneh Torah*.
> Orthodoxy for Strauss meant not the secrets of the Torah in the Maimonidean
> sense (or in the sense that Strauss understood Maimonides). Like other Jewish
> intellectuals of his generation, Strauss could not envision a return to Jewish or-
> thodoxy as the orthodox would define it; instead, like Scholem, Rosezweig, and
> Buber, he needed to redefine orthodoxy according to his own lights.

(Biale, "Leo Strauss as Weimar Jew," op. cit., p. 37).

62. For a superb and nuanced exposition, see Martin Jay, *Marxism and Totality: The Adventures of a Concept from Lukács to Habermas* (Berkeley: University of California Press, 1984); for more impatient and critical views, see Merquior and Kolakowski, op. cit.

63. There are any number of references here. For the most insightful see Dana Villa, *Arendt and Heidegger: The Fate of the Political* (Princeton: Princeton University Press, 1996) and Seyla Ben Habib, *The Reluctant Modernism of Hannah Arendt*. The literature on Arendt's politics is considerable. See, for instance, the special issue on Arendt, *Social Research*, Volume 44, Number 1 (Spring 1977); Phillip Hansen, *Hannah Arendt: Politics, History and Citizenship* (Stanford: Stanford University Press, 1993); Julia Kristeva, *Hannah Arendt*, translated by Ross Guberman (New York, Columbia University Press, 2001).

64. See Gordon, *Rosenzweig and Heidegger*, op. cit.

65. For an excellent exposition of Scholem's project, see David Biale, *Gershom Scholem*, op. cit.

66. Werner J. Dannhauser writes:

> I have become convinced of what in a previous study I could not, that Leo
> Strauss was of the party of Athens and not of the party of Jerusalem. . . . [The
> philosopher] knows by the power of his own thought that divine revelation is
> impossible. Evidently this is the final position of Leo Strauss; at least the book
> on Plato's *Laws* is his final book. . . . If [he] chose Athens over Jerusalem, and I
> think he did, one must add at once that this choice did not lead to the "un-
> stringing of the bow." Perhaps he would have argued that philosophy has its
> own built-in "magnificent tension of the spirit."

See his "Athens and Jerusalem or Jerusalem and Athens?" in Novak, ed., *Leo Strauss and Judaism*, op. cit., pp. 155–71. The quote appears on pp. 168–69. David Biale comments: "If I am correct, then the secrets of the Torah that constitute the truth of the Jewish tradition are for Strauss none other than the truths of Greek philosophy, quite possibly the esoteric meaning of Plato: From an esoteric point of view, Athens and Jerusalem are one and the same." See "Leo Strauss: The Philosopher as Weimar Jew," op. cit., p. 37.

67. On Rosenzweig's "monarchism," see Meinecke, "A Life of Contradiction," op. cit., and for a dissenting view that emphasizes the "political" nature of Rosenzweig's thought, see Pollock, "From Nation State to World Empire," op. cit.

68. See "Comments on Carl Schmitt's *Der Begriff des Politischen*," which appears as an appendix to Strauss's *Spinoza's Critique of Religion* (New York: Schocken Books, 1965), pp. 331–51. The quote appears on p. 351.

69. See "German Jews beyond *Bildung* and Liberalism: The Radical Jewish Revival in the Weimar Republic" in my *Culture and Catastrophe*, op. cit., as well as "Against Social Science: Jewish Intellectuals, the Critique of Liberal-Bourgeois Modernity, and the (Ambiguous) Legacy of Radical Weimar Theory, " in my *In Times of Crisis*, op. cit.

70. See ibid., "German Jews beyond *Bildung* and Liberalism" and the important article by Anson Rabinbach, "Between Enlightenment and Apocalypse: Benjamin, Bloch and Modern German Jewish Messianism," *New German Critique*, No. 34 (Winter 1985).

71. I owe this formulation to Jerry Z. Muller from a conversation of 22 February 2005.

72. See his complex and difficult 1962 preface to the English translation of his (1930) *Spinoza's Critique of Religion*, op. cit., pp. 1–21. Scholem saw just how difficult this would be for readers beyond the border and how much it betrayed its Weimar origins. He told Strauss that "those pages would be virtually impenetrable to an American reader." See Scholem Letter 57, 13.12. 1962, Vol. II, pp. 86–87. See, too, Letter 18, 2 June 1952; Letter 137, 21 October 1968. See, too, Strauss's important *Philosophy and Law: Contributions to the Understanding of Maimonides and His Predecessors*, trans. Eve Adler (Albany: State University of New York, 1995). The work was originally published in German in 1935. His preoccupation with Jewish and Zionist subjects during the Weimar period is apparent in the useful translations and editing of Michael Zank, *Leo Strauss: The Early Writings (1921–1932)* (Albany: State University of New York, 2002). For an excellent study of Strauss in his earlier Weimar period, see the dissertation by Eugene Sheppard, *Leo Strauss and the Politics of Exile* (University of California, Los Angeles, 2001).

73. While the Jewish population of Germany hovered around 500,000 persons, at its peak Zionist membership totaled about 9,000 members before World War I and just over 33,000 for the period between the war and 1933. (After 1933, for obvious reasons, membership rose dramatically). Even these figures may be inflated since they simply represent those who had paid the token Zion-

ist membership fee, the shekel. . . . [Moreover, a] very important segment of the
Zionist movement were the so-called *Ostjuden*, Jews from Eastern Europe.

See Stephen M. Poppel, *Zionism in Germany 1897–1933: The Making of a Jewish Identity* (Philadelphia: JPS, 1977), pp. 33, 38, and chapter 3.

74. The cases of Fromm, Löwenthal, and Buber are well known. Jonas, exceptionally, even spent a year in a Zionist agricultural training farm in Germany in 1923 before proceeding with his studies, and later, for a time, lived in Palestine/Israel. See his *Erinnerungen*, op. cit., p. 475. Unlike Jonas, Elias later tried to obscure his Zionist years. See Jörg Hackeschmidt, "Norbert Elias as a Young Zionist," *Leo Baeck Institute Yearbook* XLIX (2004), pp. 59–74.

75. See Scholem's *From Berlin to Jerusalem: Memories of My Youth*, translated from the German by Harry Zohn (New York: Schocken Books, 1980), chapters 3–5.

76. See this piece, "A Note on the Discussion on 'Zionism and Antisemitism'" in Michael Zank, ed. and trans., *Leo Strauss: The Early Writings (1921–1932)*, op. cit. See, too, the interesting unpublished article by Eugene R. Sheppard, "Raising Zionism to the Level of Antisemitism: Reflections on Leo Strauss as a Young Zionist."

77. Preface to *Spinoza's Critique of Religion*, op. cit., pp. 4–5.

78. Leo Strauss, "Zionism in Max Nordau" in *The Jew: Essays from Martin Buber's Journal, Der Jude, 1916–1918*, selected, edited, and introduced by Arthur A. Cohen, trans. Joachim Neugroschel (Alabama: University of Alabama Press, 1980), pp. 120–26. This appeared originally in *Der Jude*, VII (1922–1923), pp. 657–60.

79. See, especially, Arendt's address on receiving the Lessing Prize of the Free City of Hamburg, "On Humanity in Dark Times: Thoughts about Lessing," in her *Men in Dark Times* (New York and London: Harcourt Brace Jovanovich, 1968), pp. 3–31. The relevant quote is on p. 18.

80. The major influence on Arendt's Zionism was the German Zionist leader Kurt Blumenfeld. See their correspondence (apt indeed for the theme of this work) *". . . in keinem Besitz verwurzelt." Die Korrespondenz*, eds. Ingeborg Nordmann and Iris Pilling (Hamburg: Rotbuch Verlag, 1995).

81. The correspondence with Scholem makes both Benjamin's interest in Zionism and his hostility toward Buber very apparent. Benjamin was so opposed to Buber that he believed that Rosenzweig's reputation was "forever damaged" by dint of his co-translation of the Bible with him. See *Briefe an Siegfried Kracauer*, ed. Theodor Adorno (Marbach am Neckar: Deutsche Schillergesellschaft, 1987), p. 16n.

82. On this issue, see the reflections by Paul Mendes-Flohr, "'The Stronger and the Better Jews': Jewish Theological Responses to Political Messianism in the Weimar Re-

public," *Studies in Contemporary Jewry*, Vol. VII (1991), pp. 159–85. See especially pp. 165–69.

83. See Nahum Glatzer's introduction to his edited *Franz Rosenzweig: His Life and Thought* (New York: Schocken Books, 1953), p. xiv.

84. After the word "pin-point," Rosenzweig added "so that just one man—I, that is—can occupy it." See the letter to Gertrud Oppenheim, July 1924, in his *Gesammelte Werke* I, eds. Rachel Rosenzweig and Edith Rosenzweig-Scheinmann (Den Haag, 1979), p. 980.

85. For the comment to Koch, see Glatzer, *Franz Rosenzweig*, op. cit., p. 113, and the Letter to Ehrenburg of 19 April 1927, p. 157. See, too, Rosenzweig's comments on "Zionism" in the same volume, pp. 353–58.

86. Scholem, *From Berlin to Jerusalem*, op. cit., p. 69.

87. See, for instance, Leo Lowenthal's vivid description of such networks:

About a year after my first meeting with [Siegfried] Kracauer [around the end of World War I], he introduced me to Adorno, who was then eighteen years old. I introduced him to my friend Ernst Simon, who like myself, was studying history, *Germanistik*, and philosophy, and who won me over to a very messianic Zionism. Through Ernst Simon, Kracauer met Rabbi Nobel, then a revered figure in our Jewish circle, to whose *Festschrift*, on the occasion of his 50th birthday, Kracauer contributed. Through Nobel, Kracauer first met Martin Buber and later Franz Rosenzweig. In the spring of 1922, I introduced him to Ernst Bloch, and he in turn introduced me to Horkheimer, who was already a good friend of Adorno's.

See Lowenthal's "As I Remember Friedel," *New German Critique* (No. 54, Fall 1991), p. 6. Those very close friends Scholem and Benjamin were also friendly or at least in contact with most of these figures.

88. For one recent example of the attempt to place them in "a posthumous dialogue," see the volume edited by Dirk Auer, Lars Rensmann, and Julia Schulze Wessel, *Arendt und Adorno* (Frankfurt am Main, 2003). For the phrase "posthumous dialogue," see in this volume, Lars Rensmann "Returning from Forced Exile," op. cit., p. 171. Recently, Alfon's Söllner has suggested that—the obvious common German-Jewish dilemma and post-Nazi, post-Holocaust ruminations apart—both Arendt and Adorno were characterized by their resistance to any formal "academic" disciplines and by their common attraction to the essay form. See his *"Der Essay als Form politischen Denkens. Die Anfänge von Hannah Arendt und Theodor W. Adorno nach dem Zweiten Weltkrieg,"* *Text + Kritik* IX/05 (166/167), Hannah Arendt issue, pp. 79–91.

89. For the most recent documents on and reflections of the Arendt-Benjamin relationship, see Detlev Schöttker/Erdmut Wizisla, "*Hannah Arendt und Walter Benjamin.
Stationen einer Vermittlung*" in the Arendt issue of *Text + Kritik*, op. cit., pp. 42–57 and
the Arendt-Benjamin correspondence (pp. 58–66).

90. See Letter to Rudolf Hallo, 3 March 1922, in Franz Rosenzweig, *Briefe* (Berlin,
1935), p. 431. See also the compelling correspondence between Scholem and Strauss
that ranged from 1933 to 1973 in Heinrich und Wiebke Meier (eds.), *Hobbes' politische
Wissenschaft und Zugehörige Schriften-Briefe* (Stuttgart: J. B. Metzler, 2001), pp. 699–
772. This is Volume 3 of Strauss's *Gesammelte Schriften*.

91. Theodor Adorno to Walter Benjamin, 4 March 1938, in Theodor W. Adorno
and Walter Benjamin, *The Complete Correspondence, 1928–1940*, op. cit. Adorno's letter
is extremely insightful, liberally combining appreciation of Scholem, the man, and his
work with criticism of both. Scholem had intellectual power, he wrote, but it is

> rather strange how this power sometimes abandons him at a stretch and allows
> prejudice and the most banal observations to prevail uncontested instead. This
> is also true for his style of historical interpretation, when he explains the "explo-
> sions" of Jewish mysticism in exclusively internal theological terms, and then
> precisely for that reason violently repudiates the social connections which would
> otherwise ineluctably force themselves upon one's attention. (p. 250)

Moreover, Adorno declared, unlike his own and Benjamin's attempt to salvage the theological moment within the realm of the profane, Scholem's theology was

> a strangely linear and romantic one. . . . He himself insists upon a sort of radio-
> active decay which drives us on from mysticism, and indeed equally in all of its
> monadically conceived historical shapes and forms, towards enlightenment. It
> strikes me as an expression of the most profound irony that the very conception
> of mysticism which he urges presents itself from the perspective of the philoso-
> phy of history precisely as that same incursion into the profane with which he
> reproaches both of us. (pp. 249–50)

92. Nor am I suggesting that their Zionism, Scholem's idiosyncratic case excepted,
was a force in their later reception. The contrary may sometimes be true. Rosenzweig
may have attracted American Jewry precisely because he offered a Diasporic alternative
to Zionism, Arendt partly because of her critique of it, Benjamin because of his rejection of all simple ideological choices, and Strauss because his Zionism was subordinated
to larger matters, Jewish and non-Jewish. While their contemporary attraction lies more

in their heterodox attitudes, it was nevertheless these which drew them to Zionism in the first place.

93. I thank John Landau for guiding me in some of these formulations.

94. See Scholem's essay "Walter Benjamin" in *On Jews and Judaism in Crisis*, op. cit., p. 191.

95. Walter Benjamin to Gershom Scholem, Letter 42, 31 December 1933, *Correspondence*, op. cit., pp. 93-94.

96. See the remarkable "We Refugees" in Hannah Arendt, *The Jew as Pariah*, op. cit., pp. 55-66. The quotes appear on pp. 56, 66, respectively.

97. See Gordon, *Rosenzweig and Heidegger*, op. cit., p. 8 and his "Rosenzweig Redux," op. cit., especially pp. 1-5.

98. *Spinoza's Critique . . .* op. cit., p. 6.

99. See Elizabeth Wilcox, "Negative Identity: Mixed German-Jewish Descent as a Factor in the Reception of Theodor Adorno," *New German Critique* 81 (Fall 2000), pp. 169-87. The quotes appear on pp. 171 and 174, respectively. Wilcox goes so far as to imply that Hannah Arendt's hostility toward him was in part a function of her wariness of Adorno's partial Jewishness. She cites Arendt's comments upon hearing that when pushed to identify himself upon arrival in England in the 1930s, Adorno had declared that he was of "Non-pure 'Aryan descendance'": "[E]ven Jews would have gone along with Hitler if they had been allowed to," she wrote in a 1965 letter to Karl Jaspers. "So how can one say who would not have gone along? . . . Adorno surely would have— indeed, NB, he even tried to on the basis of his being only half Jewish, but he couldn't pull it off." Letter 373, 13 April 1965 in Hannah Arendt, Karl Jaspers, *The Complete Correspondence 1926-1969*, eds. Lotte Kohler and Hans Saner (New York; Harcourt Brace Jovanovich, 1992), trans. Robert and Rita Kimber, pp. 592-93. Arendt's comments may, indeed, as Wilcox suggests, have been prompted by her desire to find a means of defending Heidgger from Adorno's attacks. But her disdain was multilayered, and her putative insistence upon a full or authentic Jewish identity was hardly consistent with what she wrote to Jaspers earlier or how she subsequently conducted her life: "If I had wanted to be respectable I would either have given up my interest in Jewish affairs or not marry [*sic*] a non-Jewish man, either option equally inhuman and in a sense crazy." Letter 34, 29 January 1946, p. 29. Wilcox's piece is simultaneously suggestive, provocative, and problematic and merits further discussion.

100. See Arendt's piece on "Walter Benjamin 1892-1940" in *Men in Dark Times*, op. cit., p. 190.

101. The dense reflections on Kafka by Adorno, Arendt, Benjamin, and Scholem are too well known to be documented here. Rosenzweig wrote less on the author, yet at least

one of his wry statements makes the point powerfully enough. On 25 May 1927 he wrote (to Gertrud Oppenheim): "The people who wrote the Bible seem to have thought of God much the way Kafka did. I have never read a book that reminded me so much of the Bible as his novel *The Castle*, and that is why reading it certainly cannot be called a pleasure." See *Franz Rosenzweig: His Life and Thought*, ed. Nahum N. Glatzer (New York: Schocken Books, 1961), p. 160. As far as I can ascertain (although my search has not been comprehensive), Strauss is an exception to this pattern; Kafka does not appear to have figured much in his intellectual musings.

102. See *The Diaries of Franz Kafka 1914–1923*, ed. Max Brod (New York: Schocken Books, 1965), pp. 202–203, entry for 16 January 1922. The quotation continues:

> if Zionism had not intervened, it might easily have developed into a new secret doctrine, a Kabbalah. There are intimations of this. Though of course it would require a genius of an unimaginable kind to strike root again in the old centuries, or create the old centuries anew and not spend itself withal, but only then begin to flower forth.

103. See Scholem's aphoristic letter written to Zalman Schocken on the occasion of the latter's sixtieth birthday in 1937, "A Candid Word about the True Motives of My Kabbalistic Studies": "Three years, 1916–1918, which were decisive for my entire life, lay behind me: many exciting thoughts had led me as much to the most rationalistic skepticism about my fields of study as to intuitive affirmation of mystical theses which walked the fine line between religion and nihilism." Scholem added immediately that it was in Kafka that he found "the most perfect and unsurpassed expression of this fine line." See the translation of this letter in Biale, *Gershom Scholem*, op. cit, pp. 74–76. The quote appears on p. 75. The original German letter is reproduced on pp. 215–16.

104. See Scholem's "Die zionistische Verzweiflung," 19.6.1920 in *Tagebücher 1917–1923*, op. cit., p. 638.

105. See Susan A. Handelman, *Fragments of Redemption*, op. cit., p. xix. Handelman intended these comments to apply to her subjects but they apply equally well to all the figures under consideration here.

106. Scholem to Benjamin, Letter 44, early February 1934, *Correspondence*, op. cit., p. 98.

107. These thoughts were prompted by a conversation with John Landau in Jerusalem, on 18 August 2004.

108. Quoted by Rabinbach in his introduction, to the Benjamin-Scholem *Correspondence*, op. cit., p. xxv.

109. Arendt put it thus:

And Benjamin's choice, baroque in a double sense, has an exact counterpart in Scholem's strange decision to approach Judaism via the Cabala, that is, that part of Hebrew literature which is untransmitted and untransmissible in terms of Jewish tradition, in which it has always had the odor of something downright disreputable. Nothing showed more clearly—so one is inclined to say today— that there was no such thing as a "return" either to the German or the European or the Jewish tradition than the choice of these fields of study. It was an implicit admission that the past spoke directly only through things that had not been handed down, whose seeming closeness to the present was thus due precisely to their exotic character, which ruled out all claims to a binding authority.

See her essay on "Walter Benjamin," in *Men in Dark Times,* op. cit., p. 195.

110. Letter 34, Thedor Adorno to Walter Benjamin, 8.6.1935, *The Complete Correspondence,* op. cit., pp. 95–98. The quote appears on p. 97.

111. See "Against Social Science: Jewish Intellectuals, the Critique of Liberal-Bourgeois Modernity, and the (Ambigious) Legacy of Radical Weimar Theory" in my *In Times of Crisis,* op. cit., pp. 24–43 (notes pp. 205–18).

112. Letter of Arendt to Mary McCarthy, 21 December 1968, in *Between Friends: The Correspondence of Hannah Arendt and Mary McCarthy 1949–1975,* ed. Carol Brightman (New York and London: Harcourt Brace and Company, 1995), p. 231.

113. As Peter Gordon demonstrates, Rosenzweig's notions are very similar to Heidegger's. For him, the sheer fact of mortality, the nonrelational and nontransferable experience of possible death, is the conceptual instrument for exposing the falsity of idealist totalization. There is no redemption beyond death: "eternity" occurs within finitude. See *Rosenzweig and Heidegger,* op. cit., pp. 112–13.

114. See Scholem's essay, "Religious Authority and Mysticism" (first published in 1960) in his *On the Kabbalah and Its Symbolism,* trans. Ralph Manheim (New York, 1965), pp. 1–31. The quote appears on pp. 17–18.

115. Christoph Schmidt, *Der häretische Imperative: Überlegungen zur theologischen Dialektik der Kulturwissenschaft in Deutschland* (Tübingen: Max Niemeyer Verglag, 2000).

116. *From Berlin to Jerusalem,* op. cit., p. 131. The other two such sects were the Warburg Library and the "metaphysical magicians" around Oskar Goldberg. Scholem adds regarding this observation: "Not all of them liked to hear this."

117. See the entry to Scholem's Tagebuecher, 17.v.1917, *Tagebücher 1917–23,* op. cit., p. 17. This he linked to Benjamin's "fundamental insight" that the essence of the world lay in language and text. Gil Anidjar has argued that in respect of the analysis of textuality and symbol, far from agreeing with each other, "Benjamin wrote, in fact, di-

rectly against Scholem." Whereas Benjamin insisted upon the "textuality of the text (its 'form' and 'content')," Scholem's "ultimate purpose remains always to see beyond, to go beyond." See his "Jewish Mysticism Alterable and Unalterable: On *Orienting*—Kabbalah Studies and the 'Zohar of Christian Spain' in *Jewish Social Studies,* Vol. 3 (No. 1, Fall 1996), pp. 89–157, especially pp. 109–10).

118. Still, some complain of Arendt's notions of identity. Bonnie Honig has argued that her emphasis upon "Jewishness" remains too essentialist, treating it "as a univocal, constative fact. . . . Arendt relinquishes the opportunity to engage or even subvert Jewish identity performatively, to explore its historicity and heterogeneity, to dislodge and disappoint its aspirations to univocity, to proliferate its differentiated possibilities." See her "Toward an Agonistic Feminism: Hannah Arendt and the Politics of Identity," in Honig, ed., *Feminist Interpretations of Hannah Arendt* (University Park: Pennsylvania State University Press, 1995). Other feminists have argued that Arendt actually adopted a more dialectical approach that allows for both difference and solidarity: For Arendt, not

> difference, but plurality is our human condition (or, more precisely, part of our
> human condition), and although non-identity (otherness) is an important aspect of plurality, it is not all that Arendt means by that term. Plurality means
> "that we are all the same, that is human, in such a way that nobody is ever the
> same as anyone else who ever lived, lives, or will live." In other words, there is a
> dialectical tension between identity and non-identity, sameness and difference,
> at the very heart of Arendt's definition of plurality. . . . [T]his dialectic is at the
> heart of Arendt's understanding of politics as well.

See Amy Allen, "Solidarity after Identity Politics: Hannah Arendt and the Power of Feminist Theory," *Philosophy and Social Criticism,* Vol. 25, No. 1, pp. 97–118. The quotes appear on pp. 105–106. Arendt did believe that thinking now had to be done "without banisters," in a world bereft of metaphysical anchors. She also stated (in "Christianity and Revolution," in *Essays In Understanding,* op. cit., p. 155) that "[t]he truth is a rather difficult deity to worship because the only thing she does not allow her worshippers is certainty . . . and a system of certainties is the end of philosophy." For all that, "truth" was hardly abandoned as a goal.

119. Handelman, *Fragments of Redemption,* op. cit., pp. 37–40, 63–64.

120. Ibid., p. 42.

121. Letter to Zalman Schocken, "A Candid Word . . ." op. cit., p. 76.

122. See Peter Dews, "Adorno, Post-Structuralism, and the Critique of Identity" in *The Problems of Modernity,* ed. Andrew Benjamin (London and New York: Routledge, 1989), pp. 1–22. The quote appears on p. 17.

123. *Negative Dialectics,* trans. E. B. Ashton (New York: Continuum Books, 1973; originally published in German in 1966 London, 1973), p. 149.

124. Gordon, *Rosenzweig and Heidegger,* op. cit., pp. 181, 199, respectively.

125. Ibid., *Rosenzweig Redux,* op. cit., p. 33. The italics are Gordon's.

126. Dews, *Problems of Modernity,* op. cit., p. 6.

127. See the suggestive remarks by Handelman, *Fragments of Redemption,* op. cit., pp. 129–30.

128. See her "Preface: The Gap between Past and Future," in *Between Past and Future: Six Exercises in Political Thought* (Cleveland: Meridian Books, 1961), especially pp. 3–5 and, in the same volume, "Tradition and the Modern Age," especially p. 17.

129. See Handelman, *Fragments of Redemption,* op. cit., p. 341.

130. Ibid, p. 15. The quote comes from Benajmin's *Gesammelte Schriften,* op. cit., I/2, p. 681.

131. Eric Jacobson, *Metaphysics of the Profane: The Political Theology of Walter Benjamin and Gershom Scholem* (New York: Columbia University Press, 2003).

132. Thus Susan Neiman:

> It starts as a matter of tone: of everything that happens before and after argument begins. Arendt's writings are charged with theological language. It is hard to think of a twentieth century philosopher whose work as often uses concepts like "soul" and "hell" and "redemption" and "blasphemy." . . . One suspects that Arendt would have been happy to defend a literal analysis of the word "soul." Indeed, the features Arendt holds to be most definitive of the human, natality and plurality, are just those that distinguish us from the God of Abraham: He is eternal and He is one. The warning against the tendency to overstep human limits in the wrong sort of attempt to imitate God is an old one. . . . She dismisses atheists as "fools who pretend to know what no man can know."

See her piece "Theodicy in Jerusalem" in *Hannah Arendt in Jerusalem,* op. cit., pp. 65–90. The quotes appear on pp. 69–70. For a reading of Arendt's thoughts of new beginnings and natality as situated within the worldly tradition of Jewish messianic thought—as opposed to the putative worldlessness of Christianity—see Susannah Young-ah Gottlieb, *Regions of Sorrow: Anxiety and Messianism in Hannah Arendt and W. H. Auden* (Stanford: Stanford University Press, 2003), especially Part III. Arendt's messianism, ah-Gottlieb argues, was not of the traditional, utopian, or universalist but rather the "weak" kind, "because natality is the precise opposite of sovereignty: it is self-exposure, not self-assertion" (p. 139).

133. See the interesting piece by David Kaufmann, "Beyond Use, within Reason:

Adorno, Benjamin and the Question of Theology," *New German Critique* (No. 83, Spring–Summer 2001), pp. 151–73. See too his "Correlations, Constellations and the Truth: Adorno's Ontology of Redemption," *Philosophy and Social Criticism* (Vol. 26, No. 5, 2000), pp. 62–80. Of related interest is Maeve Cooke, "Redeeming Redemption: The Utopian Dimension of Critical Social Theory," *Philosophy and Social Criticism* (Vol. 30, No. 4, 2004), pp. 413–29.

134. I have examined some of these questions in "German Jews beyond *Bildung* and Liberalism," op. cit. Quote from Susan Orr, "Strauss, Reason, and Revelation: Unraveling the Essential Question" in *Leo Strauss and Judaism,* op. cit., p. 27.

135. Arendt develops this theme most systematically in her *The Human Condition* (New York: Doubleday, 1959).

136. Letter no. 4 to Werner Scholem, 13 September 1914, *Briefe* I, op. cit., p. 11.

137. See the remarkable and lengthy ruminations on the nature of time in Judaism in the entry for 17 June 1918, *Tagebuecher 1917–1923,* op. cit., pp. 235–40. The quote appears on p. 235.

138. Gordon, *Rosenzweig and Heidegger,* op. cit. See especially pp. 112–13, 185, 189.

139. For an exposition of Benjamin's view of history, see Stephane Moses, "Eingedenken und Jetzzeit: Geschichliches Bewusstein im Spätwerk Walter Benjamins," in *Memoria Vergessen und Erinnern: Poetik und Hermeneutik,* XV, eds. Anselm Haverkamp and Renate Lachmann (Munich, 1993). See, too, the excellent collection, ed. Michael P. Steinberg, *Walter Benjamin and the Demands of History* (Ithaca and London: Cornell University Press, 1996).

140. Quoted as the motto to Handelman, *Fragments of Redemption,* op. cit.

141. Entry for 19 September 1915, *Tagebücher* I, op. cit., p. 158.

142. Ibid. Entry for 23 July 1916, p. 339.

143. I have explored this more thoroughly in *Scholem, Arendt, Klemperer,* op. cit., and "The Metaphysical Psychologist," op. cit.

144. See Strauss's letter of 19 May 1933 to Löwith, in Leo Strauss, *Hobbes' politische,* p. 625. I thank Jeffrey Barash for this reference.

145. See Peter Gay, *Weimar Culture,* op. cit., and Zvi Bacharach, *The Challenge: Democracy in the Eyes of German Professors and Jewish Intellectuals in the Weimar Republic* (Hebrew) (Jerusalem: Hebrew University Magnes Press, 2000).

146. This is the general thesis of Richard Wolin's *Heidegger's Children: Hannah Arendt, Karl Löwith, Hans Jonas and Herbert Marcuse* (Princeton: Princeton University Press, 2001). For my agreement and dissent, see the review in *Journal of Modern History* 75 (No. 4, December 2003), pp. 933–35.

147. As George Kateb puts it, these were "two whose love of Greece, inflamed and me-diated by German philosophy, set them against modern democracy." See his "The Ques-tionable Influence of Arendt and Strauss," in *Hannah Arendt and Leo Strauss*, op. cit., p. 12.

148. Private communication, 15 May 1988.

149. For elaboration of these themes, see *The Crisis of Liberal Democracy*, op. cit.

150. "Jerusalem and Athens" in *Jewish Philosophy and the Crisis of Modernity*, op. cit., pp. 378–79.

151. See Albrecht Wellmer's "On Revolution" in *Hannah Arendt in Jerusalem*, op. cit.

152. See Simon Schama, "Flourishing," *The New Republic* (31 January 2005), pp. 23–30. Schama dubs this reverence "Isiaolotary" and duly notes that this has brought in its wake, especially in Britain, a certain critical, if naggingly obtuse, reaction. See especially p. 24.

153. See Lilla's "Wolves and Lambs," in *The Legacy of Isaiah Berlin*, eds. Mark Lilla, Ronald Dworkin, and Robert B. Silvers (New York: *New York Review of Books*, 2001), pp. 31–42. The quote appears on p. 32.

154. See especially Perry Anderson, "England's Isaiah," *London Review of Books*, Vol. 12 (No. 24, December 1990), pp. 3–7.

155. See Ramin Jahanbegloo, *Conversations with Isaiah Berlin* (London: P. Halban, 1992), pp. 82–83.

156. Berlin to Talmon, 13 February 1958, MS. Berlin 286, fol. 26 (papers of Sir Isaiah Berlin, Bodleian Library, University of Oxford). I thank Arik Dubnow for this reference.

157. See Berlin's long conversation with Steven Lukes in *Salmagundi* No. 120 (Fall 1998), pp. 52–135, where he declares: "In so extreme a situation, no act by the victims can (pace Miss Arendt) be condemned. Whatever is done must be regarded as fully jus-tified. It is inexpressible arrogance on the part of those who have never [been] placed in so appalling a situation to pass judgement on the decisions and actions of those who have." I thank Arik Dubnow for this reference. See, too, the biography by Michael Ig-natieff, *Isaiah Berlin: A Life* (London: Vintage, 1999), p. 253, and the notes on p. 332.

158. See Jay, "The Ungrateful Dead," *Salmagundi* 123 (Summer 1999), pp. 22–31. The quote appears on p. 25.

159. Letter to Mary McCarthy, 4/10/53, in *Between Friends*, op. cit., p. 14.

160. See Letter 71 to Mr. Southham, 15.5.1973, *Briefe III, 1971–1982*, op. cit., p. 76. This comment was not entirely accurate. For in his 1951 essay on "Jewish Slavery and Emancipation," Berlin did touch on some of these issues. It is reproduced in Norman Bentwich, ed., *Hebrew University Garland* (London: Constellation Books, 1952).

161. Ignatieff, *Berlin*, op. cit., pp. 219, 230, note no. 27, p. 328, and note 26, p. 329.

162. Jahanbegloo, *Conversations*, op. cit., pp. 31–32. Berlin declared, "I do not have the faculty which detects absolute moral rules. Somebody like Leo Strauss believes in them because he believes in a faculty which some call 'reason.' . . . I envy him. I just don't happen to have that kind of *raison*. . . . Some faculty which gives infallible truth in answer to central questions of life" (p. 109).

163. Ignatieff, *Berlin*, op. cit., p. 253.

164. Isaiah Berlin, *Flourishing: Letters, 1928–1946*, ed. Henry Hardy (London: Chatto and Windus, 2004).

165. "If reading this glorious collection of Berlin's letters," Schama comments, "is, predictably, a heady experience, it is also a hearty one. Not in the British sense of cheery muscularity (definitely not Berlin's thing), but in the sense that the letters reveal an intellectual sensibility in which an uncompromising analytical clarity was uniquely married to an unshakable faith in the decent instincts of humanity." See "Flourishing," op. cit., p. 23.

166. As Clive James asks in his excellent piece on Berlin (one from which I liberally—as it were—borrow): "If he could say so much about the preparation of the main event, but so little about the main event, how good was he on the preparation?" "Guest from the Future: Gaps and Glories in the Legacy of Isaiah Berlin," *Times Literary Supplement* (3 September 2004), pp. 3–7. The quote appears on p. 3. See, too, Timothy Garton Ash, "A Genius for Friendship," *New York Review of Books* (23 September 2004), pp. 20–25.

167. "Guest from the Future," op. cit., p. 8.

168. *Major Trends*, op. cit., p. 36. See Letter 71 to Mr. Southham, 15.5.1973, *Briefe III, 1971–1982*, op. cit., p. 76.

169. Quoted in Anthony Heilbut, *Exiled in Paradise*, op. cit., p. 86.

170. For a valuable and measured treatment of these questions, see the volume edited by Jospeh Mali and Robert Wokler, *Isaiah Berlin's Counter-Enlightenment* (Philadelphia: American Philosophical Society, 2003).

171. When Berlin comments that Georges Sorel would have roundly condemned "the metaphysics of the School of Frankfurt . . . as the latest Utopian and teleological nostrums of academic pedants, visionaries or charlatans," one can be rather certain that this was his own view too. See his 1971 piece "Georges Sorel" reproduced in his *Against the Current: Essays in the History of Ideas*, with an introduction by Roger Hausheer (Oxford: Oxford University Press, 1981), pp. 328–29.

172. I owe this insight to Moshe Halbertal, although he bears no responsibility for the use I have made of it.

173. Thus, writing on E. H. Carr's historiographical views, he comments that they

breathe the last enchantments of the Age of Reason, more rationalist than rational, with all the enviable simplicity, lucidity, and freedom from doubt or self-
questioning which characterized this field of thought in its unclouded beginnings, when Voltaire and Helvétius were on their thrones; before the Germans,
with their passion for excavating everything, ruined the smooth lawns and sym-
metrical gardens.

See the "Introduction" to his *Four Essays on Liberty* (London: Oxford University Press,
1969), p. xxvii.

174. "Wolves and Lambs," op. cit., p. 34. Lilla argues that only peripheral Enlightenment figures such as Holbach and Helvétius fitted such a picture whereas for its central thinkers like Kant, Hume, and Locke, monism was the problem not the solution.
Intolerance and homogenizing attitudes hardly applied to Lessing, Mendelssohn, and
Montesquieu (p. 36). But of course, it was out of his *liberalism* that Berlin coined this
critique, "haunted by the worry that liberalism's attachment to universal principles, dis-
covered through reason, somehow rendered it less liberal and tolerant than it ought to
be." This was the basis of Berlin's advocacy, misguided in Lilla's view, of a cultural pluralism that often resisted rational scrutiny and "drove him to the questionable company
of the Counter-Enlightenment in search of intellectual support" (p. 40).

175. Berlin's portrait of romanticism, for instance, is remarkably complex, admiring
and critical at once. Yet, again, the conclusions are comforting and liberal ones: Drawn
to its logical conclusion, he comments, romanticism "does end in some kind of lunacy";
given romanticism's doctrine of unlimited and unpredictable will, fascism too is its in-
heritor. Yet, precisely because of its assertion of a plurality of values, its denial of a single
answer to all questions, it resulted in (an unintended)

> liberalism, toleration, decency . . . appreciation for the imperfections of life;
> some degree of rational self-understanding. . . . [T]hey are the persons who
> most strongly emphasized the unpredictability of all human activities. They
> were hoist with their own petard. Aiming at one thing, they produced, fortu-
> nately for us all, the exact opposite.

See his *The Roots of Romanticism*, ed. Henry Hardy (London: Chatto and Windus, 1999).
The quotes appear on pp. 145 and 147, respectively. The work is based upon the 1965
Mellon Lectures.

176. See Avishai Margalit's illuminating analysis of Berlin's Zionism, "The Crooked
Timber of Nationalism," in *The Legacy of Isaiah Berlin*, op. cit., pp. 147–59. The quote
appears on p. 149.

177. Personal communication with Avishai Margalit, 14 December 2005. Perhaps it was this eagerness that rendered Berlin's writings less jagged and disturbing than the other figures considered in this chapter. In this respect, given Sontag's distinction, he was more of a husband than a lover. See, too, Margalit's "Tribute" to Berlin in Berlin's *The First and the Last* (New York: NYREV, Inc., 1999), pp. 107–15. There he writes:

> If anyone was at home in Oxford, Isaiah Berlin was the one. He was immensely grateful to English society for accepting him. Yet he sensed that due to his experience as an immigrant child he retained the anxiousness to please. This gave him, the great Versteher, the key for his imaginative leap for understanding what it is like to lack home. Zionism, for Isaiah, had one supreme goal: to endow the Jews with a sense of home. (pp. 110–11)

178. As Anson Rabinbach has pointed out regarding Adorno and Horkheimer's *Dialectic of Enlightenment*, what "might still be salvaged from Enlightenment in the aftermath of catastrophe was enlightenment itself, conceived as a refusal of the '*Intellectus sacrificium intellectus.*'" See the difficult but rewarding essay "The Cunning of Unreason: Mimesis and the Construction of Anti-Semitism in Horkheimer and Adorno's *Dialectic of Enlightenment*," in Rabinbach, *In the Shadow of Catastrophe: German Intellectuals between Apocalypse and Enlightenment* (Berkeley: University of California Press, 1997), pp. 166–98. The quote appears on p. 198.

179. "The German Idealism of the Jewish Philosophers (1961)," in Jürgen Habermas, *Philosophical-Political Profiles,* trans. Frederick G. Lawrence (Cambridge, Mass.: MIT Press, 1985), pp. 21–43. The quote appears on p. 42.

INDEX

Adorno, Theodor, 2, 45–46, 81–118;
American experience of, 86–87; dialec-
tical method of, 106–107; Jazz Quar-
tet, 84; and messianism, 110; as mixed-
descent, 99; on Scholem, 97, 178n91
Agamben, Giorgio, 173n58
Agnon, S. Y., 14, 94, 129n36
Aliya Hadasha, 122–123n6
Anderson, Mark, 162n148
anti-Semitism, 69–70
Arab Question, 12
Arab refugees, 29–30
Arendt, Hannah, 1, 2, 40, 47, 81–118;
American experience of, 86–87; cult
of, 82–83; and history, 109; and
liberalism, 112–113; and perfor-
mativity, 105; and Zionism, 95,
139nn119–120
Ash, Timothy Garton, 167–168n8

Bar Kochba, 13
Benjamin, Walter, 2, 40, 81–118; fame
of, 83–84, 96–97; and Jewishness, 89;
and language, 105; as Last Intellectual,
87; tragic fate of, 86; and Zionism, 95
Benjamin's Crossing, 86, 171n37
Benvenisti, Meron, 141–142n132
Berg, Nicolas, 77, 152n53, 155n70,
163nn151–152, 164n154
Bergman, Escha, 15
Bergman, Shmuel Hugo, 6, 8, 10, 13,
15–22, 36, 40; and dreams, 32; and
failure, 34–35, 42; on Statehood, 41
Berlin, 10, 14
Berlin, Isaiah, 113–118, 120n5
Bet Iksa, 17
Biale, David, 172n46, 173–174n61,
174–175n66
Bildung, 14, 15, 16, 17, 20, 63, 76, 113
binationalism, 6–44
Bloch, Ernst, 89–90
Bloom, Allan, 166–167n5
Bloom Harold, 85
Blumenfeld, Kurt, 121nn9–10, 176n80
Borges, Jorge Luis, 85
Braudel, Fernand, 52, 147–148n29
Breines, Paul, 88, 156n93, 172n54
Brit Shalom, 6–44
Broszat, Martin, 46, 162–163n151,
164n154
Brunner, Otto, 53
Buber, Martin, 8, 13, 89, 95; on State-
hood, 41; on Zionism and morality,
26–32

Carsten, Francis, 163n151
Cassirer, Ernst, 89–90
Celan, Paul, 85
Char, René, 108
Clay, Jenny Strauss, 167n6
Cohen, Ge'ulah, 139–140n121
Cohen, Hermann, 96

Collini, Stefan, 89, 151n47, 173n57
Conrad, Sebastian, 143–144n5
Conze, Werner, 53, 148n36
Crisis of German Ideology, 65
Critical Theory, 84
Cyprus, 42

Dahrendorff, Ralf, 50
Dannhauser, Werner, 174n66
Davar, 15
degeneration, 11
Dews, Peter, 106, 182n122
Diner, Dan, 72n56, 152n55,
    163–164n153
Dorpalen, Andreas, 154n70
Dreams and Delusions, 121n13
Drury, Shadia, 166n4
Dying for Jerusalem, 74

Eagleton, Terry, 86
Ehrenburg, Hans, 96
Einstein, Albert, 3, 8, 72
Einstein's German World, 77
Elias, Norbert, 93, 176n74
Elon, Amos, 119–120n4
Eurocentricism, 17–18
Eyck, Erich, 154n70

Fischer, Fritz, 144–145n12
Floud, Jean, 114
Frankel, Ernst, 50
Freud, Fania, 85, 97
Freud, Sigmund, 21, 67, 72, 85, 157n101
Freud, Jews and Other Germans, 120n7,
    143n4
Fromm, Erich, 93

Gatzke, Hans, 154n70
Gay, Peter, 4, 45–80; and criticism of
    Scholem thesis, 73; early career of,

60–61; and experience of exile, 57–59;
    Jewish self-identification of, 49–50,
    74–75, 77; name change of, 59; and
    Zionism, 74–76
Generation Exodus, 71, 119n3
German cultural history, 45–80
German Federal Republic, 51
German-Jewish dialogue, 46–47
German-Jewish history, 71ff
German Jews Beyond Judaism, 63ff, 77,
    120n6, 128n31, 156n91
German social history, 45–80
German Zionism, 93–96
Gilbert, Felix, 59, 148n35
Goldberg, Oskar, 181n116
Goldhagen, Daniel Jonah, 159–160n122
Google, 83, 169n18
Gordon, Adi, 124n14, 126n24,
    138–139n111
Gordon, Peter Eli, 85, 107–108, 110,
    170n27, 181n113
Goren, Arthur A., 122n4
Grass, Günther, 50
Greenberg, Ehud, 90, 169n19

Ha'am, Ahad (Asher Ginzberg), 7, 19,
    124n12
Habermas, Jürgen, 50, 118, 188n179
Handelman, Susan, 105, 180n105,
    182n119, 183n129, 184n140
Ha-Shomer Ha-Tzair, 8
Hazony, Yoram, 36, 138n108
Hebrew culture, 15
Hebrew Humanism, 20
Hebrew University, 14, 35–36
Heidegger, Martin, 92–93, 100
Heller, Joseph, 122n4, 124n11
Herbert, Ulrich, 146n20, 147n24
Herzl, Theodor, 16, 94, 133n71
heterodoxy, 90ff, 100–102
historicism, 102, 105
Holborn, Hajo, 59, 155n75

Iggers, George, 151n48, 154n70
Iraq War, 82
irrationalism, 24, 67, 77–78
Isenberg, Noah, 84, 169n20

Jabotinsky, Ze'ev, 36, 138n109
Jacobson, Eric, 109, 183n131
Jaffa, Harry, 109
James, Clive, 115, 116, 186n166
Jargon of Authenticity, 100
Jay, Martin, 86, 114, 119n2, 135n74,
    174n62
Jeissman, Michael, 146n21
Jenkins, Jennifer, 78, 164n157
Jens, Walter, 50
Jetztzeit, 110
Jonas, Hans, 85, 93, 166n3, 176n74
Journal of Contemporary History, 57,
    153n60
Judt, Tony, 142n133
Jung, Carl Gustav, 21
Jünger, Ernst, 92–93

Kafka, Franz, 1, 5, 94, 95, 97, 100,
    179–180nn101–102
Karavan, Dani, 83
Kehr, Eckart, 148n36
Kissinger, Henry, 60, 71
Koch, Richard, 96
Kocka, Jürgen, 46, 55, 145n15, 147n25,
    165n163
Kohn, Hans, 8, 10, 11, 12, 13, 16, 17, 21,
    31, 33; on disillusion with Zionism,
    38–39; on Zionism and Historic
    Rights, 24–26
Koselleck, Reinhart, 45, 50, 143n1,
    149–150n41
Kracauer, Siegfried, 135n74
Kreuzberger, Max, 41
Kristeller, Paul Oskar, 154n70

Labor Zionism, 9
Lagarde, Paul de, 94
Landauer, Georg, 41, 140n124
Laqueur, Walter, 2, 45–80, 83, 87; early
    career of, 60; and experience of exile,
    57–58; and experience of National
    Socialism, 68; Jewish self-identification
    of, 50, 77; name change of, 59; and
    Zionism, 73–74, 161nn140–141
Lavsky, Hagit, 43, 124n12, 125n15,
    142n134
Lazarsfeld, Paul, 86
Lehmann, Hartmut, 52–53, 145n13
Lepsius, Rainer, 50
Letter to his Father, 94
liberalism, 111ff
Lichtheim, George, 36, 41
Lichtheim, Richard, 36–37
Lilla, Mark, 113, 117, 167n6,
    172–173n54, 187n174
linguistic turn, 46
Löwenthal, Leo, 93, 176n74, 177n87
Löwith, Karl, 111
Lübbe, Hermann, 148n34

Magnes, Judah, 7, 34, 36, 122n4, 123n9,
    137n102, 139n119
Mann, Golo, 154n70
Mann, Thomas, 65
Ma'or, Zohar, 133n72
Marcuse, Herbert, 89–90
Marx, Karl, 108
Masur, Gerhard, 154n70
Meinecke, Friedrich, 47, 144n6
Mendes-Flohr, Paul, 31, 122n4, 132n51,
    133n72
Merkl, Peter, 154n70
Meyer, Gustav, 59
Michnik, Adam, 169n16
Minima Moralia, 143n2, 166n1
Moeller, Robert G., 149n38, 163n151
Momigliano, Arnaldo, 85

Mommsen, Hans, 46, 54, 148–149n37, 150nn42,45
Mommsen, Wilhelm, 148–149n37
Mommsen, Wolfgang, 46, 148–149n37
Morgenthau, Hans, 83
Moses, Dirk, 146n20
Mosse, George L., 14, 43, 45–80, 89; early career of, 60–62; and experience of exile, 57–59; and experience of National Socialism, 68; Jewish self-identification of, 49, 77; name change of, 59; and Zionism, 73–74, 160–161n136, 161n142
Mosse, Werner, 154n70, 163n151
Muller, Jerry Z., 59, 149n40
Muskeljuden, 7

Nationalism and Sexuality, 70
Negative Dialectics, 99–100
Neimann, Susan, 183n132
neoromanticism, 24
Neumann, Franz, 50
Nietzsche, Friedrich, 108, 111
Nipperdey, Thomas, 50, 164n158
Nolte, Ernst, 76
Nolte, Paul, 56, 147n25, 152n57
Nordau, Max, 74, 95
Norton, Anne, 167n7

On Jews and Judaism in Crisis, 120n6
Orient, 124n14
Origins of Totalitarianism, 95, 114, 144n8
Orlow, Dietrich, 154n70
Ostjuden, 15, 94, 129–130n39

Pachter, Henry, 85
Paret, Peter, 154n70
Paul, Gerhard, 152n57
Platt, Michael, 166n4, 168n10

political Zionism, 16, 94–95, 131n46
Politics of Cultural Despair, 65
Posen, 10
positivism, 102, 105
postmodernism, 102ff
Prague, 10, 13, 14, 94
Putnam, Hilary, 84, 170n26

Rabinbach, Anson, 175n70, 180n108, 188n178
Rahden, Till van, 152n53, 157n99
Rahel Varnhagen, 95, 119n1
Rathenau, Walther, 3, 121nn10–11
Ratzabi, Shalom, 121–122n2
Rawitsch, 10, 14
Rechavia, 14
respectability, 3, 15, 60, 70, 155n79
Ringer, Fritz, 154n70
Ritter, Gerhard, 47, 163n151
Rosen, Charles, 84
Rosenberg, Hans, 50, 59, 148n36
Rosenzweig, Franz, 2, 81–118; on exile, 99; popularity of, 84–85; and postmodernism, 107–108; tragic death of, 85; and Zionism, 95–96
Rothfels, Hans, 59, 149n38, 151n49, 154–155n70
Ruppin, Arthur, 8, 10, 11, 15, 17, 18, 19; and Brit Shalom failure, 37–38; and Hans Günther, 125n19
Ruppin, Raphael, 19
Rürup, Reinhard, 46, 56, 69

Sacred Landscape, 142n132
Said, Edward, 84, 170n24
Samuel, Edwin, 22, 133n71
Schama, Simon, 115, 186n165
Schieder, Theodor, 53, 148–149nn36–37
Schieder, Wolfgang, 46

Schlesinger, Arthur, 82, 168n10
Schmitt, Carl, 92–93
Schocken, Salman, 35, 88
Scholem, Gershom, 2, 4, 8, 10, 21; 31, 34, 81–118; aura of, 85; and changing attitudes toward binationalism, 39–41; and criticism of Ernst Simon, 41; on exilic creativity, 97–98; on history, 110; "non-dialogue" thesis of, 72ff; and opposition to World War I, 12, 94
Schorske, Carl, 79
Schulze, Winfried, 149n40
Segev, Tom, 16, 123–124n11
Sewell, William H., Jr., 55, 147n28, 148n30, 151n47
Shapira, Anita, 136n81
Shazar, Zalman, 94
Sheppard, Eugene, 112
Shira, 14
Shumsky, Dimitry, 13, 127nn27–28, 141n131
Simon, Ernst, 8, 10, 17, 35, 40; on 1948 war, 136n86, 140n122; on Statehood, 41–43
Simon, Walter, 154n70
Sittlichkeit, 16
Sonderweg, 48, 68–69, 78, 145n15, 157n99
Sontag, Susan, 81, 87, 173n60
Sontheimer, Kurt, 159n110
Sorkin, David, 164n157
Spector, Scott, 127n28
Spinoza's Critique of Religion, 97, 175n72
Star of Redemption, 116
Steinberg, Michael, 77, 164n155
Steiner, George, 89, 119n4
Stern, Fritz, 4, 45–80; early career of, 60; and experience of exile, 57; and experience of National Socialism, 68; self-identification of, 49, 74–75, 77; and Zionism, 74–75
Stern, Gabriel, 9, 123–124n11

Strauss, Leo, 2, 81–118; American experience of, 86–87; and Carl Schmitt, 92; on exile, 99; and liberalism, 111–112; and modernity, 109; and Zionism, 94–95
Straussianism, 82
Sudeten Germans, 42

Tagebuch, 15
Talbieh, 14
Talmon, Jacob, 114
theology, 109ff
Thompson, E. P., 55
Tucholsky, Kurt, 72

Ussischkin, Menachem, 15

Valentin, Veit, 59
Völkisch ideology, 24, 65–66, 69–70, 72, 133–135nn72–74
Volkov, Shulamit, 69, 157n98, 159n114, 161n136
Volksgeschichte, 53ff

Walzer, Michael, 9, 124n13
Weber, Max, 152n53
Wehler, Hans-Ulrich, 46, 51, 52, 56, 69, 79–80, 145n14, 146–147n23, 150n45, 152n54, 165nn161,163,164, 166n165
Weimar culture, 65–66, 73, 92, 130–131n45
Weimar intellectuals, 65ff, 81–118
Weininger, Otto, 21
Weiss, Yfaat, 10, 11, 34, 125n17, 125–126n22, 127–128n30
Weizmann, Chaim, 75, 124n12
Weltbühne, 15
Weltsch, Robert, 8, 10, 20, 33, 36, 41
Westjuden, 15

Wilcox, Elizabeth, 99–100, 179n99
Winkler, Heinrich, 46
Wittgenstein, Ludwig, 100
Wohlfarth, Irving, 171n38
Wolf, Heinz, 55–56, 144n11, 152n56,
    154–155n70, 158n110
Wood, Gordon, 82, 166n5
World War I, 12
Wulf, Joseph, 164n154

Yekkes, 14, 128–129n35

Zionism, 6–44, 74–76
Zionist Revisionism, 9, 36
Zipperstein, Steven, 122n3, 132n58
Zizek, Slavov, 83, 168–169n15
Zunft, 47, 50–51
Zweig, Arnold, 124n14